FIELDING
TRAVEL GUIDES

D1387538

FIELDING'S
LAS VEGAS
AGENDA

The Buzz About Fielding

Fielding Worldwide

"The new Fielding guidebook style mirrors the style of the company's new publisher: irreverent, urbane, adventuresome and in search of the unique travel experience."
—*San Diego Union Tribune*

"Individualistic, entertaining, comprehensive."
—*Consumers Digest*

"Guidebooks with attitude."
—*Dallas Morning News*

"Full of author's tips and asides, the books seem more personal and more credible than many similarly encyclopedic tomes."
—*Los Angeles Times*

"At Fielding Worldwide, adventurous might well be the order of the day."
—*Des Moines Register*

"Biting travel guides give readers a fresh look."
—*Houston Chronicle*

"For over 30 years Fielding guides have been the standard of modern travel books."
—*Observer Times*

Fielding's Las Vegas Agenda

"A concise but detailed look at the capital of glitter and gambling."
—*Atlanta Journal Constitution*

Fielding's Los Angeles Agenda

"…contains much more than the standard travel guide. The lists of theatres, sports arenas and attractions are worth the book's price by itself."
—*Baton Rouge Advocate*

Fielding's New York Agenda

"Loaded with advice…puts the whole of the Big Apple in hand."
—*Bon Appetit*

Fielding's Guide to Worldwide Cruises

"One of the year's ten best books."
—*Gourmet Magazine*

"Perhaps the best single source for unbiased cruise information."
—*The New York Times*

"To be all things to all people is impossible, but this book pretty well does it."
—*The New York Daily News*

"You can trust them [Fielding] to tell the truth. It's fun—and very informative."
—*New Orleans Times-Picayune*

"The Bible. If scarcity is any indication of quality, then this book is superb."
—*St. Petersburg Florida Times*

Cruise Insider

"One of the best, most compact, yet interesting books about cruising today is the fact-filled *Cruise Insider*."
—*John Clayton's Travel With a Difference*

Fielding's The World's Most Dangerous Places

"Rarely does a travel guide turn out to be as irresistible as a John Grisham novel. But *The World's Most Dangerous Places*, a 1000-page tome for the truly adventurous traveler, manages to do just that."
—*Arkansas Democrat-Gazette*

"A travel guide that could be a real lifesaver. Practical tips for those seeking the road less traveled."
—*Time Magazine*

"The greatest derring do of this year's memoirs."
—*Publishers Weekly*

"Reads like a first-run adventure movie."
—*Travel Books Worldwide*

"One of the oddest and most fascinating travel books to appear in a long time."

—*The New York Times*

"...publishing terra incognito...a primer on how to get in and out of potentially lethal places."

—*U.S. News and World Report*

"Tired of the same old beach vacation?...this book may be just the antidote."

—*USA Today*

"Guide to hot spots will keep travelers glued to their armchairs."

—*The Vancouver Sun*

Fielding's Borneo

"One of a kind...a guide that reads like an adventure story."

—*San Diego Union*

Fielding's Budget Europe

"This is a guide to great times, great buys and discovery in 18 countries."

—*Monroe News-Star*

Fielding's Caribbean

"If you have trouble deciding which regional guidebook to reach for, you can't go wrong with *Fielding's Caribbean*."

—*Washington Times*

"Opinionated, clearly written and probably the only guide that any visitor to the Caribbean really needs."

—*The New York Times*

Fielding's Europe

"Synonymous with the dissemination of travel information for five decades."

—*Traveller's Bookcase*

"The definitive Europe... shame on you if you don't read it before you leave."

—*Travel Europe*

Fielding's Far East

"This well-respected guide is thoroughly updated and checked out."

—*The Reader Review*

Fielding's France

"Winner of the annual 'Award of Excellence' [with Michelin and Dorling Kindersley]."

—*FrancePresse*

Fielding's Freewheelin' USA

"...an informative, thorough and entertaining 400-page guide to the sometimes maligned world of recreational vehicle travel."

—*Travel Weekly*

"...very comprehensive... lots more fun than most guides of this sort..."

—*Los Angeles Times*

Fielding's Italy

"A good investment...contains excellent tips on driving, touring, cities, etc."

—*Travel Savvy*

Fielding's Mexico

"Among the very best."

—*Library Journal*

Fielding's Spain and Portugal

"Our best sources of information were fellow tour-goers and *Fielding's Spain and Portugal*."

—*The New York Times*

Vacation Places Rated

"...can best be described as a thinking person's guide if used to its fullest."

—*Chicago Tribune*

"Tells how 13,500 veteran vacationers rate destinations for satisfaction and how well a destination delivers on what is promised."

—*USA Today*

Fielding's Vietnam

"Fielding has the answer to every conceivable question."

—*Destination Vietnam*

"An important book about an important country."

—*NPR Business Radio*

Fielding Titles

Fielding's Alaska Cruises and the Inside Passage
Fielding's America West
Fielding's Asia's Top Dive Sites
Fielding's Australia
Fielding's Bahamas
Fielding's Baja California
Fielding's Bermuda
Fielding's Best and Worst — The surprising results of the Plog Survey
Fielding's Birding Indonesia
Fielding's Borneo
Fielding's Budget Europe
Fielding's Caribbean
Fielding's Caribbean Cruises
Fielding's Caribbean on a Budget
Fielding's Diving Australia
Fielding's Diving Indonesia
Fielding's Eastern Caribbean
Fielding's England including Ireland, Scotland & Wales
Fielding's Europe
Fielding's Europe 50th Anniversary
Fielding's European Cruises
Fielding's Far East
Fielding's France
Fielding's France: Loire Valley, Burgundy & the Best of French Culture
Fielding's France: Normandy & Brittany
Fielding's France: Provence and the Mediterranean
Fielding's Freewheelin' USA
Fielding's Hawaii
Fielding's Hot Spots: Travel in Harm's Way
Fielding's Indiana Jones Adventure and Survival Guide™
Fielding's Italy
Fielding's Kenya
Fielding's Las Vegas Agenda
Fielding's London Agenda
Fielding's Los Angeles Agenda
Fielding's Mexico
Fielding's New Orleans Agenda
Fielding's New York Agenda
Fielding's New Zealand
Fielding's Paradors, Pousadas and Charming Villages of Spain and Portugal
Fielding's Paris Agenda
Fielding's Portugal
Fielding's Rome Agenda
Fielding's San Diego Agenda
Fielding's Southeast Asia
Fielding's Southern California Theme Parks
Fielding's Southern Vietnam on Two Wheels
Fielding's Spain
Fielding's Surfing Australia
Fielding's Surfing Indonesia
Fielding's Sydney Agenda
Fielding's Thailand, Cambodia, Laos and Myanmar
Fielding's Travel Tool™
Fielding's Vietnam, including Cambodia and Laos
Fielding's Walt Disney World and Orlando Area Theme Parks
Fielding's Western Caribbean
Fielding's The World's Most Dangerous Places™
Fielding's Worldwide Cruises

FIELDING'S LAS VEGAS AGENDA

By
Joyce Wiswell

Fielding Worldwide, Inc.
308 South Catalina Avenue
Redondo Beach, California 90277 U.S.A.

Fielding's Las Vegas Agenda

Published by Fielding Worldwide, Inc.

Text Copyright ©1997 FWI

Icons & Illustrations Copyright ©1997 FWI

Photo Copyrights ©1997 to Individual Photographers

3-D maps (page 34, page 98) reprinted with permission of *The Orange County Register*

FIELDING WORLDWIDE INC.

PUBLISHER AND CEO	**Robert Young Pelton**
GENERAL MANAGER	**John Guillebeaux**
OPERATIONS DIRECTOR	**George Posanke**
ELEC. PUBLISHING DIRECTOR	**Larry E. Hart**
PUBLIC RELATIONS DIRECTOR	**Beverly Riess**
ACCOUNT SERVICES MANAGER	**Cindy Henrichon**
PROJECT MANAGER	**Chris Snyder**
MANAGING EDITOR	**Amanda K. Knoles**

PRODUCTION

Martin Mancha   **Ramses Reynoso**

Craig South

COVER DESIGNED BY	**Digital Artists, Inc.**
COVER PHOTOGRAPHERS —	
Front Cover	**Las Vegas Convention & Visitors Authority**
Back Cover	**John Lawrence/Tony Stone Images**
INSIDE PHOTOS	**Catherine Gehm, W. Lyn Seldon Jr., Las Vegas Convention & Visitors Authority, Las Vegas News Bureau**
AUTHOR'S PHOTO	**Kim Reierson**
CARTOONS	***The New Yorker***

Inquiries should be addressed to: Fielding Worldwide, Inc., 308 South Catalina Ave., Redondo Beach, California 90277 U.S.A., ☎ *(310) 372-4474*, Facsimile *(310) 376-8064*, 8:30 a.m.–5:30 p.m. Pacific Standard Time.
Website: http://www.fieldingtravel.com
e-mail: fielding@fieldingtravel.com

ISBN 1-56952-149-2

Printed in the United States of America

Letter from the Publisher

In 1946, Temple Fielding began the first of what would be a remarkable new series of well-written, highly personalized guidebooks for independent travelers. Temple's opinionated, witty and oft-imitated books have now guided travelers for almost a half-century. More important to some was Fielding's humorous and direct method of steering travelers away from the dull and the insipid. Today, Fielding Travel Guides are still written by experienced travelers for experienced travelers. Our authors carry on Fielding's reputation for creating travel experiences that deliver insight with a sense of discovery and style.

Joyce Wiswell cuts through the chaos and takes you to the most exciting and offbeat places in America's fastest growing vacation destination. This savvy guide to the capital of glitter and flash offers tough but fair reviews of restaurants, hotels and attractions and even offers tips to help you improve your odds at the casinos. With *Fielding's Las Vegas Agenda*, the odds are you'll have a great trip.

The concept of independent travel has never been bigger. Our policy of *brutal honesty* and a highly personal point of view has never changed; it just seems the travel world has caught up with us.

RYP

Robert Young Pelton
Publisher and CEO
Fielding Worldwide, Inc.

Fielding Rating Icons

The Fielding Rating Icons are highly personal and awarded to help the besieged traveler choose from among the dizzying array of activities, attractions, hotels, restaurants and sights. The awarding of an icon denotes unusual or exceptional qualities in the relevant category.

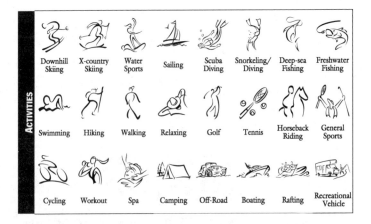

Star Ratings

Fielding rates all hotels, restaurants and attractions (with the exception of sporting activities) with a star system of one to five. Obviously, ratings are highly subjective. Keep in mind that more stars does not necessarily mean more expensive.

★ ★ ★ ★ ★	**Doesn't get any better**
★ ★ ★ ★	**Excellent**
★ ★ ★	**Good**
★ ★	**Fair to middling**
★	**Nothing to write home about**

ABOUT THE AUTHOR

Joyce Wiswell

Joyce Wiswell has been reporting on the gambling industry for more than 10 years, first as managing editor of the industry bible, *Gaming & Wagering Business Magazine*, then as a free-lance writer. Although she travels extensively throughout the islands as author of *Fielding's Bermuda* and co-author of *Fielding's Caribbean*, Las Vegas remains high on her list of favorite places.

DEDICATION

For my sister, Joanne, who loves Las Vegas as much as I do.

ACKNOWLEDGEMENTS

Many, many thanks to those who helped out with my research on the world's most unique city: Phil Hevener, publisher of *Gaming Hotline*; Tropicana casino bosses Bob Lee and Dick Darnold; the staff of the Las Vegas News Bureau; J.R. Schwartz, author of the *Official Guide to the Best Cat Houses in Nevada*; and *Las Vegas Style*; and all the dealers, bartenders, waitresses and cab drivers who enthusiastically shared their hometown knowledge.

TABLE OF CONTENTS

LIST OF MAPS

Map Legend

Essentials

- **H** Hotel
- **⚑** Youth Hostel
- **✕** Restaurant
- **S** Bank
- **☎** Telephone
- **ℹ** Tourist Info.
- **✚** Hospital
- **🍺** Pub/Bar
- **✉** Post Office
- **P** Parking
- **T** Taxi
- **S** Subway
- **M** Metro
- **M** Market
- **S** Shopping
- **C** Cinema
- **☺** Theatre
- **✈** Int'l Airport
- **✦** Regional Airport
- **★** Police Station
- **⚖** Courthouse
- **🏛** Gov't. Building
- **■** Attraction
- **🛩** Military Airbase
- **👤** Army Base
- **▬** Naval base
- **⌂** Fort
- **🏫** University
- **🏫** School

Historical

- **∴** Archeological Site
- **⚔** Battleground
- **🏰** Castle

Religious

- **✝** Church
- **🛕** Buddhist Temple
- **🛕** Hindu Temple
- **☪** Mosque
- **🔱** Pagoda
- **🕎** Synagogue

Activities

- **🏖** Beach
- **▲** Campground
- **🎪** Picnic Area
- **⛳** Golf Course
- **🛥** Boat Launch
- **🤿** Diving
- **🐟** Fishing
- **🎿** Water Skiing
- **⛷** Snow Skiing
- **🐦** Bird Sanctuary
- **🦌** Wildlife Sanctuary
- **🌲** Park
- **🏔** Park Headquarters
- **⛏** Mine
- **🗼** Lighthouse
- **🌀** Windmill
- **⚓** Cruise Port
- **⚐** View
- **🏟** Stadium
- **🏢** Building
- **🐘** Zoo
- **🌸** Garden

Monument / Museum / Ruin / Shipwreck
- **🗼** Monument
- **🏛** Museum
- **🏺** Ruin
- **🚢** Shipwreck

Physical

— — — — International Boundary	🚶 Hiking Trail
— - — - — County/Regional Boundary	▬▬ Dirt Road
PARIS ⊙ National Capital	+++++++ Railroad
Victoria ● State/Parish Capital	**RR** Railroad Station
Los Angeles ● Major City	🚢 Ferry Route
Quy Nhon ○ Town/Village	▲ Mountain Peak
— (5) — Motorway/Freeway	Lake
(163) Highway	— River
—— Primary Road	🌑 Cave
—— Secondary Road	Coral Reef
— — — Subway	Waterfall
— 🚲 — Biking Route	♨ Hot Spring

©FWI

INTRODUCTION

The Strip offers a dazzling display of candlepower.

One fine Sunday, April 2, 1995 to be exact, an old, barefoot man entered the Treasure Island, cashed his $400 Social Security check and, with the aid of a cane, hobbled over to a blackjack table. He ordered a Jack Daniel's, a Coke and a few Macanudo cigars and got down to the serious business of gambling.

It was a lucky day for Shoeless Joe, as he came to be known. He started winning and winning—and winning. Soon he was playing several hands at once with a wager of $5000 each.

By Thursday, Shoeless had won more than $1.3 million.

Despite this amazing success, the little bald man was grouchy throughout, swearing at the dealers, throwing the bones from a takeout dinner on the carpet and generally abusing the staff. He never tipped the dealers. Undeterred, the hotel comped him a suite, clothes, security guards and a limousine. It's said that one night he had the limo take him to a local park, where he slept on a bench.

Inevitably, Shoeless Joe started losing, and losing—and losing. The hotel finally kicked him out when he was down to somewhere around $40,000 or $60,000. His surliness and profanity got to be too much—though local wags say the real reason is that they feared he would lose it all and take a swan dive off the roof, which is hardly the image Las Vegas is trying to portray these days. But before Shoeless Joe left for good, he made a quick $10,000 when Steve Wynn, the hotel's owner and Las Vegas' golden boy, bought his film and video rights. (For the record, Treasure Island refuses to verify this story, but everyone knows it really happened.)

The tale is strange, but true—and that's why I love Las Vegas so much. In fact, "strange but true" should be the city's motto. A volcano that erupts each 15 minutes? Strange but true. A hotel built in the form of a pyramid, right next to the one that looks like a fantasy castle? Strange but true. Dolphins, lions and tigers in the middle of the desert? Strange but true!

Las Vegas has always been called the adult's Disneyland, but it's so much more than that. With apologies to Frank Sinatra, it is THE city that never sleeps, where the casinos never close, the dance clubs stay open till the wee, wee hours and the neon flickers and pulsates till the harsh rays of the sun drown the lights out. And where else do they broadcast radio ads for a penile pump ("for most of us, life is too short")?

But there's a whole other side to Las Vegas—sweeping vistas, ancient Indian carvings, towering canyons, cobalt-blue Lake Mead—that most visitors never see. That's a real shame, because the city has so much more to offer than the lure of quick riches and beautiful showgirls. Do yourself a real favor and spend at least a day soaking up some desert scenery far from the jingle of the slot machines.

With a total of 101,106 rooms, the vast majority in swank casino-hotels, Las Vegas has more lodging choices than any other city in the United States, perhaps the world. To help fill those ever-increasing rooms, Las Vegas has started wooing (and very successfully at that) the family market with myriad attractions that have nothing to do with getting rich quick. With most hotel rooms going for well under $100 a night and a ton of free stuff that appeals to kids, Las Vegas is a cheap family vacation—provided mom and dad stay out of the casino. Apparently they are, because room rates and buffet prices have been creeping up. The 99-cent steak-and-eggs breakfast may be history, but Las Vegas is still one of the biggest bargains in the United States.

Legalized gambling is sweeping across the United States faster than a flush beats a straight. In 1974, gambling was a $17-billion industry. Today, casinos make more than books, recorded music and movies combined. There are casinos (either corporate or Native American-owned) in more than 20 states, and, in these days of high unemployment and federal cutbacks, many more are hoping to jump on the bandwagon.

They may build gambling riverboats in Mississippi and classy casinos in Detroit, but there will always be only one Las Vegas. As people get a taste of the casino experience—in 1996, 129 million U.S. households gambled in one—they inevitably want to experience the granddaddy of them all. In fact, Las Vegas marketers say that they don't view all these new casinos as competition—they're simply a great lure to try out Sin City.

And who knows? You could be the next Shoeless Joe. Then again, keep in mind that in fiscal 1996, Clark County (in which Las Vegas sits) casinos won more than $5.84 billion, an increase of 5.1 percent over the previous year. As the casinos like to say to cover their behinds: Bet with your head, not over it.

Getting There

It's easy to get to Las Vegas, be it by air, train, bus or car.

By Air

The city's McCarran International Airport is the nation's eighth busiest and one of the nicest. Some 30.5 million passengers land here each year. It has four runways, 66 gates and is quite efficient and modern. With its stylized palm trees and large-screen TVs (on which celebrities welcome you), it's about as pretty as an airport can get. There's no doubt you're in Las Vegas: There are slot machines everywhere (but no table games).

Las Vegas is unique in that passengers don't have to stay over a Saturday night to get bargain fares, which the airlines require in virtually every other city. Even so, it's well worth your while to investigate the possibility of taking one of the charter flights that leave from most major cities. You won't have as much leeway in setting your own schedule, but the cut-rate fares nearly always beat the airlines.

Twenty-three carriers fly into Las Vegas nonstop from 61 domestic destinations, with an average of 742 daily flights. There's also nonstop service from Condor (a subsidiary of Lufthansa) from Cologne-Bonn, Germany and from Manchester, England, on Airtours.

The airport seems to be constantly expanding; current projects to lengthen two runways, expand the ticket lobby and increase parking will all be completed by 1998.

The following major carriers serve Las Vegas:

Airline Service to Las Vegas	
Air Canada	(800) 776-3000
Air Nevada	(702) 736-8900, (800) 634-6377
Alaska	(800) 426-0333
America West	(702) 736-1737, (800) 247-5692
American	(800) 433-7300

Airline Service to Las Vegas	
Continental	(702) 383-8291, (800) 525-0280
Delta	(702) 731-3111
Hawaiian	(702) 796-9696, (800) 227-7110
Northwest	(800) 225-2525
Southwest	(800) 435-9792
TWA	(702) 385-1000, (800) 221-2000
United	(702) 385-3222, (800) 241-6522
US Air	(702) 382-1905, (800) 772-4368

The airport is only one mile from the Strip, 3.5 miles from the Convention Center and five miles from downtown. A cab is expensive ($13–$17 downtown, $10 to the mid-Strip). A cheaper alternative is the shuttle run by Bell Trans (☎ *(702) 739-7990)*, which costs $3.50 to Strip hotels and $4.75 to downtown. Go to the Bell Trans booth in the baggage claim area, between doors nine and 10, for information. Bell Trans will also take you back to the airport for the same fare, but they pick you up two hours prior to flight time, which is a drag.

City	Air Mileage
Atlanta	2004 miles
Chicago	1866 miles
Dallas	1221 miles
Denver	765 miles
Honolulu	2396 miles
Houston	1484 miles
Los Angeles	288 miles
Minneapolis	1688 miles
New Orleans	1740 miles
New York City	2591 miles
Phoenix	300 miles
San Francisco	576 miles
Seattle	1204 miles
St. Louis	1621 miles
Washington D.C.	2434 miles

By Train

Amtrak (☎ *800-872-7245)* trains drop passengers off, appropriately enough, right in the basement of a downtown casino (Jackie Gaughan's Plaza Hotel), but you can start gambling right in the train station. As we went to press, the future of that Desert Wind line was uncertain; it's quite possible Las Vegas will be without passenger train service by the time you read this.

Some sample round trip fares: From Los Angeles: $77–$148 (six hours); from Denver: $184–$352 (22 hours).

By Bus

Greyhound *(☎ (800) 231-2222 and (702) 384-9561)* buses roll into the city daily from all over the United States. Passengers are dropped off at the bus station at 200 South Main Street, which is open from 5:00–1:00 a.m.

Some sample round trip fares: from Los Angeles: $62 (seven hours); from Denver: $160 (16 hours).

Getting Around

Trekking is often the mode of choice; in Las Vegas, you walk and gawk at the same time. Las Vegas Boulevard South (the Strip) experiences constant gridlock on the weekends; you're often better off hoofing it than taking a cab or a bus. It's especially easy to get around on foot downtown, where the casinos are smaller and much closer together than on the Strip.

Folks who drive or bus to Las Vegas welcome the sight of a desert snack stand.

By Bus

The public transportation system is **Citizens Area Transit** *(downtown at 300 N. Casino Center Blvd.,* ☎ *(702) 228-7433)*, known locally as CAT. Buses operate from 5:30–1:30 a.m. The exception is Route 301, which traverses the Strip, which runs 24 hours. Buses come each 10 to 15 minutes. All routes operate weekdays, weekends and holidays. Transfers, good for one hour past the time of arrival, are free; just ask your driver for one when you pay the fare. You can pick up a schedule at any 7-Eleven.

The fare is $1 for all routes except the 301 and 303 (which also do the Strip), which cost $1.50. Senior citizens, kids five–17 and disabled persons pay 50 cents. Children under five ride free. Exact change is required.

By Trolley

The CAT-run Strip Shuttle *(Route 301)* runs 24 hours. The fare is $1.50 for adults. See above.

The privately owned **Las Vegas Strip Trolley** (☎ *(702) 382-1404)* runs up and down the Strip each 15 minutes or so from the Sahara to the Hacienda. It runs from 9:30–2 a.m. and costs $1.30 per ride—exact change required. Since it stops at every major hotel (including the Las Vegas Hilton, which is off the Strip), sit back and expect a long ride. The CAT makes fewer stops, so it's quicker.

By Monorail

An elevated, electric monorail links the Strip hotels. It takes just four minutes for the mile-long trip, and it's free. The schedule was not firm at press time, but it's expected to run 24 hours.

By Taxi

There are tons of cabs out there, but they don't come cheap. It costs $2.20 just to get in and $1.50 each mile thereafter, plus 35 cents for each minute of waiting time. You can catch one easily at any hotel's main entrance; it's a lot harder to flag one down, as they are not permitted to stop along the Strip to pick passengers up (some do anyway, of course).

Las Vegas Cab Companies	
A-North Las Vegas Cab	☎ *(702) 643-1041*
A Vegas Western Cab	☎ *(702) 736-6121*
ABC Union Cab	☎ *(702) 736-8444*
Ace Cab	☎ *(702) 736-8383*
Checker/Star/Yellow Cab	☎ *(702) 873-2227*
Desert Cab	☎ *(702) 376-2687*
Nellis Cab	☎ *(702) 252-0201*
Western Cab	☎ *(702) 736-8000*
Whittlesea Blue Cab	☎ *(702) 384-6111*

By Rental Car

Unless you plan to see some of the surrounding desert (which I recommend), you really don't need to rent a car.

You can travel in style in a Corvette convertible ($169–$189 a day at **Rent a Vette**) or in shame in a beat-up old clunker ($21.95 a day at **Rent a Wreck**). Most mid-range cars go for about $30 a day, but the rates do vary, so shop around. And be sure to check your own car insurance policy to see if it covers rental cars (most do). That'll save you big bucks over buying the rental agencies' outrageously priced insurance. You must have a major credit card to rent a car, though **Ladki International** (☎ *(702) 597-1100)* accepts cash deposits of about $400 in lieu of a card—after running a $15 non-refundable credit check.

Car rental companies

A Abbey	☎ *(702) 736-4988*
A Fairway	☎ *(702) 369-7216*
A Lloyd's	☎ *(702) 736-2663*
AA Auto Rentals	☎ *(702) 893-1333*
Airport	☎ *(702) 732-8282, (800) 221-4447*
Alamo	☎ *(702) 737-3111, (800) 327-9633*
Allstate	☎ *(702) 736-6147, (800) 634-6186*
Avis	☎ *(702) 261-5591, (800) 831-2847*
Brooks	☎ *(702) 735-3344, (800) 634-6721*
Budget	☎ *(702) 736-1212, (800) 527-0700*
Dollar	☎ *(702) 739-8408, (800) 826-0991*
Enterprise	☎ *(702) 795-8842, (800) 325-8007*
Fairway	☎ *(702) 369-8533*
Hertz	☎ *(702) 736-4900, (800) 654-3131*
Ladki	☎ *(702) 597-1100*
National	☎ *(702) 261-5391, (800) 227-7368*
Payless	☎ *(702) 798-0025, (800) 729-5377*
Practical	☎ *(702) 798-0025, (800) 233-1663*
Rebel	☎ *(702) 597-1707, (800) 346-4222*
Rent a Vette	☎ *(702) 736-8016, (800) 372-1981*
Rent a Wreck	☎ *(702) 474-0037, (800) 227-0292*
Sav-Mor	☎ *(702) 736-1234*
Sears	☎ *(702) 736-8066, (800) 527-0700*
Thrifty	☎ *(702) 736-4706, (800) 367-2277*
U.S.	☎ *(702) 798-6100, (800) 777-9377*
Value	☎ *(702) 733-8886, (800) 468-2583*

By Limousine

Impress your friends with your own chauffeur-driven stretch limo. The going rate is about $48 per hour, with a one-hour minimum.

Las Vegas Limousines

Bell Trans	☎ *(702) 385-5466*
Las Vegas Limousines	☎ *(702) 739-8414* *(only to and from the airport)*
Lucky 7	☎ *(702) 739-6177*

INTRODUCTION

Las Vegas Limousines

Presidential   ☎ *(702) 731-5577*

Parking

Traffic may be brutal at times, but parking is always easy. Most of the casino-hotels have major self-parking garages, and virtually all have free valet parking (just be sure to tip the guy a dollar or two when he fetches your car). The only problem with taking advantage of the valet is that you'll sometimes wait a long time to get your car back, especially after a big show. For some reason, very few hotels provide benches to sit on while you wait.

Climate

Las Vegas averages 294 days of sunshine per year, with an average yearly rainfall of just 4.19 inches. The city is smack in the middle of the desert, 2174 feet above sea level, and summer temperatures often top 100 degrees. It's a dry heat, but it's still brutal. Spring and fall are relatively short, with temperatures in the 70s, while the winter months usually have daytime temps in the 50s and 60s.

AVERAGE TEMPERATURES				
Month	Temperature	Humidity	Precipitation	Sun
	min./max	a.m./p.m.	inches	%
Jan.	33/56	41/30	.50	77
Feb.	37/67	36/26	.46	80
Mar.	42/68	30/22	.41	83
Apr.	49/77	22/15	.22	87
May	59/87	19/13	.22	88
June	68/98	15/10	.09	92
July	75/104	19/15	.45	87
Aug.	73/101	14/18	.54	88
Sept.	65/94	23/17	.32	91
Oct.	53/81	25/19	.25	87
Nov.	41/66	33/27	.43	80
Dec.	33/57	41/33	.32	77

What to Wear

Casual clothes go just about anywhere except for the gourmet restaurants—even there you'll often get away with "dressy casual" duds (no jeans or T-shirts). Sadly, the old tradition of puttin' on the ritz at night has given way to denim and running shoes, but it's still fun to dress up and I recommend covering yourself in sequins—the more outrageous the better—at least one night.

Winter nights are quite cool, so bring a jacket.

Media

Las Vegas has two daily newspapers, the *Sun* and the *Review-Journal;* the latter is the better. There are also several weeklies and a ream of free magazines published for tourists that are well worth picking up; many have discount and two-for-one coupons. Of these, I like *Today in Las Vegas* and *Tour Guide of Las Vegas* the best; they're both crammed with information on shows, restaurants and attractions. Keep in mind, though, that these giveaways rely heavily on their advertisers, so they describe everything as the biggest, the brightest, the best. Seldom is heard a discouraging word—and the money keeps flowing all day.

For a REAL look at the politics and intrigue behind the tables, subscribe to Phil Hevener's *Gaming Hotline (P.O. Box 81645, Las Vegas, NV 89180)*, a bi-weekly newsletter that details the latest developments in the ever-changing industry. It ain't cheap— $350 a year or $195 for six months—but it is the last word in Las Vegas. Hevener also publishes the more consumer-oriented *Las Vegas Style (5087 S. Arville, Las Vegas, NV 89118; ☎ (800) 897-1691 or (702) 871-8202)*, a monthly magazine chock-full of articles with an insider's perspective. Subscriptions are $28 per year.

FM Radio Stations		
Name	**Freq.**	**Format**
KCEP	88.1	Contemporary
KNPR	89.5	National Public Radio (news and classical)
KILA	90.5	Christian
KUNV	91.5	Jazz, Alternative
KOMP	92.3	Album-oriented Rock
KBGO	93.1	Oldies
KMXB	94.1	Contemporary
KDVC	94.3	Traffic/weather
KWNR	95.5	Country
KKLZ	96.3	Classic Rock
KXPT	97.1	Alternative
KLUC	98.5	Top 40
HWHY	98/99	Contemporary
KMZQ	100.5	Contemporary
KFM	102	Country
KEDG	103.5	Alternative
KJUL	104.3	Nostalgia
KVBC	105.1	News & Talk

FM Radio Stations

Name	Freq.	Format
KOOL	105.5	Oldies
KDVQ	105.7	Traffic/weather
KSNE	106.5	Contemporary
KXTE	107.5	Howard Stern & Alternative

AM Radio Stations

Name	Freq.	Format
KDWN	720	News, Sports, Talk
KXNT	840	News, Sports, Talk
KORK	920	Big Band
KNEWS	970	News
KKVV	1060	Christian Talk
KLAV	1230	Talk
KDOL	1280	Spanish
KRLV	1340	Talk, Sports
KENO	1460	Sports Talk

Major Network TV Stations

Name	Affiliate	Channel
KVBC	NBC	3
KVVU	Fox	5
KLAS	CBS	8
KLVX	PBS	10
KTNV	ABC	13

Major Cable TV Stations

Name	Channel
USA	16
ESPN	19
CNN	20
Disney	28
A & E	32
Showtime	51
CMAX	53
HBO 1	54

Tips on Tipping

The definition of TIPS means "to ensure prompt service," but nowadays tipping is virtually mandatory in many situations. Las Vegas is no exception, and everyone accepts tips happily.

Tip Chart	
Bartenders	*$1-2 per round, even when the drink is free.*
Bellmen:	*$1-2 per bag.*
Change Persons:	*Grease their palms with at least $5 and they may steer you to a hot machine. If it hits, fork over 10 percent of the jackpot for the good advice.*
Cocktail Waitresses:	*At least $1 each time she brings you a drink, whether or not it's free.*
Dealers:	*This is completely optional, but a good dealer has earned a tip. Most people place a bet for them (half or equal to their own bet) on occasion, or toss them a chip when leaving the table.*
Poker Dealers:	*Each time you win a pot, tip $1 or so.*
Doormen:	*$1-2 a bag when checking into the hotel; $1 if he hails you a cab.*
Keno Runners:	*A dollar or so every few games played; more if you're winning.*
Limo Drivers:	*5-20 percent of the total fare.*
Maids:	*$1-2 per day. At least $1 each time you order up an iron or extra towels.*
Masseurs:	*15-20 percent.*
Pool Attendants:	*$1-2 if he or she gets you a lounge chair.*
Room Service:	*Some add the gratuity to the bill, others don't, so be sure to ask. 15-20 percent is the average.*
Showroom Maître d':	*Most shows now assign seats, so there's no need to tip unless you want something better. In that case, slip him at least $10 and as high as $50 or $100.*
Skycaps:	*$1-2 per bag.*
Taxi Drivers:	*When the fare is under $10, tip $1 and change. Over $10, give 15 percent.*
Tour Guides:	*$1 or $2 at the end of the trip.*
Valet Parking:	*$1-2.*
Wait Staff:	*15-20 percent.*

LOCAL LINGO	
Toke:	*A tip.*
Comp:	*Free or complimentary.*
RFB Comp:	*Free room, food and beverage.*

LOCAL LINGO	
In Red:	A comped person's name usually appears in red ink on a maitre d's reservation chart.
Marker:	An IOU owed the casino by a gambler playing on credit.
Shooter:	The person rolling the dice at craps.
Shoe:	The container from which cards are dealt at the tables.
Stickman:	The dealer who moves the dice around on a craps table with a hook-shaped stick.
Drop Box:	A locked box on the gaming tables into which the dealers deposit paper money.
Boxman:	The craps dealer who sits over the drop box and supervises bets and payoffs.
Pit Boss:	The casino boss who oversees table dealers.
Eye in the Sky:	That decorative glass on the walls and ceiling is actually one-way mirrors. You're being watched and videotaped at all times.
Whale:	An ultrahigh roller.

The People

The city of Las Vegas is home to 401,703 souls, while surrounding Clark County totals 1.1 million—and the numbers keep growing. Between 4000 and 6000 people move into Clark County monthly, and it's expected that the county will hit two million residents within 15 years. Some 40 percent come from California. It's a young town: the median age is just 33.1 years and nearly 25 percent of the population is under 18, while just 10.5 percent are over 65. The median household income is a healthy $30,986. Most folks work in the tourism and service industry, followed by the military at Nellis Air Force Base and the Nevada Test Site. Unemployment is about 5.3 percent.

Three-quarters of the county's population are of European descent, followed by Hispanics (11.2 percent), African- and Asian-Americans (9.3 percent), Pacific Islanders (7 percent) and Native Americans (1 percent). The city has the 11th largest school district in the country, with 184 primary and secondary schools and more than 156,000 students. Nevada residents pay the third-lowest state taxes in the U.S. and no state income tax.

Money magazine rates Las Vegas 43rd in the top 300 "best places to live in America," based on criteria including crime rate, clean water and air, good health care, strong government and low taxes.

Visitors interested in Las Vegas' ethnic groups can contact one of the following:

Native Americans

Las Vegas Paiute Tribe	☎ *(702) 386-3926*
Las Vegas Indian Center	☎ *(702) 647-5842*

Hispanics

Latin Chamber of Commerce	☎ *(702) 385-7367*
NV Assn. of Latin Americans	☎ *(702) 382-6252*
El Mundo	☎ *(702) 649-8553*

African-Americans

NV Black Chamber of Commerce	☎ *(702) 648-6222*
Black Business Directory	☎ *(702) 646-4223,* ☎ *(800) 425-4223*
NAACP	☎ *(702) 646-1662*

Asians

Asian Chamber of Commerce	☎ *(702) 367-4810*
Filipino American Federation	☎ *(702) 383-6933*
Thailand Nevada Assn.	☎ *(702) 735-0005*
Japanese American Club	☎ *(702) 382-4443*
Las Vegas Korean Assn.	☎ *(702) 252-4750*

Visitors

Some 30 million people visited Las Vegas in 1996, a 2.2 percent increase over 1995. Though the city added 10 percent more rooms, occupancy averaged 90.4 percent, a 2.4 percent gain over the previous year.

Las Vegas is the seventh most popular destination for foreign travelers visiting the United States, beating out Washington D.C., Chicago and Boston.

Convention Facilities

Conventions are big business in Las Vegas. More than 3.3 million people come to town for 2400 conventions each year. The biggest by far is COMDEX, an annual computer show that attracts some 190,000 delegates each November.

With 1.3 million square feet of exhibit space, the Las Vegas Convention Center is America's largest single-level convention facility. It was originally built in 1959 and had a neat flying saucer-like rotunda, but that was razed a few years ago for today's ultramodern facility. It's located just a few blocks off the Strip, next to the Las Vegas Hilton.

Groups also meet near downtown at Cashman Field Center, which has 98,000 square feet of exhibit space, a 1950-seat auditorium and a 10,000-seat baseball stadium. And virtually every large casino-hotel has tons of meeting space.

Business and fraternal groups that met for years in Las Vegas are finding it harder to get large blocks of rooms. As more families pour into town for a cheap vacation, the casinos want customers that spend their free time at the tables, not in the theme parks.

Churches

The city has more than 500 churches and synagogues representing more than 40 faiths. Las Vegas used to have the distinction of having more churches per capita than anywhere else in the world, but that title may not fit now that the population has grown so rapidly.

Liquor

Not surprisingly, the city has some of the most liberal liquor laws in the country. There are no closing hours for liquor sales or consumption, and the casinos supply gamblers with all the free drinks they can gulp. The legal drinking age is 21.

Hospitals

Las Vegas has several hospitals. As in other cities, call 911 in emergencies. For non-emergencies, call the **Clark County Medical Society** (☎ *702-739-9989*) for a doctor referral and the **Clark County Dental Society** (☎ *702-435-7767*) for a dentist.

Major Hospitals

Sunrise Hospital and Medical Center
> *3186 South Maryland Parkway*
> ☎ *(702) 731-8000*

Desert Springs Hospital
> *2075 East Flamingo Road*
> ☎ *(702) 733-8800*
> 24-hour emergency room

Meadows Hospital
> *2075 East Flamingo Road*
> ☎ *(702) 735-2537*

Montevista Hospital
> *5900 West Rochelle Avenue*
> ☎ *(702) 364-1111*

Valley Hospital Medical Center
> *620 Shadow Lane*
> ☎ *(702) 388-4000*
> 24-hour emergency room

University Medical Center
> *1800 West Charleston Blvd.*
> ☎ *(702) 383-2000*
> 24-hour emergency room

Time Zone

Las Vegas is on Pacific time; if it's noon in New York, it's 9 a.m. in Nevada.

Area Code

The area code for Nevada is 702.

Establishing Credit

If you have a big bankroll (say, $10,000) but don't want to carry that much cash, see the casino credit manager and fill out an application. He'll check your bank account to verify you really have the dough to gamble with. If so, you sign markers (IOUs) with the pit boss each time you get money.

Be warned, though, that under law the casino must report all cash transactions that exceed $10,000 in each 24-hour period. You'll have to supply your name, address and driver's license or passport each time you get more than $10,000. Known as Reg 6, this U.S. Department of Treasury law makes casino owners see red and has driven many a high roller off shore.

Getting Comped

Each year, the casinos give out more than a half-billion dollars worth of comps. Freebies are not just for the high rollers; anyone who gambles can get their share. Slot players should always join the slot clubs offered by virtually every casino; credit points good for discounts and free meals add up fast, and some clubs, like the Tropicana, even give cash back.

The first thing to do is ask the pit boss to rate you. He'll keep track of how much your bets average and how long and quickly you play. Generally you need to put in at least four hours a day to qualify for anything.

If you're placing $5 and $10 bets at the tables, you can score low-level comps like breakfast in the coffee shop and drinks at the bar. Betting $10-$25 per hand gets a coffee shop dinner, buffet and a casino rate on your room (generally half off the rack or published rate).

Betting $25 to $100 per hand? Expect tickets to the show, comps to the gourmet restaurant and a free room.

You'll need a bankroll of at least $10,000 and bets of at least $100 per hand for the coveted RFB treatment, which means free room, food and beverages, as well as good tickets to the show and deferential treatment by the pit boss.

The highest of rollers have casino credit lines of more than $1 million. The last thing these people need are freebies, but they're among the most demanding when it comes to getting their egos stroked. The casinos happily oblige with gigantic suites, personal limos, expensive gifts and generally the best of everything. Who says money can't buy happiness?

Activities for Nongamblers

Don't despair nongamblers, there is plenty to do in Las Vegas without risking a dime.

Major Non-Casino Properties

Alexis Park

All accommodations are in plush suites, and there's even tennis courts, a putting green and great pool at this upscale spot.

St. Tropez

Another all-suite property, this one has a 24-hour pool and a Strip shuttle.

Residence Inn by Marriott

Located right across from the Convention Center, so a good choice for travelers attending a show.

Quality Inn Sunrise Suites

A free shuttle ferries you over to the Strip or Convention Center.

Shop Till You Drop

If you're staying in a major hotel, it is sure to have a shopping mall. Other choices:

Forum Shops at Caesars

You'll have to exit through the casino, but it's worth the hassle to explore this elegant, Roman-themed mall.

Fashion Show Mall

Not as glitzy as the above, but very pleasant, with lots of good dining choices.

Belz Factory Outlet

Not only are you saving money by not gambling, you'll really make a killing at these brand-name outlet shops.

Las Vegas Factory Outlets

The same as above, but this one is open air.

(For more, see page 165.)

Visit a Museum

Yes, they do exist in Las Vegas (and we're not just talking about the Guinness World of Records Museum).

King Tut's Tomb (Luxor)

A remarkable recreation of the boy king's final resting place, exactly as it was rediscovered in 1922.

Las Vegas Art Museum

Western art and works by locals are showcased at this fine gallery.

Las Vegas Natural History Museum

An easy place to while away a few hours among the interesting exhibits on wildlife and the desert.

Clark County Heritage Museum

The history of the area, pre- and post-gaming, is well covered.

Debbie Reynolds' Movie Museum

The actress' vast collection of memorabilia is displayed throughout the casino and in a multimedia show.

Liberace Museum

You can't come to Las Vegas without experiencing some kitschkitsch-kitsch; you'll find all that and more at this giant tribute to the flamboyant entertainer.

(For more, see page 126.)

Get Out of Town!

A number of beautiful sites within an easy drive will give you new respect for Las Vegas.

Red Rock Canyon

Dramatic cliffs and pristine nature, just minutes from the Strip.

Mount Charleston

It's a whole other world up here among the fragrant pines and cool breezes.

Lake Mead

Rent a boat, drop a fishing line or just snooze on the beach at the nation's largest man-made lake.

River Rafting

The folks at Black Canyon River Raft tours will make your day with their ultra-relaxing, wonderfully scenic rafting trips.

Valley of Fire

This state park is renowned for its red sandstone rock formations and Indian petroglyphs.

Floyd Lamb State Park

Not on the grand scale of Valley of Fire, but a scenic desert oasis just 20 minutes from the Strip.

(For more, see page 183.)

The Excalibur is very family friendly.

Activities for Kids

These days, Las Vegas is a bit of a paradox. The city has added a ton of attractions designed to appeal to mom, dad and the kids, yet it still is predominantly a playground for adults. Many of the lavish production shows tame their act down a bit for the 7:30 edition, billed for families, but often the humor, costumes and dancing are still too risqué for many children (the Riviera's "Splash" comes to mind). Shows that work well for kids, such as MGM's "EFX" and Mirage's "Siegfried and Roy"), are so expensive that the average family will be hard-pressed to come up with the cash for just 90 minutes of entertainment.

To top it off, one of the biggest problems for hapless parents is trying to keep an eye on their kids among the crowds. Excalibur and Circus Circus were designed specifically for families, but are usually so crowded that parents will have a coronary keeping the kids in tow.

Now that we've covered all the negatives, the fact remains that Las Vegas can be a great destination for families, and a bargain to boot. Though rates are higher than ever, hotel rooms are still extremely reasonable compared to other resort destinations. Buffets are still a bargain, and the city constantly teems with free entertainment. Even the theme parks have free admission, and there's enough to do and see at MGM Grand Adventures for free that you won't have to shell out too many bucks for the rides—assuming you can keep the kids away from the overpriced souvenir stands.

Family-Friendly Production Shows

The following shows are especially recommended for families. For more details, see the extended listings in "The Shows" chapter.

King Arthur's Tournament (Excalibur)

What could be more kid-friendly than a raucous atmosphere that encourages yelling, screaming and bad table manners? Good for kids of all ages.

EFX (MGM Grand)

It's a steep ticket price, but those who can afford it will treat their kids (and themselves) to a highly imaginative and often astounding show. May be too scary for kids under five.

An Evening in Vienna (Excalibur)

Tickets are very reasonable for this afternoon show that showcases the beauty of white Lipizzaner stallions.

Jubilee! (Bally's)

This kitschy production show has enough oohs and ahhs to keep kids over 10 amused, though the occasional sexual content may make their parents squirm.

Legends in Concert (Imperial Palace)

Children into music should enjoy this high-energy celebrity impersonator show; leave those under 10 with a sitter.

Caesars Magical Empire (Caesars Palace)

Teens will love it, but don't bring your picky eaters—dinner, included in the high ticket price, is decidedly gourmet. Open only to those over age 12.

Siegfried & Roy (Mirage)

This overrated, over-the-top magic show still has its charms, and kids will be enthralled by the showy illusions and white tigers—if their parents can afford the steep price of admission.

Country Tonite (Aladdin)

Kids can be as rowdy as they want at this high-spirited, contagiously fun salute to country music.

Country Fever (Golden Nugget)

Children over 10 are welcome but pay full fare, though the $22.50 price is quite reasonable for the rollicking good time this show guarantees.

American Superstars (Stratosphere)

"Michael Jackson," "Madonna," "Gloria Estefan" and other talented impersonators put on a good, reasonably priced show that will appeal to kids who like music.

Lance Burton: Master Magician (Monte Carlo)

Burton's low-key charisma may be lost on younger tykes, but teenage girls will fall hopelessly in love.

Mystere (Treasure Island)

Kids over 10 will love this enchanting, surrealistic circus; those younger may not appreciate its beauty.

Free Things for Kids

Pirate Show (Treasure Island)

Come early for a good view of this nightly (weather permitting) live battle.

MGM Grand Adventures (MGM Grand)

There's a reasonable charge for the rides, but it's easy to spend lots of time just soaking up the atmosphere and street entertainment at this theme park.

Fremont Street Experience (downtown)

Before you tuck the little ones into bed, treat them to this dazzling light show.

Kidd Marshmallow Factory Tour (Henderson)

Tasty as well as educational, with free samples at the end.

White Tiger Habitat (Mirage)

One or two of Siegfried and Roy's rare white tigers are on constant display. There's also a cool aquarium in the hotel lobby and the erupting volcano out front.

Hotels to Keep Kids Happy

Excalibur

The Fantasy Faire area has tons of stuff to keep tykes busy, from games and rides to free entertainment.

Luxor

There's a high-tech amusement arcade and interactive rides on the attractions level.

MGM Grand

Beside the theme park, there's a large midway-style arcade.

Circus-Circus

All that's missing is the ocean at the boardwalk-themed attraction with Skee Ball and other games.

Event the tightest family needs time apart. That's when it's time to call a baby-sitter. Check with your hotel concierge, the Yellow Pages, or the following:

Baby-sitters

Various locations, Las Vegas.

The kids getting you down? Need to spend some quality time in the casino? These agencies can help: **Around the Clock Child Care** (☎ *365-1040*), **Cinderella Careskool** (☎ *732-0230*), **Grandma Thompson's Romp'n Play** (☎ *735-0176*), **Las Vegas Baby-sitting Service** (☎ *791-7045*), **Nanny's & Granny's** (☎ *364-4700*) and **Precious Commodities** (☎ *871-1191*). Most are cleared through the FBI, sheriff and health departments, and are insured and bonded—but be sure to ask. Rates vary.

Crime

Surprisingly enough in a city driven by cash and greed, Las Vegas does not have a major crime problem. The biggest threat to tourists are pickpockets, so you're best off carrying your money in your front pocket or in a fanny-pack on your waist, with the zipper in front. Never hang your purse off a chair; if you're shooting craps and want to place it on the floor, wrap the strap a few times around your ankle, or ask someone you trust to hold your bag while you play.

Pickpockets are especially troublesome on jammed city buses and around crowded attractions such as the pirate show at Treasure Island. In these situations, thieves often work in pairs—one bumps you, and while you're distracted, the other picks your pocket. Keep alert!

Tourists also get ripped off in sex scams, detailed in the chapter "Sex for Sale."

As with any large city, use common sense: don't flash large bills around; keep your money and valuables in your in-room safe or at the front desk; don't walk down dark streets late at night; never give out your room number; be wary of too-friendly strangers.

A Brief History

Las Vegas ("the meadows" in Spanish) was founded on May 5, 1905 and is today the largest American city founded in the 20th century. But use of the area dates back hundreds of years; the Paiute Indians lived here for centuries and Mexicans traveling on the Old Spanish Trail stopped in Las Vegas because of its natural springs and meadows in the 16th century.

In 1855, Mormon followers of Brigham Young tried to colonize Las Vegas, but crop failures caused the mission to fail.

The town first made its mark when it was chosen as a railroad crossroads in the late 1800s. But it wasn't until the 1930s that much happened. In 1931, the Nevada Legislature legalized gambling to finance public education, and that same year, construction began on Hoover Dam, which created more than 5000 jobs in the middle of the Great Depression. The legislature was busy that year: it also approved a six-week divorce law, making Nevada the only place to go for a quickie divorce.

The first casino-hotel opened in 1941, the El Rancho, followed in 1946 by the Flamingo, a grand affair built by Benjamin "Bugsy" Siegel that opened on Christmas Day to dismal failure. In retaliation, the mob rubbed him out—but they should have waited awhile, as the place soon became a huge hit. After World War II, development started in earnest.

Howard Hughes came to town in 1967 and threw enough money around to end up owning six casino-hotels, the airport and most of the land. That marked the beginning of the end of the mob era, and today Las Vegas is owned by deep-pocketed corporations instead of shifty gangsters—though the debate on mob influence still rages.

Today, Las Vegas is the fastest-growing city in America. The city proper is 84 square miles surrounded by Clark County, which at 7910 square miles, is about the size of Massachusetts.

Information

The **Las Vegas Convention & Visitors Authority** provides tourists with handy maps and brochures. Contact them at *3150 Paradise Road, Las Vegas, NV 89109*, or call ☎ *(702) 892-7575*. The fax number is *(702) 892-2824*.

The **Nevada Commission on Tourism** can help supply information on the surrounding area. They're at *Capital Complex, Carson City, NV 89104*; ☎ *(800) 638-2321*.

Insider's Tip

It's amazing how far a smile and a "thank you" will get you in Las Vegas. Most tourists are amazingly rude (probably because they're losing), and employees really respond to simple courtesy.

WHERE TO STAY

The glitter of Las Vegas lights up the desert night.

Las Vegas is basically divided into two areas: the Strip (Las Vegas Boulevard South) and downtown. Each has its own personality. Before we get into that, note that Las Vegas has occupancy rates in the high 90 percentile, with many weekends 100 percent sold out. (Every single room may not actually be occupied, but they always hold a large block for high-rollers.) Book early! If you're having a hard time getting a room, try one of these identical-sounding reservations agencies: **Las Vegas Tourist Bureau**, ☎ *(800) 522-9555;* and **Las Vegas Reservation Systems**, ☎ *(800) 233-5594.* They often have blocks of rooms even when the front desk is saying no room at the inn, and the service is free.

Two old-time casino-resorts came down in 1996, marking the end of an era. The Sands, which opened in 1952 and was known as "Queen of the Strip" and home of the Rat Pack, has been imploded to make way for a new 6000-room resort called the Venetian. The venerable Hacienda, opened in 1957, was also imploded to make way for the upcoming Four Seasons hotel.

WHERE TO STAY

A Note About Rates

Staying at a Las Vegas hotel is kind of like taking a flight—everyone is paying a different rate. Room rates change *continuously*. You could call at 10 a.m. and be quoted a rate of $60, call back at noon and be told $55 and call a third time and be charged $70. That's why the room rates quoted here show such a wide range.

It's well worth shopping around, especially on the weekdays. For a Tuesday in February, I was quoted $65 at Bourbon Street and $70 at Harrah's. Discouraged by these high rates and on a tight budget, I booked a room at the low-frills Center Strip Inn for $35. But just for the hell of it, I called Treasure Island, far superior to the three above, and got in for only $50.

Mega Resorts

With nine of the world's 10 largest hotels, Las Vegas is obviously under the assumption that bigger is always better. Since it seems the larger the property, the harder people fall for it, many folks think this is apparently true. The mega-resorts certainly offer a wealth of advantages: huge casinos, lots of dining choices, something happening at all hours and generally fanciful pools. But what comes with all these frills are their biggest downfall—nonstop crowds. If you're sharing a hotel with three to five thousand other guests, don't expect room service in a jiffy and be prepared to queue up forever at the front desk, restaurants and valet. If you're intent on getting tan, you'll have to hurry to the pool to snag a well-placed lounge chair before the hundreds of other sun worshippers beat you to it.

One last note: Be sure to take advantage of express checkout (where you leave a credit card imprint and they mail you a statement), or you'll wait hours for the privilege of checking out.

Casino-Hotels

The vast majority of accommodations in Las Vegas are in hotels with casinos on the first floor. They run the gamut from the highest of quality (Caesars, Desert Inn) to solid, middle-of-the-road value (Stardust, Flamingo Hilton, Imperial Palace) to tacky motel-style lodging (Casino Royale, Westward Ho). Unless noted, all have several restaurants, pools and 24-hour action in the casino.

All-Suite Hotels

The city's smattering of all-suite hotels attract mainly upper-level business executives who have to be in Las Vegas but would just as soon be in Boise. The atmosphere at these properties is generally sophisticated and low-key, with a notable absence of gambling. Alexis Park is by far the nicest, with the rates to match.

Motels

Some of the motels listed here are quite decent, offering clean and comfortable rooms at reasonable rates. However, it's often possible to score a room at a more deluxe property for virtually the same price.

Cheap Motels

Las Vegas' cheap motels are quickly becoming extinct. In 1995, the Desert Rose, which offered budget lodging on the Strip for some 40 years, became the latest to succumb to the fact that no-frills motels have become dinosaurs in this town of cartoon castles and pyramid-shaped resorts. Unless you really don't mind paper-thin walls, carpeting from the Truman administration and lumpy mattresses, there's no reason to stay in a motel when the casino-hotels offer such competitive rates, especially on weekdays.

RV Parks

Those who own recreational vehicles know that they're the cheapest way to travel. There are a number of RV parks where these happy campers can hook up their home-away-from-home and see the city sights. Several are connected to casino-hotels, giving patrons the best of both worlds.

The Strip: See It To Believe It

If it's your first trip to town, you'll probably be happiest on the Strip. This is where the pirates battle, the volcano erupts, one hotel looks like a cartoon castle and another the skyline of New York. All of the mega-resorts are located on the Strip, starting at the far south at the Luxor and running down a few miles to the Sahara. (Las Vegas Boulevard continues far north of the Sahara, right into downtown.) The biggest drawback to the Strip is that the hotels are all so huge that it's a real hike to get from one to another. Some places like Caesars and the Excalibur have people-movers to whisk you in—but you're on your own when it comes to getting out. The traffic is also horrendous and you're often better off walking, even far distances, rather than paying for a cab that's stuck in gridlock.

The intersection of Las Vegas Boulevard and Flamingo Road is known as the "Four Corners," and is a great place to stay, with Caesars, Bally's, Barbary Coast, the Mirage, Harrahs, Treasure Island, the Flamingo Hilton and other smaller casinos within a relatively easy walk. Another good cluster is farther south at the corner of Las Vegas Boulevard and Tropicana, home of the MGM Grand, Tropicana, New York-New York and Excalibur, with the Luxor a block away.

Those two popular areas have—finally!—been connected via an electric monorail that goes from the MGM Grand to Bally's.

It takes just four minutes for the mile-long trip, and it's free! It runs 24 hours. It's hoped that eventually, the downtown, Convention Center and airport will all be similarly linked.

Mega-Resorts

Excalibur Hotel   **$59–$250**   ★ ★ ★

3850 Las Vegas Boulevard, Las Vegas, 89119, *(800) 937-7777, (702) 597-7777, FAX: (702) 597-7009.*

Located at the southern strip, across from the Tropicana. Double: $59–$250.

This cartoon replica of a European castle often sacrifices quality to serve the vast hordes that fill its 4000-plus rooms and eat 20,000 meals a day in its seven theme restaurants. A great place for kids, provided their parents can keep track of them among the crowds, it has a Renaissance Faire atmosphere with jugglers, fools and "street" performers. There's tons going on at all hours, and most of it is geared toward families. The King Arthur's Tournament dinner show—in which you eat with your hands and cheer on live jousters—is an especially big hit with kids. The lower level has carnival and video games, roving performers and two fantastic "magic motion" theaters that take kids (of all ages) on a wild and wooly ride on a runaway train, out-of-control race car or giant Ferris wheel. Accommodations are just average and the two bare-bones pools barely handle all the splashing kids. On the plus side, the restaurants are all reasonably priced and the giant casino is quite pleasant. I especially like the video-poker bar set right in the middle of the casino, beneath a huge tree. Unless you're really into crowds, avoid this place like the plague during weekends and holidays—it'll seem like hours just to work your way through the casino to the pool. The Excalibur is one of the city's most popular hotels and it frequently sells out, so make your reservations early. And pity the poor staff, forced to wear some of the most absurd uniforms ever seen! A new people-mover connects Excalibur with its next-door neighbor, Luxor. Amenities: conference facilities. 4032 rooms. Credit cards: A, CB, DC, D, MC, V.

Las Vegas Hilton   **$95–$275**   ★ ★ ★ ★ ★

3000 Paradise Road, Las Vegas, 89109, *(800) 732-7117, (702) 732-5111, FAX: (702) 794-3611.*

Located adjacent to the Convention Center, near the Strip. Double: $95–$275.

Located next to the Convention Center and a 10-minute walk from the Strip, most guests at the Las Vegas Hilton are business travelers. The hotel also gets a fair share of high-rollers, especially since adding three suites—at the cost of $40 million—the largest of which totals a whopping 15,000 square feet. All have their own pool, butler, workout room and media center. Guest rooms for the rest of us peons range from very nice to very elegant and all have views. The Hilton is like a small city, very self-contained with 12 restaurants, a big showroom and lounge, tons of convention space, six tennis courts and a nine-hole putting green. The hotel recently acquired a championship golf course to add to its already impressive facilities. When it's time for dinner, you'll be overwhelmed with choices. I especially love the serene Japanese garden in Benihana Village, but if you don't have a

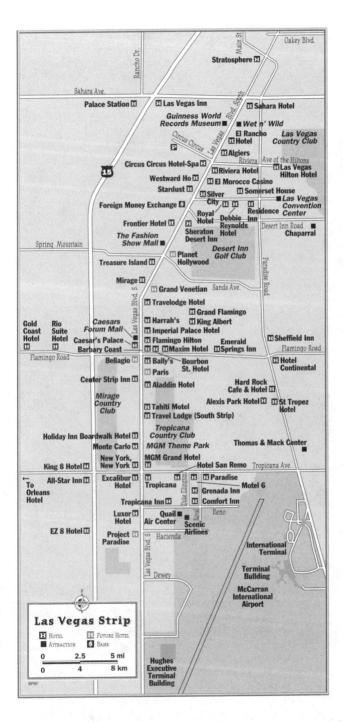

Oakey Blvd.

Rancho Dr.

Main St

Stratosphere H

Sahara Ave.

Palace Station H

H **Las Vegas Inn**

H **Sahara Hotel**

Las Vegas Blvd South

Guinness World Records Museum ■

■ **Wet n' Wild**

Circus Circus

El Rancho H **Hotel**

Las Vegas Country Club

P

H **Algiers**

Riviera *Ave of the Hiltons*

Circus Circus Hotel-Spa H

H **Riviera Hotel**

H **Las Vegas Hilton Hotel**

15

Westward Ho H

H **El Morocco Casino**

Stardust H

H **Silver City**

H **Somerset House**

■ *Las Vegas Convention Center*

Foreign Money Exchange $

H H H **Residence Inn**

Royal Hotel H

Debbie Reynolds Hotel

Desert Inn Road ■ **Chaparral**

Frontier Hotel H

Sheraton Desert Inn H

The Fashion Show Mall ■

Desert Inn Golf Club

Spring Mountain

Treasure Island H

H **Planet Hollywood**

Paradise Road

Mirage H

H **Grand Venetian** *Sands Ave.*

H **Travelodge Hotel**

Gold Coast Hotel H

Rio Suite Hotel H

H **Grand Flamingo**

Caesars Forum Mall

H **Harrah's**

H **King Albert**

Caesar's Palace ■

H **Imperial Palace Hotel**

Barbary Coast ■

H **Flamingo Hilton**

Emerald Springs Inn

H **Sheffield Inn**

Flamingo Road

Flamingo Road

Bellagio H

H H **Maxim Hotel**

Center Strip Inn H

H **Bally's**

Bourbon St. Hotel

H **Hotel Continental**

H **Paris**

Mirage Country Club

H **Aladdin Hotel**

Hard Rock Cafe & Hotel H

H **Tahiti Motel**

Alexis Park Hotel H

H **St Tropez Hotel**

H **Travel Lodge (South Strip)**

Holiday Inn Boardwalk Hotel H

Tropicana Country Club

Monte Carlo H

MGM Theme Park

Thomas & Mack Center ■

King 8 Hotel H

New York, New York H

MGM Grand Hotel H

Hotel San Remo *Tropicana Ave.*

← To Orleans Hotel

All-Star Inn H

Excalibur Hotel H

H **Tropicana**

Duke Ellington

H ■ **Paradise**

Motel 6

H **Grenada Inn**

Tropicana Inn H

H **Comfort Inn**

Koval

Reno

Luxor Hotel H

Quail Air Center ■

EZ 8 Hotel H

Project Paradise

Scenic Airlines

Las Vegas Blvd. S.

Hacienda

International Terminal

Terminal Building

Dewey

McCarran International Airport

N

Las Vegas Strip

H HOTEL   H FUTURE HOTEL

■ ATTRACTION $ BANK

0   2.5   5 mi

0   4   8 km

Hughes Executive Terminal Building

©FWI

yen for Asian food, American, Italian, English, French and Mexican eateries await, among others. The prices in the restaurants are generally higher than other casino-hotels, maybe because most guests are on expense accounts. With its shimmering glass chandeliers and plush seats for slots players, the casino is one of the nicest and most elegant in town, as is the Hilton's nightclub with its classy art deco touches. Because it is well off the Strip, the casino stays quiet. The pool area, perched on an eight-acre deck on the third floor, is nice but rather stark. The nearby full-service health club is simply fabulous. In fact, most everything is fabulous at this very upscale enclave—though its sheer size may put off some. Elvis fans will appreciate the shrine to the King just off the front entrance and should ride in elevator number one, which goes to floors 15-30. It has a little door built specifically so he could travel directly from his suite to the showroom without getting mobbed by screaming fans. (Elvis had an eight-year exclusive run at the hotel, back when it was called the International, with 837 consecutive sold-out shows.) Though the hotel has long eschewed themes, it has added a "Star Trek" attraction that offers "the ultimate simulated ride surpassing anything of its time" (see "Attractions") and a futuristic-themed casino adjacent. Amenities: conference facilities. 3174 rooms. Credit cards: A, CB, DC, D, MC, V.

Pyramid power presides over the Luxor's Egyptian splendor.

Luxor   **$69–$159**   ★★★★

3900 Las Vegas Boulevard South, Las Vegas, 89119, ☎ (800) 288-1000, (702) 262-4000, FAX: (702) 597-7455.
Located next to the Excalibur. Double: $69–$159.

Just when it seemed Las Vegas could not get more outlandish, along came the Luxor, a giant black pyramid with a somewhat menacing look. It opened in 1993 and had its problems—the inside of the casino-hotel did not come close to matching its outside grandeur—so the property bravely took a big swallow and spent millions redesigning. The results are fabulous, and those who may have been turned off by Luxor in the past should give it a second look. The earlier design left those entering the casino stuck between floors, having to decide whether to go up or down; the redo has opened the area up, luring patrons straight into the casino through a life-sized replica of the

Temple of Ramses II. The overall look is open and airy, though the casino still suffers from relatively low ceilings. The lobby area is also much improved; there's a great new casino lounge called Nefertiti's, and the new Oasis Spa, a 12,000-square-foot plush facility for exercise and treatments. Guestrooms are large (465 square feet for standards, and up to 1100 square feet for Jacuzzi suites) and situated around the perimeter of the pyramid, overlooking the atrium. (Unfortunately, a few unhappy gamblers have taken a swan dive off the top.) There are also the new rooms in the new "ziggurat"-shaped 22-story towers, which brings Luxor's room count to 4427, making it the second-largest hotel in the country (after MGM Grand). The large casino is nice and enhanced with Egyptian touches, but it's the upper attractions level that makes Luxor worth a visit, especially if you're traveling with kids. Features include the "In Search of the Obelisk" interactive trilogy, a new IMAX theater, a high-speed arcade and the excellent King Tut museum (relocated from the lower level). The pool is adequate but rather plain. With its eight restaurants and moving walkway that connects it to the Excalibur, it's quite possible to stay here and never venture outside. 4427 rooms. Credit cards: A, CB, DC, D, MC, V.

The world's largest hotel, the MGM Grand, offers a theme park and a casino the size of four football fields.

MGM Grand Hotel Casino   **$69–$259**   ★ ★ ★ ★

3900 Las Vegas Boulevard South, Las Vegas, 89109, ☎ *(800) 929-1112, (702) 894-7111, FAX: (702) 891-1112.*   ❙❙❙❙

Located across from the Tropicana and Excalibur. Double: $69–$259.

"Grand" is indeed the operative word at this hotel, the world's largest with 5000 rooms. In fact, you'll get sick of the word, as everyone keeps ordering you to "have a grand day." (The staff is overwhelmingly cheerful.) Everything is on a huge scale and it's all quite impressive, but rather annoying if you're staying here—it's just TOO big. Count on spending lots of time wandering around lost among the throng of fellow guests and curiosity seekers, and if you're trying to find someone, forget about it. MGM has undergone some changes since opening in late 1993. A 30-month, $250-million master plan (underway at press time) is changing the overall theme to the "City of Entertainment." The most noticeable change is the redesign of Emerald City. Now it's known as Studio Walk and aims to recreate a Hollywood sound stage. That giant lion out front guarding the entrance at Las Vegas Boulevard and Tropicana is also set to be replaced. Guestrooms are nice but rather standard; like most of the competition, money is poured into the public areas, not the rooms. Except, that is, for the three presidential mega-suites for mega-rich high rollers and entertainers starring in the showroom. Each is 6040 square feet and has four master bedrooms, 21 phones (including one in the private elevator), Chanel No. 5 toiletries, a kitchen with a private chef who cooks meals to order, a bartender to whip up martinis, and nearly every other token of decadent living you can imagine. The 10 restaurants run the gamut from Wolfgang Puck's Cafe to the new Brown Derby; there's also a fast-food court and tons of lounges and boutiques. Sporting facilities include a large and very nice pool, a full-service health club and four tennis courts. Out back is the much-ballyhooed theme park, a great place to while away the hours with about a dozen major rides, stage shows and street performances (see "Attractions" for details). There's also a supervised Youth Center and a carnival-style arcade to keep kids amused, but their harried parents will have a hard time keeping an eye on the tykes among the ever-present crowds. My advice: Come to look, but stay elsewhere—unless, of course, you're rich and famous enough to score a presidential suite. Amenities: conference facilities. 5005 rooms. Credit cards: A, CB, DC, D, MC, V.

The Mirage's amazing volcano erupts every 30 minutes, stopping traffic on Las Vegas Boulevard.

Mirage   **$79–$380**   ★ ★ ★ ★ ★

3400 Las Vegas Boulevard South, Las Vegas, 89109, ☎ (800) 456-4564, (702) 791-7111, FAX: (702) 791-7446.

Located between Caesars and Treasure Island. Double: $79–$380.

This is the most elaborate resort in Las Vegas, with an indoor rainforest and jungle, tigers, sharks and dolphins, and, most extraordinarily, a "volcano" that erupts every 30 minutes, stopping traffic on Las Vegas Boulevard. It is owned by Steve Wynn, the man with the golden touch whose holdings also include the Golden Nugget and Treasure Island. Whatever Wynn does, he does right—and the Mirage is certainly no exception. The outside is dominated by palm trees, fountains and that much-loved volcano. Inside is a mini rainforest, a huge tank that houses sharks and other fishes, a habitat that displays the white tigers used in the over-hyped Sigfried and Roy show, and a huge, crowded casino. Other facilities include nine restaurants, an elegant health club and an off-site championship golf course. (Steve Wynn also owns his own golf course, considered the most beautiful in town, but it's only open to the highest of rollers invited personally by the man himself.) Guest rooms were recently redone to the tune of $54 million, wisely changed from a tropical, almost blinding decor to elegant, subdued and expensive furnishings. The suites—which start at $400—are quite nice, too. One of the Mirage's best assets is its pool, the best in town even if it is a rip-off of the Tropicana's. It's simply enormous, with a rocky and palm-studded island in the center, an area for lap swimmers, small water slides and whirlpools, all beautifully landscaped and enhanced by the sound of rushing water from the several falls. You have to show your room key just to walk around the pool—that's how elaborate it is. If you're really into spending money or impressing your date, rent one of the pretty blue canvas pool-side cabanas, which cost $85 per day and come with cable TV, telephone, rafts, a newspaper and snacks. Behind all that, and only accessible after paying a fee, is the dolphin habitat, which (to the dismay of animal rights advocates) houses seven Atlantic bottleneck dolphins and the new "Secret Garden." On the plus side, the creatures were gleaned from captivity, not the wild, and at least they're spared jumping through hoops or performing in any way. Still, it makes you worry that the next mega-resort will insist on live elephants for attention. The Mirage isn't cheap, and neither is its casino; most table limits are pretty high, so if you're on a budget, stay and gamble elsewhere. But don't miss the volcano, which "erupts" each 30 minutes from dusk to midnight. Amenities: conference facilities. 3049 rooms. Credit cards: A, CB, DC, D, MC, V.

Monte Carlo $60–$200   ★★★★

3770 Las Vegas Boulevard South, Las Vegas, ☎ (800) 311-8999, (702) 736-6000, FAX: (702) 730-7275.

Located on the Strip, next to New York-New York. Double: $60–$200.
The Monte Carlo added a touch of elegance to the Strip when it opened in June 1996. Rather than the hokey themes that are all the rage, this resort, owned by the Circus Circus team, strives for a Monaco feel (at more affordable prices); its design is based on the famous Place du Casino. There's lots of marble, arches, chandeliered domes, ornate fountains and stained-glass faux skylights, all giving the place an upscale feel. Guest rooms have marble and granite finishes, brass fixtures and turn-of-the-century decor. The lushly landscaped pool area is great, with a misting system, waterfalls, a children's pool, a wave pool and the Easy Rider water ride, which duplicates a slow-moving river. The grounds also include four lighted tennis courts and a health spa and exercise room. The six restaurants include a micro-brewery. Magician Lance Burton performs nightly in the plush show-room. Those into outlandish themes may not appreciate the understated Monte Carlo. 3002 rooms. Credit cards: A, DC, D, MC, V.

New York-New York　　　$89–$129　　　★★★★

3155 West Harmon Avenue, Las Vegas, ☎ *(800) 693-6763, (702) 740-6969, FAX: (702) 740-6510.*

Located on the Strip, across from the MGM Grand. Double: $89–$129.

Just opened in early 1997, New York-New York is a great addition to Las Vegas' already remarkable skyline. Designed to resemble its namesake, the property consists of 12 hotel towers that are about a third the size of the actual Manhattan architecture they mimic. The tallest tower replicates the Empire State Building, and there's also a 150-foot-high Statue of Liberty, a 300-foot-long replica of the Brooklyn Bridge and other New York landmarks such as the Chrysler Building and the Soldiers & Sailors Monument. Guest rooms have 63 different decor themes. It's really impressive! Looping throughout the entire facade is the Manhattan Express, a heart-stopping roller coaster (see "Attractions"). The fun continues inside, with the giant casino themed into various areas of Manhattan, including Wall Street, Central Park, Park Avenue and Times Square. The food court, designed to recall Little Italy, is wonderfully atmospheric with its authentic store fronts, brownstone buildings, fire escapes, balconies and little touches like laundry lines and spray-painted graffiti. Though the casino is nearly the size of two football fields, excellent signage makes getting around easy—a real plus. It's all quite something to see, but realize everyone else wants to see it too, so the crowds can be overwhelming (another authentic slice of the Big Apple). For recreation, there's a health spa and fitness center and a rather disappointing outdoor pool—not a great place to relax, since the roller coaster goes screaming by right overhead. The Coney Island Emporium has family attractions such as midway-style games, bumper cars, high-tech video games and a fiber-optic light show. Start spreading the news: This $640-million property, a joint venture of MGM Grand and Primadonna Resorts, is a real winner. 2035 rooms. Credit cards: A, D, MC, V.

Stratosphere　　　$39–$229　　　★★★★

2000 Las Vegas Boulevard South, Las Vegas, ☎ *(800) 998-6937, (702) 380-7777, FAX: (702) 383-4755.*

Located on the northern Strip. Double: $39–$229.

The Stratosphere, which replaced the old kooky Vegas World when it opened in April 1996, is the tallest building west of the Mississippi; you'll see it looming 1149 feet in the air, dwarfing the rest of the hotels. It's a pretty cool place, and a ride to the top (see "Attractions") is an absolute must for the sweeping, 360-degree views; waits of an hour are not uncommon, especially at night. A dinner in the revolving gourmet restaurant, Top of the World, on the 106th floor, is highly recommended. To get to the tower you pass, naturally, through the large casino and then a decent shopping mall with prices a lot more reasonable than most hotel outlets. The casino is typical looking and very busy; it's hard to get change to play the slots—many of which promise 98 to 100 percent returns. There's a small pool on the 24th floor, with a bigger and better one possibly on the way, though that's uncertain, as the property was in Chapter 11 bankruptcy at press time. Guest rooms are standard but adequate. 1500 rooms. Credit cards: A, D, MC, V.

The pirate battles at Treasure Island attract gawkers in droves.

Treasure Island   **$59–$249**   ★ ★ ★ ★ ★

3300 Las Vegas Boulevard South, Las Vegas, 89109, ☎ *(800) 944-7444, (702) 894-7111, FAX: (702) 894-7414.*

Located at the heart of the Strip, next to the Mirage. Double: $59–$249.
The official name is Treasure Island at the Mirage, but the two are really completely separate properties. Since its opening in 1993, Treasure Island has fast become one of my favorite hotels·in Las Vegas. I love the facade, designed to resemble a 17th-century Caribbean village with lots of palm trees, fountains and lagoons. The big attraction here is the live sea battles out front on "Buccaneer Bay" in which crafty pirates sink a huge British frigate, much to the crowd's delight. (Come early or you'll never catch even a glimpse of this free show; see "Attractions" for details.) It's fun inside, too, with the pirate theme carried throughout the large casino and public areas. Guest rooms are quite attractive; the best ones give you a bird's-eye view of the pirate show, so request that when you check in. There's a large range of restaurants from gourmet to surprisingly affordable (and good) Mexican fast food, lots of shopping, a full health club with spa facilities, two wedding chapels and a quite decent pool with a neat waterslide. The Treasure Island has a really good feel to it; the dealers and bartenders are very friendly and seem to take a lot of pride in their establishment. The small Battle Bar is a great place to sit and play video poker; adjacent is a cozy and intimate piano lounge, where you can catch a glimpse of the pirate battle through the windows. On the other side of the casino, the huge Doubloon Saloon draws lots of locals with its great bands and D.J. dancing. There's little not to like here, save the crowds who pour in after the pirates are done battling. Ahoy! Amenities: conference facilities. 2900 rooms. Credit cards: A, CB, DC, D, MC, V.

Casino-Hotels

Aladdin Hotel & Casino   **$45–$195**   ★ ★ ★

3667 Las Vegas Boulevard, Las Vegas, 89109, ☎ *(800) 634-3424, (702) 736-0111, FAX: (702) 734-3583.*
Located north of Bally's. Double: $45–$195.
This star-crossed property, where Elvis and Priscilla tied the knot, teeters in and out of bankruptcy. Part of the problem is the location;

Fielding **LAS VEGAS**

NEW YORK, NEW YORK
(EXTERIOR)

EMPIRE STATE BUILDING (1931) Dubbed "Most famous building in the world"

CENTURY APARTMENTS (1931) Twin towers define Central Park West skyline

LIBERTY PLAZA (1974) Nicknamed "Glass Box"

SHRIVELLED APPLE
Anchor buildings in condensed Las Vegas skyline are approximately one-third actual size .

LEVER HOUSE (1952) Ultramodern, minimalist style built by soap maker

55 WATER STREET (1971)

SEPARATE HOTELS?
Skyscraper facades: A Single hallway on each floor runs through the high rises connecting them. Art deco interior themes change to separate four main buildings: Chrysler, Empire State, Century and New Yorker.

NEW YORK CITY PUBLIC LIBRARY

PORTE COCHERE Passenger drop-off

SOLDIER'S AND SAILOR'S MONUMENT

ELLIS ISLAND

DETAILS, DETAILS, DETAILS
Statue of Liberty torch door handles. Geometric, streamlined Art Deco motif carried throughout design of casino and hotel.

NEW YORKER HOTEL
(1930)

MUNICIPAL BUILDING
(1914) Inspired Stalinist-era Moscow skyscrapers

CHRYSLER BUILDING
(1930) Stainless steel beauty snatched world's tallest structure title from Eiffel Tower

SEAGRAM BUILDING
(1958) Austere lines topped all records for cost-per-square foot

CBS BUILDING
(1965) Nicknamed "Black Rock"

CITY STREETSCAPE

MANHATTAN EXPRESS ROLLER COASTER
Barrel-rolling, loop-de-looping cyclone-esque coaster weaves around skyscrapers, dips into casino's Little Italy.
• Tallest point: **203 ft.**
• Biggest drop: **144 ft.**
• Top speed: **67 mph**
• Cost: **$5 per ride**
• Ride time: **4 minutes**

BROOKLYN BRIDGE
Vegas: 300 feet long, 50 feet tall, 4 months to build
NYC: 1595 feet long, 277 feet tall, 16 years to build

GRAND CENTRAL STATION

STATUE OF LIBERTY
Vegas: 150 feet, 150 tons
NYC: 305 feet, 225 tons

Las Vegas Blvd.

NEW YORK, NEW YORK

WHERE TO STAY

Cost: $460 million
Rooms: 2035
Opening: Jan. 3, 1997
Parking spaces: 4000
Owner: MGM Grand Inc./Primadonna Resorts

FRONT DESK
Bronze paneling with etched mirror

CONEY ISLAND ARCADE:
Carnival barkers man midway, hi-tech games

AMERICA

IL FORNAIO

EMPIRE BAR
Revolving "Big Apple" mirror ball

Gaming tables

HAMILTON'S

SHOPS

CENTRAL PARK
Casino: 84,000 square feet
Gaming tables: 71
Slot machines: 2400

New York Checkered Cab limousine

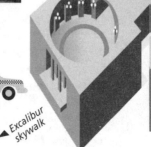

▲ Excalibur skywalk

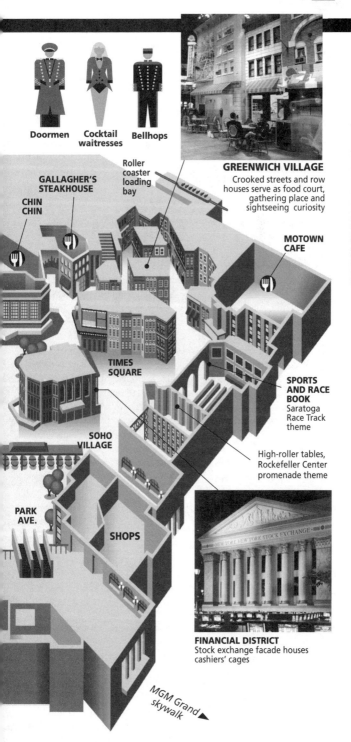

Doormen

Cocktail waitresses

Bellhops

GREENWICH VILLAGE
Crooked streets and row houses serve as food court, gathering place and sightseeing curiosity

Roller coaster loading bay

GALLAGHER'S STEAKHOUSE

CHIN CHIN

MOTOWN CAFE

TIMES SQUARE

SPORTS AND RACE BOOK
Saratoga Race Track theme

High-roller tables, Rockefeller Center promenade theme

SOHO VILLAGE

PARK AVE.

SHOPS

FINANCIAL DISTRICT
Stock exchange facade houses cashiers' cages

MGM Grand skywalk ▲

while the Aladdin is right on the Strip, a block north of Bally's, it's not surrounded by much, and most folks like to stay right in the heart of things. To help lure folks to the casino, the hotel is undergoing a $750-million, two-year renovation that will add a European-style casino. The current casino is of a good size and nicely decorated, and usually stays quieter than its Strip counterparts—a definite plus. The hotel's six restaurants, nightly lounge entertainment and long-running show, "Country Tonite," keep patrons busy. There are also three tennis courts and an indoor swimming pool for recreation. Accommodations are divided between rooms in the older garden section and the newer tower. Units in the tower are decorated in pastel colors, offer better views and are a much better bet. Amenities: conference facilities. 1100 rooms. Credit cards: A, CB, DC, D, MC, V.

Bally's $85–$225   ★ ★ ★ ★

3645 Las Vegas Boulevard South, Las Vegas, 89109, *(800) 634-3434, (702) 739-4111, FAX: (702) 739-4432.*

Located at the heart of the Strip. Double: $85–$225.

The location is great: just a tad off the Strip catty-corner from Caesars Palace and within walking distance of the Mirage and Treasure Island. This is also the spot where the new monorail from the MGM starts. Everything about Bally's is large and grand, including the lobby with its pianist at the entrance, its mural of celebrity faces behind the registration desk and its statues, chandeliers and velvet sitting areas. There's also a huge casino, two showrooms and a mall with 45 stores. Its Sunday brunch is considered the best in town. Guest rooms are luxurious with fine wood furnishings, sitting areas and large tile and marble combination baths. Rooms on the upper floors are more expensive but have better views. Guests can work out in the luxurious health spa (one of the city's best) swim laps in the Olympic-size pool and chase the ball on 10 all-weather tennis courts. Their long-running production show "Jubilee!" is Las Vegas' most elaborate. A lot of Bally's business comes from the meetings and convention market, so many guests are dressed in business garb as opposed to the jeans and T-shirts that dominate most places. This lends a touch of class to an already classy place. The only complaints here are about the long walks from rooms to elevators—but then, that's true for most every place in town. Amenities: conference facilities. 2813 rooms. Credit cards: A, CB, DC, D, MC, V.

Barbary Coast $75–$200   ★ ★ ★ ★

3595 Las Vegas Boulevard South, Las Vegas, 89109, *(800) 634-6755, (702) 737-7111, FAX: (702) 737-6304.*

Located at the heart of the Strip. Double: $75–$200.

This is a small, somewhat luxurious hotel located on the Strip next to the Flamingo Hilton. Boasting a 19th-century theme with dark wood and stained glass murals in the casino, the hotel caters primarily to high rollers. Some of the rooms have canopied, four-poster beds and lots of white lace, but are often hard to book as the management reserves them for regular customers. However, all accommodations are very nicely done with velvet furniture, a period desk and pretty Victorian-style touches. Its gourmet restaurant, Michael's, is a favorite of local power-mongers. Less-connected types can ride the escalator to the basement, where a McDonald's awaits.

The classy Barbary Coast is a great choice for those turned off by the mega-resorts, but who still want to be in the heart of things. The lack of a pool is a definite liability, though guests can take a free shuttle to another hotel and splash about there. 200 rooms. Credit cards: A, CB, DC, Y, MC, V.

Bourbon Street   **$40–$175**   ★ ★ ★

120 East Flamingo Road, Las Vegas, 89109, ☎ (800) 634-6956, (702) 737-7200, FAX: (702) 794-3490.
Located just off the Strip, across from Bally's. Double: $40–$175.
Because of its central location (just off the Strip behind the Barbary Coast and across from Bally's), this small hotel is a good choice for those who'd rather spend their money in the casino than on the room. The biggest drawback is the lack of a pool, although guests can swim at the nearby Maxim. The Victorian-themed casino is small and slightly dingy, but a very talented New Orleans jazz band helps liven things up considerably. The rooms are large and surprisingly pleasant; most can be had for about $85 on the weekends. Much more manageable than the mega-resorts (and cheaper than the similar Barbary Coast), but short on luxury. Amenities: private spas, conference facilities. 170 rooms. Credit cards: A, CB, DC, D, MC, V.

The glory that was Rome was never as glorious as the Las Vegas version at Caesars Palace.

Caesars Palace   **$89–$500**   ★ ★ ★ ★ ★

3570 Las Vegas Boulevard South, Las Vegas, 89109, ☎ (800) 634-6661, (702) 731-7110, FAX: (702) 731-6636.
Located at the heart of the Strip, north of the Mirage. Double: $89–$500.
Besides being one of the most luxurious hotels in Vegas, Caesars is a tourist attraction in its own right. With its marble statuary, Roman arches, breast-plated Roman soldier standing guard and half-clad waitresses, guests feel they are back in Rome's glory. Guest rooms come in an astounding variety of configurations and decor, but even the most basic—if such a word can be used to describe Caesars—are spacious and lovely. Many have canopy beds, Jacuzzi tubs or self-standing spas, giant armoires and large-screen TVs; all have luxurious

toiletries in the bath. Some also have round beds with mirrors above. Suites run the gamut from elegant duplexes to villas near the pool. There are also 14 "Fantasy Suites," available only to the highest of rollers, that encompass 4500 square feet and have four bedrooms, a "fantasy sky" accented with fiber optics, a huge stereo system complete with karaoke machine, and giant whirlpool tubs. The only drawback to the rooms—and in my book, it's a big one—is the ugly cement casing that covers many of the windows. It lets the sun in but kills any decent view. Many of the rooms look only onto another tower; the cement offers privacy, but it also shuts out the sun and gives a somewhat oppressive feeling. Another drawback is the very convoluted room numbering system—be sure to pay attention to which elevator takes you to your room, or you'll spend a lot of time lost. A 29-story tower, under construction at press time, will add 1130 guest rooms and suites and a new 20,000-square-foot health spa and fitness center. Completion is scheduled for early 1998. Also planned farther into the future are chariot races held in the middle of a mock Roman hill town in a new retail, restaurant and entertainment area called Circus Maximus. The Olympic-size pool area, enlarged to 4.3 acres by April 1998, is pretty and understated in this land of waterfalls and volcanoes. There are also six tennis courts and a health spa for keeping in shape. Caesars' adjacent Forum Shops, probably the most fanciful shopping mall in the nation, is not to be missed. It carries on the Roman theme splendidly and even has a "sky" that changes each 15 minutes. The hotel's nine restaurants and bars offer great variety; I especially like Cleopatra's Barge, a cozy and romantic lounge tucked off the casino. Action in the elegant casino matches the high room rates—low rollers will be happier playing elsewhere, but everyone loves to spend at least a little time in this Las Vegas landmark. Amenities: handball, private spas, conference facilities. 2600 rooms. Credit cards: A, CB, DC, MC, V.

Casino Royale Hotel $45–$85   ★★

3419 Las Vegas Boulevard South, Las Vegas, 89109, ☎ *(800) 854-7666, (702) 737-3500, FAX: (702) 737-1973.*
Located at the heart of the Strip, across from the Mirage. Double: $45–$85.

Frankly, this place is something of a dump—but the location, across from the Mirage and close to Treasure Island, Caesars, Bally's and many other fine spots—makes it worth a look if you're watching every cent. They do have a pool, casino and coffee shop, but that's about it in the way of niceties. 160 rooms. Credit cards: A, MC, V.

Circus Circus Hotel $39–$79   ★★★

2880 Las Vegas Boulevard South, Las Vegas, 89109, ☎ *(800) 634-3450, (702) 734-0410, FAX: (702) 734-2268.*
Located on the lower Strip, across from the Riviera. Double: $39–$79.

This huge, family-oriented hotel and casino has a cheery, decidedly low-market circus theme. The public areas are crowded and very, very noisy, and the casino caters to low-rollers. Accommodations, recently renovated, are just adequate; the motel-style furnishings are enhanced (or ruined, depending on your outlook) by the balloons and circus horses painted on the walls. The cheap rates keep this place packed, and if you can't get a room here, they'll help find you space at another bargain locale. Free entertainment consists of live circus acts daily from 11 a.m. to midnight under the concrete pink and white big top (don't forget to look up to see the trapeze artists), and there's a colorful midway area with video and carnival games and a pizzeria on the second tier that's great for kids. The Grand Slam Canyon Adventuredome out back (see "Attractions") is perfect for families and especially welcome on blistery summer days. The hotel added a new, 1000-room tower in late 1996. Circus Circus serves its market of cash-strapped families well, but singles, businesspeople and serious gamblers will be a lot happier elsewhere. The company also owns the Luxor and Excalibur, which also cater to families but with a bit more panache (and higher rates). Amenities: family plan. 3700 rooms. Credit cards: A, CB, DC, D, MC, V.

Continental Hotel and Casino   **$35–$95**   ★ ★

4100 Paradise Road, Las Vegas, 89109, ☎ *(800) 634-6641, (702) 737-5555, FAX: (702) 737-9276.*
Located one mile from the Strip. Double: $35–$95.
This low-rise property has basic rooms and facilities, including a pool in a nice garden setting. There's a 24-hour restaurant and occasional live entertainment in the lounge. Not too much to recommend it by, but not too bad, either. It shuttles gamblers over to the Strip, a mile away. 367 rooms. Credit cards: A, DC, D, MC, V.

Debbie Reynolds' Hotel and Casino   **$49–$175**   ★ ★ ★

305 Convention Center Drive, Las Vegas, 89109, ☎ *(800) 633-1777, (702) 734-0711, FAX: (702) 734-7548.*
Located a half-block off the Strip, near the Stardust. Double: $49–$175.
Actress Debbie Reynolds says she's spent a lifetime collecting motion picture memorabilia and years looking for a place to display it. Well, she finally found that place in the former Paddlewheel Hotel, located just a short walk from the Convention Center and the Strip. Her hotel/museum opened in June 1993 and features guest rooms with floor-to-ceiling windows, America's first Motion Picture Museum (see "Attractions"), two restaurants, two bars and the Star Theatre starring Reynolds herself and special guest performers. The casino is remarkably small by Las Vegas standards but nicely accented with interesting movie memorabilia such as Edward G. Robinson's pipe collection and hats worn by Vivian Leigh in *Gone with the Wind*. This spot attracts an older, low-key crowd. At press time, the hotel had filed for bankruptcy, so unless a new owner takes over, the future of this resort is uncertain. 197 rooms. Credit cards: A, DC, D, MC, V.

Flamingo Hilton   **$69–$205**   ★ ★ ★

3555 Las Vegas Boulevard South, Las Vegas, 89109, ☎ *(800) 732-2111, (702) 733-3111, FAX: (702) 733-3528.*
Located in the heart of the Strip. Double: $69–$205.
This is the first of the big casino-type hotels in Vegas; it was built in 1946 by the gangster Bugsy (Ben) Siegel and featured in the film *Bugsy*. Nothing remains of that era today (Hilton bought the hotel in the 1970s), though a restaurant is named after the founder. The Flamingo has a great location—surrounded by Bally's, the Imperial Palace, Harrah's and the Mirage. Facilities include nine restaurants, a

sushi bar, a full health club, a large pool and four tennis courts. There are two production shows on indefinite engagement and nightly entertainment in the lounge. Guest rooms vary between older accommodations in the garden unit and the more deluxe (and expensive) tower rooms, some of which offer great views of the Strip. The casino is enormous and easily navigated. A reliable standard, but the Flamingo has been upstaged by its flashier neighbors. It's gaudier and less expensive than its sister property, the Las Vegas Hilton, though the latter is far superior. Amenities: conference facilities. 3642 rooms. Credit cards: A, CB, DC, D, MC, V.

Frontier Hotel & Casino   **$35–$95**   ★ ★ ★

3120 Las Vegas Boulevard South, Las Vegas, 89109, *(800) 634-6966, (702) 794-8200, FAX: (702) 794-8326.*
Located on the northern Strip, across from the Desert Inn. Double: $35–$95.

Though it is outclassed by its Strip neighbors, the Frontier recently added a large block of mini-suites and renovated its casino, improving it somewhat. Decorated in a southwestern style, the rooms are spacious and a bargain by Vegas standards, and the location, across from the Desert Inn and near the Stardust, is handy. Amenities include two tennis courts, a nice pool area, several dining establishments and frequent live entertainment. Frontier employees have been on strike since December 1991, and no end is in sight. Though the picketers keep a relatively low profile, you still may have to pass them to get into the hotel, and there have been occasional altercations. This could be reason alone to stay elsewhere. Amenities: balcony or patio, family plan, conference facilities. 986 rooms. Credit cards: A, CB, DC, MC, V.

Gold Coast Hotel   **$55–$75**   ★ ★ ★

4000 West Flamingo Road, Las Vegas, 89103, ☎ *(800) 331-5334, (702) 367-7111, FAX: (702) 367-8575.*
Located one mile west of the center Strip. Double: $55–$75.

The Gold Coast, a favorite with locals, offers simple and inexpensive guest rooms in Spanish decor. The appeal of this hotel is the casino and the 24-hour entertainment downstairs. It boasts a huge country-western dance hall (largest in the state, in fact) and 72 lanes of bowling. There are also two movie theaters and free child care for harried parents. Frequent shuttles transport guests to the Strip, a few minutes away. A good, family-oriented choice. Amenities: family plan, conference facilities. 750 rooms. Credit cards: A, CB, DC, D, MC, V.

Hard Rock Hotel   **$85–$300**   ★ ★ ★ ★ ★

4455 Paradise Road, Las Vegas, 89109, ☎ *(800) 473-7625, (702) 693-5000, FAX: (702) 693-5010.*
Located a few blocks off the Strip. Double: $85–$300.

The Hard Rock Hotel opened in March 1995, and quickly became the hippest place in town. Its owners poured $100 million into this place, which is astounding considering there are only 340 rooms, which is tiny by Las Vegas standards. Built next to the Hard Rock Cafe, the hotel's guest rooms are really special, each uniquely decorated with rock and roll memorabilia and adorned with French doors that actually open to the outside. The casino is really cool, with piano-shaped roulette tables, gaming chips with appropriate rock song titles ("You Got Lucky" by Tom Petty on the $100 ones), and, of course, tons of memorabilia, from Pearl Jam's surfboard to jackets worn by Jimi Hendrix and Lenny Kravitz. The casino is also politically correct—an oxymoron if ever there was one—with an ambitious recycling program, non-toxic, biodegradable cleaning products used by the housekeeping staff, and "morally correct" slot machines whose proceeds go to rainforest conservation foundations. The property also includes a pretty pool area with a sandy beach, pool with piped-in underwater music and lots of tropical foliage. You can rent a pool cabana for $65–$95 but book early—they always sell out. There's also "The Joint," a 1200-seat concert venue books hot acts (the Eagles and Sheryl Crow played at the grand opening). So what if the well-off-the-Strip location stinks? This place is HOT! 340 rooms. Credit cards: A, CB, DC, D, MC, V.

The Hard Rock Hotel has quickly become a favorite with the 20–40's crowd.

Harrah's   **$50–$259**   ★ ★ ★ ★

3475 Las Vegas Boulevard South, Las Vegas, 89109, ☎ (800) 634-6765, (702) 369-5000, FAX: (702) 369-6014.
Located at the heart of the Strip. Double: $50–$259.
Formerly the Holiday Casino/Holiday Inn, this venerable hotel is right in the heart of the action. A major renovation has changed the paddlewheel facade to an European look. The large casino, recently expanded to more than 100,000 square feet, is shaped to resemble a Mississippi riverboat, and does a brisk business with the middle-market crowd. Accommodations vary with standard hotel furnishings and TVs with movies in most guest rooms. The Captain's Tower offers better rooms, bigger baths and better views—especially of Caesars Palace and eruptions of the Mirage volcano—but all the rooms are clean and comfortable. A new 671-room tower opened in mid 1997. There are five restaurants, several bars, a showroom, nightly entertainment, a good health spa, a shopping arcade—in short, everything you expect from a full-service operation. It's just not terribly exciting, but that's a plus for some people. This facility is kept in excellent condition but seems a bit overpriced considering the competition. Amenities: health club, conference facilities. 2334 rooms. Credit cards: A, CB, DC, D, MC, V.

Holiday Inn Casino Boardwalk   **$49–$149**   ★★★

3750 Las Vegas Boulevard South, Las Vegas, 89109, ☎ (800) 635-4581, (702) 735-1167, FAX: (702) 739-8152.
Located a block south of the MGM. Double: $49–$149.

The Boardwalk has been around since the 1960s, but just became affiliated with Holiday Inn in 1994, when all its guest rooms were extensively renovated. The recently expanded hotel has two pools, and guests without kids can request a "cabana room," which is on the first floor and opens right onto the pool deck. A new and improved (or at least larger) casino debuted in June 1995. Most rooms are under $85. Decent enough but overpriced, and no comparison to the mega-resorts. Don't be fooled by the roller coaster out front—it's only for show. 654 rooms. Credit cards: A, CB, DC, D, MC, V.

Hotel San Remo   **$89–$149**   ★★

115 East Tropicana Avenue, Las Vegas, 89109, ☎ (800) 522-7366, (702) 597-6020, FAX: (702) 739-7783.
Located behind the Tropicana. Double: $89–$149.

Since it is located off the Strip, the crowds are smaller and the hotel is relatively quiet—for Las Vegas. The rooms are nicely decorated with hardwood furnishings, patterned wallpaper and small balconies, a real rarity. The garden rooms have views of the pool, the hotel's only recreational facility. The hotel is no longer part of the Ramada chain. Considering its off-the-beaten-path location, the rates are no bargain, and the casino, which strives for a European feel, is rather dull. The MGM and Tropicana are close by and better buys. Amenities: conference facilities. 711 rooms. Credit cards: A, CB, DC, D, MC, V.

Imperial Palace   **$49–$129**   ★★★

3535 Las Vegas Boulevard South, Las Vegas, 89109, ☎ (800) 634-6441, (702) 731-3311, FAX: (702) 735-8328.
Located at the heart of the Strip. Double: $49–$129.

The mid-Strip location is great and the pool area is nice, but everything looks a bit tired at this Asian-motif casino. The hotel does big business with group travelers, so prepare to see a lot of name tags. Car buffs appreciate the auto museum, which charges admission to see its 200 vintage cars, some owned by the famous and infamous (see "Attractions"). Guest rooms vary from low-rise motel-style units to newer tower rooms and a few fantasy rooms with mirrored ceilings and 300-gallon tubs. All have Asian touches and small combination baths. Many also have balconies, a rare treat. Elevators can be annoyingly slow. Dining options keep with the hotel's middle-market clientele, though the long-running show, "Legends in Concert," is great fun. Other facilities include a health spa and eight cocktail lounges. Locals were appalled when the hotel's owner, Ralph Engelstad, was fined $1.2 million several years ago by the state gaming commission as an embarrassment to the industry—it seems he had a propensity for throwing Hitler theme parties. Some believe the hotel is built in the shape of a swastika, but a local news station deemed the design "inconclusive" after flying over the hotel in a helicopter. Not a first choice by any means, but an okay spot for those who like to be in the heart of the action. Amenities: exercise room, balcony or patio, conference facilities. 2700 rooms. Credit cards: A, CB, DC, MC, V.

Maxim Hotel $42–$96 ★ ★ ★

160 East Flamingo Road, Las Vegas, 89109, *(800) 634-6987, (702) 731-4300, FAX: (702) 735-3252.*
Located two bocks off the Strip. Double: $42–$96.
Although the guest rooms in the Maxim are overly decorated with silver foil wallpaper and carpet on the walls, the hotel is a great value and one of the best off-Strip hotels. It's an efficient operation with a friendly staff, and offers an attractive casino with good lighting, a pool and a shopping arcade. The Strip is an easy walk away. Amenities: conference facilities. 800 rooms. Credit cards: A, MC, V.

Palace Station Hotel $49–$109 ★ ★ ★

2411 West Sahara Avenue, Las Vegas, 89102, *(800) 634-3101, (702) 367-2411, FAX: (702) 367-2478.*
Located two blocks west of the Strip. Double: $49–$109.
By expanding the casino and adding a restaurant and a new tower of guest rooms, the Palace Station, which is themed to resemble a turn-of-the-century train station, has begun attracting the attention of more tourists. The guest rooms are small but attractively furnished. The staff is friendly and there's a first-class entertainment lounge. There are several good and varied restaurants serving everything from Brazilian lobster tails to tacos, and extras include a free shuttle to the Strip. Popular with locals, but its location—just off the 1-15 and rather removed from the Strip—makes it a hard sell for tourists. 1030 rooms. Credit cards: A, CB, DC, D, MC, V.

Quality Inn Hotel & Casino $49–$59 ★ ★

377 East Flamingo Road, Las Vegas, 89109, *(800) 634-6617, (702) 733-7777, FAX: (702) 369-6911.*
Located one mile from the Strip. Double: $49–$59.
Located a mile from both the Convention Center and the Strip, this Quality Inn puts guests up in mini-suites with wet bars and refrigerators. There's a small casino on site, as well as a pool, restaurant, and lounge. It will shuttle you over to the Strip for free. 370 rooms. Credit cards: A, CB, DC, D, MC, V.

Riviera Hotel $35–$250 ★ ★ ★

2901 Las Vegas Boulevard South, Las Vegas, 89109, ☎ *(800) 634-6753, (702) 734-5110, FAX: (702) 794-9663.*
Located near Circus Circus and the Stardust. Double: $35–$250.
The Riviera is one of the Strip's oldest resorts, and it shows its age, though a 1997 guestroom renovation to the tune of $15 million helps somewhat. There's lots to do here, with four showrooms and some of Las Vegas' best talent. Request a room in the newer tower, as they are better furnished and have better views. All the rooms are spacious with cherry wood furnishings, floral wallpaper and marble sinks with brass fittings, but the corner rooms near the elevator can be noisy. The popular two-story lanai units are large and close to the pool. Facilities include two tennis courts, a full health club, a large free-form pool, a wedding chapel, seven restaurants and six bars. Despite all that, the Riviera is just okay, having been overshadowed by the newer hotels. The whole place is a bit of a maze and it's easy to lose your way. The location, right in the heart of the northern Strip, is a definite plus. Amenities: conference facilities. 2071 rooms. Credit cards: A, CB, DC, MC, V.

Royal Hotel & Casino   **$45–$85**   ★ ★

99 Convention Center Drive, Las Vegas, 89109, *(800) 634-6118, (702) 735-6117, FAX: (702) 735-2546.*

Located two blocks from the Convention Center. Double: $45–$85.

This older hotel (1970) is just a block off the Strip. It offers motel-style accommodations (with shag carpeting and balconies) and low-frills amenities. The property has a pool and two restaurants, but not much else. The small casino stays quiet. Hardly a first, or even second, choice. 236 rooms. Credit cards: A, CB, DC, D, MC, V.

Sahara Hotel & Casino   **$85–$115**   ★ ★ ★

2535 Las Vegas Boulevard South, Las Vegas, 89109, *(800) 634-6666, (702) 737-2111, FAX: (702) 791-2027.*

Located on the northern Strip. Double: $85–$115.

Located at the end of the Strip near downtown, the Sahara dates all the way back to 1956, making it practically an antique. The guest rooms vary greatly in quality, and are not luxurious, but are comfortable for the price. In the budget rooms (set in low garden wings), expect budget accommodations. The Sahara offers a large, dated casino, showroom, a good buffet and other restaurants, two swimming pools and a shopping arcade, but it's a few notches down from the city's nicer hotels. Strictly for the undemanding middle market. Amenities: conference facilities. 2035 rooms. Credit cards: A, CB, DC, D, MC, V.

Sheraton Desert Inn   **$89–$220**   ★ ★ ★ ★ ★

3145 Las Vegas Boulevard South, Las Vegas, 89109, *(800) 634-6906, (702) 733-4444, FAX: (702) 733-4676.*

Located across from the Frontier and Stardust. Double: $89–$220.

Though it is small compared to other Strip hotels, the Desert Inn is a resort in the true sense of the word. It's understated and without a theme, and the casino is smaller, quieter and much more dignified than most others in town. Accordingly, it attracts lots of high rollers, and there is a noticeable dearth of slot machines. Rooms vary widely from standards to luxurious suites and pool-side villas; all are well appointed and plush. Many have balconies and some even have patios. New in 1997 are a nine-story tower of mini-suites and some spiffy poolside villas. Recreational facilities abound out back. There are 10 tennis courts, a luxurious health club with expensive pampering services, lots of Jacuzzis scattered about the pretty grounds, a new lagoon-style pool and the crown jewel: a gorgeous, 18-hole PGA golf course, with, as you'd imagine, astoundingly high greens fees. A country club feeling prevails. Happily, the hotel has backed off plans that would have transformed it into a 4000-room mega-resort—this place works just fine the way it is, and its 1997 $200-million expansion/renovation keeps it that way. Lots of little touches keep the DI classy, such as the uniformed attendants that keep the restrooms supplied with hand lotion and hair spray. The coffee shop is just like everyone else's, but serves veggie burgers—try finding THAT anywhere else. Those serious about their blackjack, roulette, craps and baccarat need look no further. Amenities: conference facilities. 712 rooms. Credit cards: A, CB, DC, D, MC, V.

Stardust Resort   **$32–$150**   ★ ★ ★

3000 Las Vegas Boulevard South, Las Vegas, 89109, ☎ (800) 634-6757, (702) 732-6111, FAX: (702) 732-6257.
Located south of the Desert Inn. Double: $32–$150.
The Stardust is one of the hotels that comes to mind when you think of Las Vegas; it's been around since 1958 but has changed considerably in that time—it even got rid of its great old Jetsons-style sign a few years ago in favor of a ubiquitous neon one. The Stardust did add some neat water sculptures out front, though, whose water hypnotically leaps from fountain to fountain—very mesmerizing, especially if you've taken advantage of the free drinks. Guest rooms vary in quality, from motel-like units in the back to the more expensive rooms in the newer tower, which are decorated in modern dark tones. Suites have Jacuzzi tubs in the bedroom, while the ground-floor Chateau rooms open onto the pool, a plus for families. (On the minus side, the pool is very plain.) The showroom is home to the excellent "Enter the Night" production show (see "The Shows"), while the lounge is given over to a Rod Stewart look- and soundalike who wows the crowds with "Maggie May" nightly. The casino is absolutely huge and always hopping, and appeals mostly to middle-rollers. One unique touch: Each afternoon (except Tuesday) from 1 to 4, you can get your picture taken with an authentic showgirl in full regalia ($5 for a 6 x 8). Guests at the Stardust won't go hungry—there are six themed restaurants and a 24-hour coffee shop. Recreational facilities are limited to the pool, though guests are welcome at a nearby health club. This is a very adequate property, but little signs of cheapness— plastic glasses in the guestrooms, mini-beers in the casino—are a real turnoff. Amenities: conference facilities. 2340 rooms. Credit cards: A, CB, DC, D, MC, V.

Town Hall Casino Hotel   **$35–$74**   ★ ★

4155 Koval Lane, Las Vegas, 89109, ☎ (800) 634-6541, (702) 731-2111, FAX: (702) 731-1113.
Located near the Strip, behind Bally's. Double: $35–$74.
Everything is pretty basic at this small Day's Inn casino-hotel located behind Bally's. It has a pool and piano bar, but that's about it. You'll have to walk over to the Strip for excitement. Only worth considering if everything else is sold out, though the rates are reasonable. 360 rooms. Credit cards: A, CB, MC, V.

Tropicana Resort & Casino   **$49–$159**   ★ ★ ★ ★

3801 Las Vegas Boulevard South, Las Vegas, 89109, ☎ (800) 634-4000, (702) 739-2222, FAX: (702) 739-2469.
Located across from the MGM and Excalibur. Double: $49–$159.
This 900-acre resort is a "tropical island" with a huge pool area (its best feature) boasting lagoons, grottoes, waterfalls, a neat slide, ducks and swans and fountains. There's even a special area where high-rollers can tan without having to rub elbows with the teeming masses. The casino is striking with its $1 million, leaded-glass ceiling, but it's gotten a bit tacky lately due to the posting of cheap advertising signs. In fact, the entire Tropicana—one of Las Vegas' oldest hotels—seems to be sliding downhill, which makes me sad; this was my favorite hotel for years. It is nearly impossible to score a free drink in the casino— last time I was there, a waitress charged me $3.50 for a beer, despite

the fact that I was playing a $1 video poker machine (unheard of!). There's also the incredibly obnoxious talking elevators that will drive you crazy if you spend more than a night here. On the plus side, the dealers are friendly and helpful. The guest rooms, located in far-apart towers, are quite nice, but like everything else, maintenance is getting shoddy. Those in the near tower have Victorian-style decor; the others have a tropical, rattan look. (Some also have mirrors over the bed.) There are also old motel-style units out back that are best avoided. Connecting the two towers is a free "Wildlife Walk" that showcases exotic birds (See "Attractions".) The Victorian tower is close to the casino but far from the pool; the other tower has the opposite problem. Prepare for long walks wherever you end up. The Trop's on-site comedy club is a hoot, and the restaurants are generally excellent. Once off all by itself at the very southern end of the Strip, the Trop is now surrounded by the MGM Grand, Excalibur, Luxor and New York-New York. Because of its wonderful pool, which is surpassed only by the Mirage's, the Trop is still one of the best choices during warm weather months. But it's increasingly becoming passé. Amenities: private spas, conference facilities. 1970 rooms. Credit cards: A, CB, DC, D, MC, V.

Vacation Village Hotel $35–$175   ★★★

6711 Las Vegas Boulevard South, Las Vegas, 89119, ☎ *(800) 338-0608, (702) 897-1700, FAX: (702) 361-6726.*
Located south of the Strip. Double: $35–$175.
Vacation Village is a friendly, informal hotel providing budget accommodations and basic amenities, all in a southwestern style. Facilities include four restaurants, five bars and lounges, live entertainment, a casino and a nice pool with a great desert view. It's a good value but a long, long way from Strip action. Amenities: conference facilities. 313 rooms. Credit cards: A, CB, DC, D, MC, V.

Westward Ho $37–$76   ★★

2900 Las Vegas Boulevard South, Las Vegas, 89109, ☎ *(800) 634-6803, (702) 731-2900, FAX: (702) 731-6154.*
Located near the Stardust. Double: $37–$76.
This older, '60s-style casino-motel is dated and has been far, far surpassed by most properties in town—though the rates and location are decent, with lots within walking distance. It has four pools and several bars and restaurants; the nondescript casino is devoted mainly to slot machines. Not a first (or even second) choice, but adequate enough when rooms are tight. 777 rooms. Credit cards: MC, V.

All-Suite Hotels

Alexis Park Resort $95–$175   ★★★★

375 East Harmon Avenue, Las Vegas, 89109, ☎ *(800) 582-2228, (702) 796-3300, FAX: (702) 796-4334.*
Located two blocks from the Strip. Double: $95–$175.
This upscale resort hotel, located off the Strip, offers plush suites that range from deluxe to luxurious. Since there's no casino on the premises, the usual Las Vegas frenzy is absent. A casino can easily be found right across the street, however, at the Hard Rock Hotel and Casino—a real plus, as there used to be no gambling within an easy walk. The hotel used to offer shuttle service to the Strip, but has dis-

continued that nicely since the Hard Rock opened. The Alexis attracts lots of upscale business travelers and hosts many business functions in its 13 meeting rooms. All accommodations are in suites of at least two rooms; some have Jacuzzis and/or fireplaces. The grounds, which include a putting green and two restaurants, are quite lovely and provide a real respite from this bawdy city. There are also two tennis courts, a health club and two restaurants. Not the place for partyers or singles, but ideal for those who have to be in Las Vegas, but would rather be anywhere else. Amenities: secluded garden atmosphere, private spas, conference facilities. 500 rooms. Credit cards: A, CB, DC, D, MC, V.

Blair House Suites   **$45–$125**   ★★

344 East Desert Inn Road, Las Vegas, 89109, ☎ *(800) 553-9111, (702) 792-2222, FAX: (702) 792-9042.*
Located across from the Desert Inn Golf Course. Double: $45–$125.
Located between the Convention Center and the Strip, the small Blair House is a decent choice for those on an extended stay (inquire about special rates). All accommodations are in one-bedroom suites with kitchens. Facilities are limited to a pool, but there's lots within walking distance. 224 rooms. Credit cards: A, CB, DC, D, MC, V.

Carriage House   **$89–$275**   ★★★

105 East Harmon Avenue, Las Vegas, 89109, ☎ *(702) 798-1020, FAX: (702) 798-1020.*
Located a half-block off the Strip. Double: $89–$275.
This quiet, older hotel offers a rooftop restaurant and lounge, sundeck and free transportation to the Strip, a half-block away. Accommodations are in studios and one- and two-bedroom suites with kitchenettes or full kitchens. A nice enough spot, but considering the rates and off-Strip location, you may as well stay in a full-service casino-hotel. 150 rooms. Credit cards: A, DC, D, MC, V.

Holiday Inn Crowne Plaza   **$79–$109**   ★★★

4255 Paradise Road, Las Vegas, 89109, ☎ *(800) 465-4329, (702) 369-4400, FAX: (702) 369-3770.*
Located across from the Continental. Double: $79–$109.
This newer all-suite hotel has no casino, which may appeal to those wishing to avoid the hustle-bustle atmosphere of Las Vegas. Accommodations are two-room suites with wet bars, coffeemakers and refrigerators. The Strip is an easy walk away. Formerly the Howard Johnson Plaza-Suite Hotel, it has a pool, restaurant and cocktail lounge. Amenities: exercise room, conference facilities. 201 rooms. Credit cards: A, CB, DC, D, MC, V.

Residence Inn by Marriott   **$95–$219**   ★★★

3225 Paradise Road, Las Vegas, 89109, ☎ *(800) 331-3131, (702) 796-9300, FAX: (702) 796-3000.*
Located across from the Convention Center. Double: $95–$219.
Since this hotel is located across from the Las Vegas Convention Center, it caters mostly to extended-stay business travelers. There is no restaurant but the hotel offers a free Continental breakfast, newspaper, and an evening hospitality hour. Each unit is a suite with a fully equipped kitchen. The Strip is a long block away. Amenities: conference facilities. 192 rooms. Credit cards: A, DC, D, MC, V.

St. Tropez Suite Hotel $95–$300 ★★★

455 East Harmon Avenue, Las Vegas, 89109, ☎ (800) 666-5400, (702) 369-5400, FAX: (702) 369-1150.
Located across from the Hard Rock Hotel. Double: $95–$300.

A good choice for those who want to stay a bit removed from the Strip's hubbub, the St. Tropez is across from the new Hard Rock Casino-Hotel and two long blocks from both the Strip and Convention Center. Accommodations are in junior, one-bedroom and presidential suites, all with coffeemakers and minibars. Some of the more elaborate layouts also have Jacuzzis and balconies. Guests get complimentary breakfast and two cocktails daily. Amenities include a nice pool that's open 24 hours, several restaurants and a shuttle to the Strip. Nice, but the nearby Alexis Park, built on the same sophisticated non-gaming concept, is better. Amenities: exercise room. 149 rooms. Credit cards: A, CB, DC, D, MC, V.

Sunrise Suites $40–$85 ★★★

4575 East Boulder Highway, Las Vegas, 89121, ☎ (800) 221-2222, (702) 434-0848, FAX: (702) 434-2419.
Double: $40–$85.

This newer all-suite hotel has a southwestern theme. Each unit has a kitchenette with refrigerator and microwave. It's near the Convention Center and Strip, and offers a courtesy shuttle to both. There's a barbecue and picnic area on-site, and for those who can't get enough, video poker in the lobby. Amenities: conference facilities. 305 rooms. Credit cards: A, CB, DC, D, MC, V.

Hotels

Courtyard by Marriott $80–$140 ★★★

3275 Paradise Road, Las Vegas, 89109, ☎ (800) 321-2211, (702) 791-3600, FAX: (702) 796-7981.
Located adjacent to the Convention Center. Double: $80–$140.

This residential-style hotel near the Convention Center offers the usual reliable amenities of a Marriott. Rooms have work desks and coffeemakers, and the entire facility is geared more toward business travelers than gamblers. There's a restaurant and bar on site, but no casino. Other features include a pool, Jacuzzi, and gym. A good choice for those who shun the noisy casino-hotels, but the rates seem a tad high for Las Vegas. The Strip is two blocks away. Amenities: exercise room, conference facilities. 149 rooms. Credit cards: A, CB, DC, D, MC, V.

Motels

Best Western Mardi Gras $50–$120 ★★★

3500 Paradise Road, Las Vegas, 89109, ☎ (800) 634-6501, (702) 731-2020, FAX: (702) 733-6994.
Located two blocks from the Convention Center. Double: $50–$120.

The Mardi Gras is a quiet property with standard guest rooms and mini-suites with comfortable, reliable trappings. The Strip is three long blocks away, so the free shuttle bus, which operates daily from 7 a.m. to 11 p.m., comes in handy. Niceties include in-room coffee, free continental breakfast on weekdays, a beauty salon, a decent pool and a slot casino. Fine if you're watching your bucks—most times rooms are well under $100—but best-suited to families and business folks who need to be near the Convention Center. Amenities: conference facilities. 315 rooms. Credit cards: A, CB, DC, MC, V.

Best Western McCarran Inn $65–$140   ★★★

4970 Paradise Road, Las Vegas, 89119, ☎ *(800) 626-7575, (702) 798-5530, FAX: (702) 798-7627.*
Double: $65–$140.
The McCarran Inn features an atrium lobby and offers its guests a complimentary breakfast and newspaper on weekdays, and free daytime transportation to the airport, a half-mile away. A pleasant enough spot, but the Strip and Convention Center are both too far away to walk comfortably, and the shuttle linking these areas is too sporadic to count on. You're better off at a motel closer to the action. Amenities: conference facilities. 98 rooms. Credit cards: A, CB, DC, D, MC, V.

Emerald Springs Holiday Inn $70–$200   ★★★

325 East Flamingo Road, Las Vegas, 89109, ☎ *(800) 732-7889, (702) 732-9100, FAX: (702) 731-9784.*
Located behind Bally's, two blocks off the Strip. Double: $70–$200.
This Holiday Inn has a nice hacienda-style facade and art-deco lobby with a fireplace in the pleasant sitting area. Accommodations are extra large; half have combined living and sleeping areas while the rest are full suites with separate bedrooms. All come equipped with coffeemakers, refrigerators and hair dryers. Facilities are limited to a pool and cafe. They'll shuttle you over to the Strip for free. Decent. Amenities: conference facilities. 150 rooms. Credit cards: A, DC, D, MC, V.

Fairfield Inn by Marriott $50–$80   ★★

3850 Paradise Road, Las Vegas, 89109, ☎ *(800) 228-2800, (702) 791-0899, FAX: (702) 791-0899.*
Located near the Strip and the Las Vegas Hilton. Double: $50–$80.
This small motel is a mile from the Convention Center and near the Strip and Las Vegas Hilton. Its reasonable rates make it a nice alternative to the casino-hotels, but don't expect much in the way of excitement. Continental breakfast and morning newspaper are complimentary, as are local phone calls (not bad when you consider that many hotels charge $1 per call). Amenities: conference facilities. 129 rooms. Credit cards: A, DC, D, MC, V.

La Quinta Motor Inn $50–$80   ★★

3782 Las Vegas Boulevard South, Las Vegas, 89109, ☎ *(800) 531-5900, (702) 739-7457, FAX: (702) 736-1129.*
Located a block from the Aladdin. Double: $50–$80.
Located right on the Strip, this Spanish-style motor inn offers up a free continental breakfast. There's a pool on site and a 24-hour restaurant adjacent, but not much else. Free local phone calls are a nice touch. 114 rooms. Credit cards: A, CB, DC, MC, V.

Cheap Motels

Center Strip Inn $50–$250   ★

3688 Las Vegas Boulevard South, Las Vegas, 89109, ☎ *(800) 777-7737, (702) 739-6066, FAX: (702) 736-2521.*
Located near the MGM. Double: $50–$250.
This is a pretty bare-bones motel, though it does have a pool, and coffeemakers in the very basic rooms. The location is decent; you can

walk to the MGM, Excalibur and Tropicana easily, with Caesars and the Mirage just a bit farther to the north. 137 rooms. Credit cards: A, CB, DC, D, MC, V.

Comfort Inn Central   **$65–$95**   ★

211 East Flamingo Road, Las Vegas, 89109, ☎ *(800) 228-5150, (702) 733-7800, FAX: (702) 733-7353.*
Located across from the Maxim. Double: $65–$95.

The Strip is one and half blocks away from this basic motel; you don't have to go that far to gamble, as the Maxim is right across the street. The Comfort Inn has a pool, and serves a complimentary continental breakfast. But you can do better for the price. 120 rooms. Credit cards: A, CB, DC, D, MC, V.

Somerset House   **$40–$50**   ★★

294 Convention Center Drive, Las Vegas, 89109, ☎ *(702) 735-4411, FAX: (702) 735-0817.*
Located one block from the Convention Center and Strip. Double: $40–$50.

The three-story motel offers budget accommodations convenient to those with business at the Convention Center. Rooms are basic, but do include coffeemakers; most also have kitchenettes. Facilities are limited to an Olympic-size pool. 104 rooms. Credit cards: A, CB, MC, V.

Travelodge South Strip   **$49–$99**   ★

3735 Las Vegas Boulevard South, Las Vegas, 89102, ☎ *(800) 578-7878, (702) 736-3443, FAX: (702) 736-1356.*
Located half-block south of the Aladdin. Double: $49–$99.

This small motor inn is within walking distance of the MGM, Tropicana, New York-New York and Excalibur—that's about it's only selling point. Rooms are very spartan, and there's nothing on site but a pool. 128 rooms. Credit cards: A, DC, D, MC, V.

RV Parks

Circusland RV Park   **$16–$18**   ★★★

500 Circus Circus Drive, Las Vegas, 89109, ☎ *(800) 634-3450, (702) 734-0410, FAX: (702) 734-2268.*
Located behind Circus Circus. Double: $16–$18.

A convenient location—right off the Strip behind the massive Circus Circus Hotel and Casino—make this older RV park stand out. Facilities include 421 hookups, laundry and showers, pool, Jacuzzi and convenience store. Great for families, as Circus Circus and its indoor amusement park, Grand Slam Canyon, cater to kids and those watching every cent. Credit cards: A, CB, DC, D, MC, V.

Sam's Town RV Resort   **$16–$16**   ★★★★

5111 Boulder Highway, Las Vegas, 89122, ☎ *(800) 634-6371, (702) 456-7777, FAX: (702) 454-8014.*
Located a few miles from the Strip. Double: $16.

Sam's Town has two RV parks, one next to its large hotel and casino that has a two-week maximum stay, and one across the street, where you can stay for up to six months (☎ *(800) 897-8696, ex. 1310,* for details on the latter). The two have a total of 500 hookups, as well as laundry and shower facilities, a pool and a recreation room—plus all the amenities (including a bowling alley) at the recently expanded hotel and casino. Credit cards: A, CB, DC, D, MC, V.

Downtown: Where All the Lights Are Bright

Downtown Las Vegas, where the locals hang out, is more compact and less glamorous than the uptown Strip.

Downtown Las Vegas is just a few miles north of the Strip, but worlds apart in atmosphere. With the notable exception of the Golden Nugget, the hotels here are old, tired and dated, bringing to mind a washed-up showgirl who still insists on squeezing into spandex and caking on the makeup. The themes of the Strip are scoffed at here—there's serious gambling going on in the small, low-frills casinos with claustrophobically low ceilings.

The Fremont Experience has helped to change that image—or at least make it a bit more palatable. That multimillion dollar project opened in late 1995, has transformed downtown's main thoroughfare into a festive area under a five-block-long canopy. There is an amazing light show nightly with lots of neat sound effects.

Downtown may be a poor stepsister to the Strip, but it has considerable charms. Everything is close together, so it's easy to casino hop (you can even bring your drink). Hotel rooms are generally cheaper and easier to snag. The gaming limits are lower, and you'll find a lot of locals at the tables. And the lights really are brighter—Fremont Street ain't called Glitter Gulch for nothing. If you've never stayed downtown and have done the Strip, give it a try.

The Fremont has been a landmark since 1956.

Casino-Hotels

Binion's Horseshoe   **$28–$60**   ★★★

128 East Fremont Street, Las Vegas, 89101, ☎ *(800) 622-6468, (702) 382-1600, FAX: (702) 384-1574.*

Double: $28–$60.

Built in 1965, Binion's harks backs to Las Vegas' early days, and attracts a loyal following of locals who come to play poker—its annual "world series" is famous—and splurge on the no-limit gaming. This Las Vegas institution is tired and dated, its accommodations surpassed by the myriad newer resorts in town. But the casino—a true thowback with its low, low ceilings and low, low frills—attracts lots of locals and is great fun. Craps players especially like the eight tables— a huge amount for the size of the casino—and 10 times odds (which gets expensive when the dice are cold). There's a swimming pool on the roof with great views of the desert, but it's open only in the warmer months. You may not want to stay here—the rooms are certainly nothing to get excited about—but do drop into the casino for a true look at what Las Vegas was like before all the deep-pocketed corporations moved in. And check out the display of 100 $10,000 bills—that's a cool million bucks behind that glass. Amenities: conference facilities. 379 rooms. Credit cards: A, CB, D, MC, V.

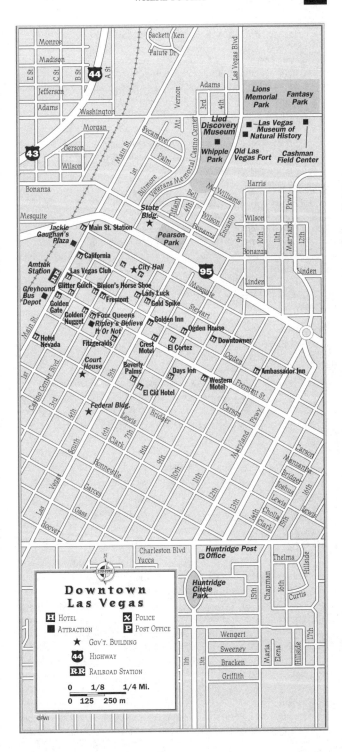

Downtown
Las Vegas

H HOTEL   **X** POLICE

■ ATTRACTION   **P** POST OFFICE

★ GOV'T. BUILDING

44 HIGHWAY

RR RAILROAD STATION

0   1/8   1/4 Mi.

0   125   250 m

Boulder Station   **$29–$189**   ★★★

4111 Boulder Highway, Las Vegas, 89121, ☎ *(800) 683-7777, (702)*
432-7777, FAX: (702) 432-7730.
Located a few miles off the Strip. Double: $29–$189.
This $85 million resort opened in August 1994. The theme is a 19th-
century railroad station, and the property includes a huge casino and
five restaurants that run the gamut from steak and seafood to Mexican
to Italian. It's located on the east side of town, off highways 95-93,
two minutes from downtown. This is a good place for slot players
with sensitive lungs—more than 2000 machines are found in a non-
smoking area. Rates are usually well under $100. 300 rooms. Credit
cards: A, CB, DC, D, MC, V.

California Hotel   **$50–$80**   ★★

12 Ogden Avenue, Las Vegas, 89101, ☎ *(800) 634-6255, (702) 385-*
1222, FAX: (702) 388-2610.
Located a block from Fremont Street. Double: $50–$80.
This older, quiet hotel with a newer tower section is a nice alternative
to some of the seedier downtown properties. Guests should definitely
avail themselves of the safes in the motel-style rooms. The hotel's
large casino stays relatively uncrowded, which can't be said for the
other downtown hotels. Pleasant enough, but nothing special.
There's an RV park out back. 650 rooms. Credit cards: A, DC, D, MC, V.

Fitzgerald's   **$38–$90**   ★★★

301 East Fremont Street, Las Vegas, 89101, ☎ *(800) 274-5825, (702)*
388-2400, FAX: (702) 388-2181.
Located in the heart of downtown. Double: $38–$90.
Like most of its downtown neighbors, the Irish-themed Fitzgerald's
(lots of green everywhere) is tired and dated. The casino is always
crowded, though, with those attracted by the low-minimum tables.
Facilities include three restaurants (including an uninspired buffet),
three bars and frequent live entertainment. There's also an exercise
room and Jacuzzi, but no pool. This place is nothing special, but
acceptable if you want to be downtown and save some bucks. Amenities: conference facilities. 650 rooms. Credit cards: CB, DC, D, MC, V.

Four Queens   **$48–$59**   ★★★

202 East Fremont Street, Las Vegas, 89101, ☎ *(800) 634-6045, (702)*
385-4011, FAX: (702) 387-5133.
Located in the heart of downtown, next to the Golden Nugget. Double:
$48–$59.
A strictly middle-of-the-road, but recently improved, downtown
hotel built mainly to accommodate visitors to its casino. The rooms
are comfortable with king or double beds, but TVs get local stations
only. Some suites have their own Jacuzzis. The lounge downstairs
often offers top-quality entertainment. The casino is something of a
throwback—among the low-limit tables is a vending machine selling
cards and dice formerly used in casino play. There's also the world's
biggest slot machine, which stands 10 feet tall and 15 feet wide, and
can be played by six people at once. Lots of locals here, especially in
the nightly (except Saturday) video poker tournaments, which start at
6 p.m. The buy-in is $20; first place wins $250. There are three restaurants and four bars, but, alas, no pool. Rumor has it that the ashes
of a compulsive gambler are stashed somewhere in the casino, his

former haunt. Amenities: family plan, conference facilities. 700
rooms. Credit cards: A, DC, D, MC, V.

Golden Nugget $59–$300 ★★★★★

129 East Fremont Street, Las Vegas, 89101, ☎ *(800) 634-3454, (702)
385-7111, FAX: (702) 386-8362.*
Located in the heart of downtown. Double: $59–$300.

One of the most elegant and well-maintained hotels in Las Vegas, the
Golden Nugget really stands out in comparison to its lower-heeled
downtown neighbors. All is brass and gold in the upscale casino, and
the floral-accented guest rooms are unusually attractive. Even the
hallways are pretty! Each tower has a separate check-in, so lines can be
shorter than at other hotels. Unfortunately, the pool area is oddly set
just off the main lobby, placing bathers in full view of passers-by—
hard to understand the reasoning behind that. The health club is simply gorgeous and one of the best in town. There are lots of choices
when it comes time to eat, including several gourmet rooms and the
casual California Pizza Kitchen, which is always excellent. Service is
excellent and friendly, and the hotel is blessedly free of hokey
themes—although many come by to gawk at the world's largest gold
nugget (61 pounds, 11 ounces) on display off the lobby. One of Las
Vegas' classiest acts by far and a real standout in its downtown location. Even if you don't stay here, plan an evening in the elegant
casino. Amenities: family plan, conference facilities. 1907 rooms.
Credit cards: A, CB, DC, MC, V.

Jackie Gaughan's Plaza $30–$140 ★★★

One Main Street, Las Vegas, 89101, ☎ *(800) 634-6575, (702) 386-
2110, FAX: (702) 382-8281.*
Located at the heart of downtown. Double: $30–$140.

If you arrive in Las Vegas via Amtrak, you can depart at this hotel and
walk directly into its casino. Located next to the Greyhound station,
which makes it perfect for the budget-minded traveler, the hotel
offers a three-acre casino and the only tennis courts downtown.
There's also a large pool, another downtown rarity. Guest rooms were
recently remodeled and are fairly decent, but this older hotel, formerly the Union Plaza, shows its age. Food at the Centerstage Restaurant is nothing to rave about, but the views of Glitter Gulch are
priceless. Amenities: tennis, family plan, conference facilities. 1037
rooms. Credit cards: A, CB, DC, MC, V.

Lady Luck Casino Hotel $40–$80 ★★★

206 North Third Street, Las Vegas, 89101, ☎ *(800) 523-9582, (702)
477-3000, FAX: (702) 477-3002.*
Located downtown. Double: $40–$80.

The Lady Luck offers comfortable guest rooms and small Jacuzzi
suites. The newer 25-story tower has the nicest rooms, but the ones
in the old low-rise wing aren't too bad, either. All have refrigerators,
radios, and full-length mirrors in addition to the usual amenities.
Facilities are limited to a pool and several restaurants (gourmet, Chinese, buffet, coffee shop), but the service is very good and the informal atmosphere quite friendly. This is one of the better downtown
hotels, with a large and happening casino with—gasp!—large picture
windows, something you're hard pressed to find anywhere else. Fre-

mont Steet is a short walk away. Amenities: private spas. 796 rooms.
Credit cards: A, CB, DC, MC, V.

Las Vegas Club   **$40–$50**   ★ ★

*18 East Fremont Street, Las Vegas, 89101, ☎ (800) 634-6532, (702)
385-1664, FAX: (702) 387-6071.*
Located in the heart of downtown. Double: $40–$50.
Locals like this downtown casino-hotel for its liberal blackjack rules
and casual casino. A $17-million expansion in late 1996 added a 16-
story tower and more casino space. Guest rooms are on the small side,
but relatively soundproof and nicely decorated in a southwestern
style. Sports buffs appreciate the huge collection of memorabilia,
mostly devoted to baseball (there's even the Dugout Restaurant), but
with a democratic sprinkling of basketball and boxing mementos as
well. Like most of its downtown counterparts, there's no pool. Good
value. 415 rooms. Credit cards: A, CB, DC, D, MC, V.

Sam Boyd's Fremont   **$36–$52**   ★ ★ ★

*200 Fremont Street, Las Vegas, 89101, ☎ (800) 634-6182, (702) 385-
3232, FAX: (702) 385-6229.*
Located in the heart of downtown. Double: $36–$52.
This friendly, informal downtown landmark hotel dates to Las Vegas'
stone age—1956. It offers budget accommodations and good food. A
decent enough choice if you want to stay downtown and spend your
money in the casino, not on the room. But don't expect too much—
not even a pool. A locals' favorite. 452 rooms. Credit cards: A, CB, DC, D,
MC, V.

Showboat Hotel   **$49–$69**   ★ ★ ★

*2800 East Fremont Street, Las Vegas, 89104, ☎ (800) 634-3484, (702)
385-9123, FAX: (702) 385-9238.*
Located at Fremont Street and Boulder Highway. Double: $49–$69.
Located on Boulder Highway, about 10 minutes from the Strip and
close to downtown, the Showboat is famous for its sports complex
that boasts a 106-lane bowling alley and occasional professional boxing and wrestling matches. The rooms are simply furnished and
motel-like, but still quite pleasant. The lower floor garden units have
sliding-glass doors that open onto the pool area, a nice touch. Decorated in a Mississippi riverboat theme, the casino is popular with locals
and includes a large bingo hall. Excellent value. Amenities: conference
facilities. 491 rooms. Credit cards: A, CB, DC, MC, V.

Cheap Motels

Days Inn Downtown   **$36–$175**   ★ ★

*707 East Fremont Street, Las Vegas, 89101, ☎ (800) 325-2344, (702)
388-1400, FAX: (702) 388-9622.*
Located two blocks from casino center. Double: $36–$175.
This 30-year-old motel is decent enough if you can't get a room elsewhere. Facilities are limited to a pool, restaurant, lounge and slot
casino. 147 rooms. Credit cards: A, CB, DC, D, MC, V.

Travelodge Downtown   **$40–$50**   ★

*2028 East Fremont Street, Las Vegas, 89101, ☎ (800) 578-7878, (702)
384-7540, FAX: (702) 384-0408.*
Located downtown near casino center. Double: $40–$50.

WHERE TO STAY

The name says it all: it's a Travelodge and it's downtown, but not in the heart. There's a pool but nothing else; you'll have to eat out. No reason to stay here, unless you're really stuck. 58 rooms. Credit cards: A, CB, DC, D, MC, V.

RV Parks

Sam Boyd's California Hotel RV Park $12–$12   ★ ★ ★

12 Ogden Avenue, Las Vegas, 89109, *(800) 634-6255, (702) 388-2602, FAX: (702) 388-2610.*
Located downtown, behind the California Hotel. Double: $12.
Stay right in the heart of downtown and enjoy all the amenties of the adjacet California Hotel & Casino. Facilities include 222 hookups, laundry and showers, pool, Jacuzzi and convenience store. Credit cards: A, CB, DC, MC, V.

And Elsewhere

Several casinos are located a bit off the beaten path, which is a real liability for those who like to hop from one casino to another. The best of the bunch (and one of my favorites overall) is the Rio Suites, located at the I-15 and Flamingo Road. Boomtown, a few miles south of the Strip and just off the I-15, is also quite decent. I don't recommend either for a first trip to Las Vegas, though, since it's much more fun to be right in the thick of things either on the Strip or downtown.

Casino-Hotels

Boomtown   **$45–$75**   ★ ★ ★ ★

3333 Blue Diamond Road, Las Vegas, 89139, *(800) 588-7711, (702) 263-7777, FAX: (702) 896-5635.*
Located south of the city on the I-15. Double: $45–$75.
Boomtown, which just opened in May 1994, is themed to the rafters—so themed, in fact, that when you call its 800 number, "John Wayne" is the recorded voice giving voice-mail instructions. It's all in great fun, and it really works. In and out, everything resembles an old west mining town, from the rail tracks overhead to the country-western bands crooning in the casino lounge, to the comfortable, Victorian-style guestrooms. Appropriately enough, guests striking out in the casino can try their luck panning for gold at a special attraction. Kids are kept happy at the pair of pools, video arcade and "Nashville U.S.A." musical extravaganza. I like this place a lot, but the locale—right on the I-15 freeway several miles from the Strip—is a definite liability. There's nothing close enough to walk to, though Red Rock Canyon is a short drive. Amenities: conference facilities. 300 rooms. Credit cards: A, CB, DC, D, MC, V.

Orleans   **$49–$350**   ★ ★ ★ ★

4500 West Tropicana Avenue, Las Vegas, *(800) 675-3267, (702) 365-7111, FAX: (702) 365-7499.*
Located several miles west of the strip. Double: $49–$350.
Opened in late 1996, the Orleans has quickly become a locals' favorite—evidenced by how hard it is to find a space in the giant parking lot. The nicely appointed, 92,000-square-foot casino has a Mardi

Gras theme and is quite friendly; they even give out free beads at the change booths. Upstairs is a 70-lane bowling center and an elegant wedding chapel; by September 1997 a 12-screen movie theater will open as well as a child-care center. Guest rooms are surprisingly lovely and have the feel of a small suite, with a separate siting area with sofa, high-quality New Orleans-style furnishings, brass headboards and large baths. Six restaurants and a plush, 827-seat headliner theater complete the scene. A free shuttle links the hotel to the Strip and sister property, the Gold Coast. Because it is far off the beaten path with virtually nothing within walking distance, the Orleans isn't for everyone, but it's a great property just the same. 840 rooms. Credit cards: A, CB, DC, D, MC, V.

Rio's off-the-strip location appeals to many.

Rio Suites Hotel   **$95–$150**   ★★★★★

3700 West Flamingo Road, Las Vegas, 89103, ☎ *(800) 752-9746, (702) 252-7777, FAX: (702) 253-6090.*

Located a few long blocks from the Strip. Double: $95–$150.

The Rio has become the hip, happening place for Las Vegas' hip, happening young people, and it's easy to see why. The location is not the greatest for tourists—the Strip is a few long blocks away (too far for a comfortable walk), but the Rio is easily accessible by car, which can't be said for the Strip hotels. The casino, with its tropical Brazilian theme, is really pleasant, and the hotel's many restaurants win lots of awards in local newspaper polls. Especially notable is the dazzling Carnival World Buffet, which, unfortunately, is always mobbed (see "Restaurants" for more details). Guest rooms are quite nice and comfortable, and all have floor-to-ceiling windows with great views, but I wouldn't go so far as to call them suites (which to me means two rooms), as the hotel does. Each is quite large—600 square feet—and includes a large sofa, refrigerator and coffeemaker, big-screen TV and a small canopy over the bed. The bi-level penthouse suites, which are rented out for $850 when not occupied by high rollers, are really something with grand pianos, wet bars, dining rooms, whirlpool tubs, enormous bathrooms and tiny closets with telephones for private calls. Up the sweeping stairway is a loft-type bedroom—really classy!

The new Masquerade Village, opened in February 1997, is designed to create an ongoing carnival atmosphere with the Masquerade Show in the Sky, which features three complete parades and live performances. Guests can participate by traveling on a float in complete costume. The new Masquerade Tower has 1037 suites, bringing Rio's room total to 2563. While the pool area won't win any architectural or landscaping awards, it's notable for its "beach"—that's real sand on which to loiter or play volleyball. Occasionally the Rio has concerts out here with the likes of Kenny Loggins or Fleetwood Mac, and if you show up early enough, you can rent a lounge chair or float upon which to groove to the music. Each Tuesday during the warm months there is a beach party; $4 admission buys you two drinks and music by a local band. Summertime also sees lots of locals cheering on the volleyball tournaments held on the "beach." Club Rio, the hotel's circular nightclub, is a big hit with thirty-something locals who like the spread-out seating and D.J. dancing. Men pay a $10 cover, while women get in for free. The dinner show is popular as well. I just love this place, but, as noted, the location is a bit of a drag if you're into casino hopping. The Rio does offer a shuttle to both the MGM and the Fashion Show Mall (next to the Treasure Island) from 10 a.m. to 11 p.m. on weekdays and until 1 a.m. on weekends, while a cab to the Mirage costs only about $5. After touring this property, I vowed to stay here next time I'm in town. Trust me—you'll love it too. Amenities: exercise room, conference facilities. 2563 rooms. Credit cards: A, CB, DC, D, MC, V.

Sam's Town is a family-oriented Old West themed hotel.

Sam's Town $50–$100   ★ ★ ★

5111 Boulder Highway, Las Vegas, 89122, ☎ *(800) 634-6371, (702) 456-7777, FAX: (702) 454-8014.*

Located seven miles from the Strip. Double: $50–$100.

This family-oriented, Old West-style hotel reopened in May 1994 following a big expansion. Amenities include a large casino (the second largest in town) and sports book, free continental breakfast, seven restaurants, a 56-land bowling center, a huge and lively western dance hall, and what they claim is the largest western wear shop west of the Mississippi. There's also a pretty indoor park with waterfalls and footpaths that at night comes alive with laser light shows and dancing fountains. (See "Attractions.") Sam's Town is a local favorite and a very fun place to visit with its country-western bands and friendly staff, but the location, well off the Strip, makes it somewhat problematic for those who like to casino hop. Sam's Town does, however, offer a shuttle to both the Strip and Downtown. 650 rooms. Credit cards: A, CB, DC, D, MC, V.

Santa Fe Hotel $49–$89   ★ ★ ★

4949 North Rancho Drive, Las Vegas, 89130, ☎ *(800) 872-6823, (702) 658-4900, FAX: (702) 658-4919.*

Located off the I-95, 10 miles northwest of the Strip. Double: $49–$89.

Located far from the Strip, the Santa Fe is a small hotel decorated in a warm, southwestern style. Besides a good buffet and restaurant, and a large casino and live entertainment in the lounge, there's a hockey-sized ice skating rink and a bowling alley. So how come there's no pool? This place is nice, but its far-off-the-beaten-path locale is a real liability. On the other hand, you can snag a room on most weekends for about $60. Amenities: conference facilities. 200 rooms. Credit cards: A, CB, DC, D, MC, V.

RV Parks

Boomtown RV Resort $18–$20   ★ ★ ★

3333 Blue Diamond Road, Las Vegas, ☎ *(800) 588-7711, (702) 263-7777, FAX: (702) 896-5635.*

Located south of the Strip on the I-15. Double: $18–$20.

This RV park is attached to the very nice Boomtown Hotel and Casino, which opened in May 1994. Each space is serviced with phone and cable TV hookups, and can handle 20, 30 and 50 amp power. There are runs for pets, picnic and barbecue areas, and, of course, all the amenities that come with the excellent fun hotel and casino. For further details, see the Boomtown entry under "Casino-Hotels." Credit cards: A, CB, DC, D, MC, V.

Boulder Lakes RV Resort $19   ★ ★ ★ ★

6201 Boulder Highway, Las Vegas, 89122, ☎ *(702) 435-1157, FAX: (702) 435-1125.*

Located nine miles from the Strip. Double: $19.

This park provides more of a resort feel and peaceful location than those closer into town. There's no Strip shuttle, although nearby casinos occasionally offer one to their establishments. The grounds include 417 hookups, laundry and shower facilities, four pools, five Jacuzzis, a clubhouse and a convenience store. Weekly rates are $124. Credit cards: A, CB, DC, D, V.

Good Sam's Hitchin' Post $18 ★★★

3640 Las Vegas Boulevard North, Las Vegas, 89115, ☎ *(702) 644-1043.*
Located near Nellis Air Force Base. Double: $18.

It's a good half-hour to the Strip from this RV Park near Nellis Air
Force Base. It doesn't offer a shuttle, but a public bus stops just out
front. Facilities include 195 hookups, laundry and showers, pool, 30
and 50 amp hookups and in-park propane deliveries. NOTE: No RVs
older than 1980 accepted. Weekly rates are $108. Credit Cards: Not
Accepted.

KOA Kampgrounds $28 ★★★

4315 Boulder Highway, Las Vegas, 89121, ☎ *(702) 451-5527, FAX:*
(702) 434-8729.
Located five miles east of the Strip. Double: $28.

It costs a lot more than more conveniently located RV parks, but
KOA can usually be relied upon for immaculate grounds. The 300-
hookup site has laundry and shower facilities, pool, Jacuzzi, a recreation room and a free evening shuttle to the Strip. Credit cards: A, CB,
DC, D, MC, V.

"No, I don't know where your pirate shirt is."

Drawing by Victoria Roberts; ©1995 The New Yorker Magazine, Inc.

WHERE TO EAT

Diners may choose between breakfast at $1.49, or a mega-buffet that could feed an army.

Many visitors to Las Vegas never venture outside the hotels for a meal. It's certainly easy enough not to—every hotel has at least a coffee shop (I love the vegetarian burgers at the Desert Inn), and the mega-resorts each have five or six varied restaurants within their walls. But it's well worth the extra effort to try a few independent eateries as well, usually located far from the madding crowds (in atmosphere if not geographically). The closing hours listed here for each restaurant signify the latest you can come in and order dinner.

Buffet Style

The city is almost as famous for its buffets as it is for its slot machines. Virtually every casino-hotel has one; for years, they were regarded as loss leaders—a way to get people in the door to gamble before or after their cheap meal. (You *always* have to walk through the casino to get to the buffet.) The buffets are still an incredible bargain, but prices have gone up as Las Vegas cultivates the family market. That's because most people with kids in tow do very little gambling, and hotels are seeking ways to raise the bottom line everywhere—even at the lowly buffet.

The only drawback with buffets are their inevitable lines—it seems the cheaper the cost, the longer the wait. This is especially true at Rio Suite's Carnival World Buffet, widely considered the best in town. The lines are huge but the payoffs ample. If you have the patience to queue up for an hour or so, you'll be rewarded with an amazing meal at an astounding price.

Downtown

Fremont Paradise Buffet   **$$**   ★★★
200 East Fremont Street, Las Vegas, 89101, ☎ (702) 385-3232.
Buffet cuisine.
Lunch: 11 a.m.–3 p.m., prix fixe $7.
Dinner: 4–10 p.m., prix fixe $10.
Decent all the time, and the Seafood Fantasy is especially good. That costs $14.95 and takes place on Tuesday and Sunday from 4–10 p.m. and Friday from 4–11 p.m. They also have a champagne brunch on Sunday from 7 a.m.–3 p.m. for $8.95. Credit cards: A, CB, DC, D, MC, V.

Golden Nugget's Buffet   **$$**   ★★★★★
129 East Fremont Street, Las Vegas, 89101, ☎ (702) 385-7111.
Buffet cuisine.
Lunch: 10:30 a.m.–3 p.m., prix fixe $8.
Dinner: 4 p.m., prix fixe $11.
One of Las Vegas' better buffets. Sundays are given over to a champagne buffet that costs $10.95 and lasts from 8 a.m.–10 p.m. Credit cards: A, CB, DC, D, MC, V.

Lady Luck's Buffet   **$**   ★★★★
206 North 3rd Street, Las Vegas, 89101, ☎ (702) 477-3000.
Buffet cuisine.
Lunch: 11 a.m.–2 p.m., prix fixe $5.
Dinner: 4–10 p.m., entrées $9.
A downtown favorite, with shrimp, crab and prime rib at dinner as well as ethnic specialties. Credit cards: A, CB, DC, MC, V.

Molly's Country Buffet   **$**   ★★★
301 East Fremont Street, Las Vegas, 89101, ☎ (702) 388-2400.
Buffet cuisine.
Lunch: 11:30 a.m.–4 p.m., prix fixe $5.
Dinner: 5–10 p.m., prix fixe $8.
This country-style buffet features traditional fare such as pork chops, corn on the cob, fried chicken and braised short ribs. The restaurant is open 24 hours if you come too late for the buffet, and offers up one of the very few remaining 99-cent breakfasts (hotcakes or biscuits and gravy). There's brunch each Saturday and Sunday from 8 a.m. to 4 p.m. for $7.99. Credit cards: CB, DC, D, MC, V.

Showboat's Captain's Buffet   **$**   ★★★
2800 Fremont Street, Las Vegas, 89104, ☎ (702) 385-9104.
Buffet cuisine.
Lunch: 10 a.m.–3:30 p.m., prix fixe $5.
Dinner: 4:30–10 p.m., prix fixe $7.
After pigging out, you can burn off all (some?) of those calories at the Showboat's 106-lane bowling alley. Thursday and Friday evenings are

given over to the "Seafood Spectacular," which runs from 4:30–10 p.m. and costs $7.95. The weekend brunch costs $6.45 and runs from 8 a.m.–3 p.m. Credit cards: A, CB, DC, MC, V.

The Strip

After the fabulous buffet at The Mirage, guests can walk off calories along garden pathways.

Aladdin Marketplace **$** ★★★

3667 Las Vegas Boulevard South, Las Vegas, 89109, ☎ *(702) 736-0111. Buffet cuisine.*
Lunch: 10:30 a.m.–3 p.m., prix fixe $6.
Dinner: 4–10 p.m., prix fixe $7.
Lots of fresh fruits, vegetables and pastries to compliment the usual assortment of chicken, meat and fish dishes. There's also a carving station. Credit cards: A, CB, DC, D, MC, V.

Bally's Big Kitchen **$$** ★★★★★

3645 Las Vegas Boulevard South, Las Vegas, 89109, ☎ *(702) 739-4111. Buffet cuisine.*
Brunch: 7:30 a.m.–2:30 p.m., entrées $9.
Dinner: 4–10 p.m., prix fixe $13.
One of the best buffets in town, Bally's serves up brunch daily with such niceties as caviar, lobster and cognac omelettes. The dinner buffet is highlighted by additional Chinese cuisine. Patrons go right into the kitchen (hence the name) to pick out their own fresh-cooked food. Bally's Sterling Brunch ($49.95) is arguably Las Vegas' best. Served Sundays in the Steakhouse, it has lots of high-quality items such as lobster ravioli, roast lamb and smoked salmon. 9:30 a.m.–2:30 p.m. Credit cards: A, CB, DC, D, MC, V.

Bally's Sterling Brunch **$$$** ★★★★★

3645 Las Vegas Boulevard South, Las Vegas, 89109, ☎ *(702) 739-4111. Buffet cuisine.*
Widely considered one of the city's best Sunday brunches, this extravaganza is held each week in the Steakhouse Restaurant from 9:30 a.m.–2:30 p.m. Specialties include smoked salmon, roast lamb, roulades of sole, lobster ravioli and cooked-to-order waffles and eggs. The champagne flows freely, too. $49.95 plus tax. Features: own baking. Credit cards: A, CB, DC, D, MC, V.

Boulder Station's The Feast $ ★★★

4111 Boulder Highway, Las Vegas, 89121, ☎ (702) 432-7777.
Buffet cuisine.
Lunch: 11 a.m.–2:30 p.m., prix fixe $6.
Dinner: 4–10 p.m., prix fixe $8.
All the usual yummies at this hotel's buffet, as well as some specials
such as crayfish and mussels and "action stations" where chefs whip
up items to order. Boulder Station also offers a Sunday champagne
brunch from 7 a.m.–3:30 p.m. for just $6.95. Credit cards: A, CB, DC, D,
MC, V.

Bourbon Street Buffet $ ★★★

120 East Flamingo Road, Las Vegas, 89109, ☎ (702) 737-7200.
Buffet cuisine.
Lunch: 10:30 a.m.–2 p.m., prix fixe $4.
Dinner: 5–10 p.m., prix fixe $9.
Everything from salads to seafood, sandwiches to steaks. There's also
brunch, featuring made-to-order omelettes, from 10:30 a.m.–2 p.m.
on Saturday and Sunday for $6. Credit cards: A, CB, DC, D, MC, V.

Buffet of Champions $$ ★★★★★

3000 Paradise Road, Las Vegas, 89109, ☎ (702) 732-5111.
Buffet cuisine.
Lunch: 11 a.m.–2:30 p.m., prix fixe $9.
Dinner: 5–10 p.m., prix fixe $13.
Traditionally one of the city's most reputable buffets, with prices to
match. It also gets my vote for silliest buffet name. Breakfast and
lunch are served on weekdays only. Kids eat for half-price. An elabo-
rate champagne brunch ($11.99) is offered on Saturday and Sunday
from 8 a.m.–2:30 p.m. Credit cards: A, CB, DC, D, MC, V.

Caesars Palace's Palatium $$ ★★★★★

3570 Las Vegas Boulevard South, Las Vegas, 89109, ☎ (702) 731-7110.
Buffet cuisine.
Lunch: 11:30 a.m.–3:30 p.m., prix fixe $9.
Dinner: 4:30–10 p.m., prix fixe $14.
Breakfast and lunch are served Monday through Friday at this elegant
buffet with a lavish food display and a carving station. On Saturdays,
there's the Olympiad Brunch from 8:30 a.m.–3:30 p.m. ($13.35),
while Sundays are given over to the champagne brunch ($15.00), a
quite elaborate and tasty spread. Credit cards: A, CB, DC, D, MC, V.

Celebrity Cafe $ ★★★

305 Convention Center Drive, Las Vegas, 89109, ☎ (702) 734-0711.
Buffet cuisine.
One of the more reasonably priced Sunday brunches at only $7.95.
Choose from the buffet or order from a special menu. 10 a.m.–3 p.m.
Afterward, check out the hotel's new Motion Picture Museum (see
"Attractions"). Credit cards: A, DC, D, MC, V.

Circus Circus Buffet $ ★★

280 Las Vegas Boulevard South, Las Vegas, 89114, ☎ (702) 734-0410.
Buffet cuisine.
Brunch: Noon–4 p.m., prix fixe $4.
Dinner: 4:30–11 p.m., prix fixe $5.
You can build your own sundae at this "Plate of Plenty" buffet, one
of the cheapest-priced in town. Friday is a seafood buffet. Credit cards:
A, CB, DC, D, MC, V.

Continental's Florentine $ ★★

4100 Paradise Road, Las Vegas, 89109, ☎ *(702) 737-5555.*
Buffet cuisine.
Lunch: 11 a.m.–3:45 p.m., prix fixe $4.
Dinner: 6–10 p.m., prix fixe $6.
One of the cheapest buffets in town. The additional crab leg buffet,
served daily from 6 –10 p.m., is well worth the $12.95 charge. Credit
cards: A, DC, D, MC, V.

Desert Inn Sunday Brunch $ ★★★★

3145 Las Vegas Boulevard South, Las Vegas, 89109, ☎ *(702) 733-4434.*
Buffet cuisine.
One of the better Sunday brunches, with cooked-to-order omelettes
and waffles, carved-to-order prime ribs, smoked fish and lots of sinful
desserts. Served from 9 a.m.–2 p.m. in the Crystal Showroom.
$10.95, $7.95 for kids under 12. Under 3 free. Credit cards: A, CB, DC,
D, MC, V.

Excalibur's Round Table Buffet $ ★★★

3850 Las Vegas Boulevard South, Las Vegas, 89109, ☎ *(702) 597-7777.*
Buffet cuisine.
Lunch: 11 a.m.–4 p.m., prix fixe $5.
Dinner: 4–11 p.m., prix fixe $6.
This is a huge spread with knights and armor thrown in for effect. As
they describe it, "this massive buffet takes you back to days of old
when the masses ate in expansive dining halls." Hmmm.... Credit cards:
A, CB, DC, D, MC, V.

Flamingo Hilton's Buffet $$ ★★★★

3555 Las Vegas Boulevard South, Las Vegas, 89109, ☎ *(702) 733-3111.*
Buffet cuisine.
Lunch: Noon - 2:30 p.m., entrées $8.
Dinner: 4:30–10 p.m., prix fixe $10.
This buffet is in the Paradise Garden Restaurant, a pretty room that
overlooks the pool area. Buffet offerings vary daily. Friday 4:30–10
p.m. is the Seafood Spectacular at $9.95. Credit cards: A, CB, DC, D, MC, V.

Gold Coast Buffet $ ★★★

4000 West Flamingo Road, Las Vegas, 89103, ☎ *(702) 367-7111.*
Located a mile west of the Strip.
Buffet cuisine.
Lunch: 11 a.m.–3 p.m., prix fixe $4.
Dinner: 4–10 p.m., prix fixe $6.
Lots of hot and cold specialties, and a free cocktail with each meal.
Wednesday nights feature seafood for $7.95. Sunday brunch takes
place from 8 a.m.–3 p.m. and costs just $4.95. Credit cards: A, CB, DC,
D, MC, V.

Harrah's Galley Buffet $ ★★★★

3475 Las Vegas Boulevard South, Las Vegas, 89109, ☎ *(702) 369-5000.*
Buffet cuisine.
Lunch: 11 a.m.–4 p.m., prix fixe $6.
Dinner: 4–11 p.m., prix fixe $8.
Items vary daily at this elaborate spread, which always features at least
35 items at each meal. Credit cards: A, CB, DC, D, MC, V.

Imperial Palace's Emperor's Buffet $ ★★★

3535 Las Vegas Boulevard South, Las Vegas, 89109, ☎ *(702) 731-3311.*
Buffet cuisine.

WHERE TO EAT

Lunch: 11:30 a.m.–4 p.m., prix fixe $6.
Dinner: 5–10 p.m., prix fixe $7.

The Emperor's Buffet features baron of beef among the many choices. The hotel also offers the Imperial Buffet, which offers brunch on weekdays from 8 a.m.–3 p.m. ($5.95) and a roast sirloin buffet from 5 p.m.–10 p.m. for $7.95. There's a champagne brunch on Saturday and Sunday ($6.95) from 8 a.m.–3 p.m. Credit cards: A, CB, DC, MC, V.

Luxor's Manhattan Buffet $ ★★★
3900 Las Vegas Boulevard South, Las Vegas, 89119, ☎ *(702) 262-4000.*
Buffet cuisine.
Lunch: 11 a.m.–4 p.m., prix fixe $6.
Dinner: 4–10 p.m., prix fixe $8.

Lots of international entrées at this large buffet. You can choose from a number of dining rooms with big-city themes. Children 10 and under are half-price; kids under 4 are free. Credit cards: A, CB, DC, MC, V.

MGM Grand Sunday Brunch $$ ★★★★
3900 Las Vegas Boulevard South, Las Vegas, 89109, ☎ *(702) 891-7777.*
Buffet cuisine.

The Grand (what else?) Champagne Brunch features such mouth-watering items as filet mignon, prime rib, rack of lamb and eggs benedict. There's also a complete seafood bar. 9 a.m.–2 p.m. in the Brown Derby. $28.95 adults, $10.95 kids 6-12 and kids 5 and under free.

Credit cards: A, CB, DC, D, MC, V.

MGM Grand's Oz Buffet $ ★★★★
3799 Las Vegas Boulevard South, Las Vegas, 89109, ☎ *(702) 891-1111.*
Buffet cuisine.
Brunch: 7 a.m.–2:30 p.m., prix fixe $6.
Dinner: 4:30–10 p.m., prix fixe $8.

It's a different theme each day at this lavish setup featuring food from around the world. Credit cards: A, CB, DC, D, MC, V.

Maxim's Grand Buffet $ ★★★
160 East Flamingo Road, Las Vegas, 89109, ☎ *(702) 731-4300.*
Buffet cuisine.
Brunch: 9 a.m.–3 p.m., prix fixe $8.
Dinner: 4–10 p.m., prix fixe $6.

The typical brunch and dinner offerings daily, with roast baron of beef a specialty at dinner. There's a Saturday and Sunday champagne brunch form 9 a.m.–3 p.m. for $10.95. Credit cards: A, MC, V.

Mirage Buffet $$ ★★★★★
3400 Las Vegas Boulevard South, Las Vegas, 89109, ☎ *(702) 791-7111.*
Buffet cuisine.
Lunch: 11 a.m.–2:45 p.m., prix fixe $9.
Dinner: 3-9:30 p.m., prix fixe $13.

The Mirage does everything well, and its buffet is no exception. The breakfast and lunch prices are higher than most, but so's the quality. The Sunday brunch ($14, 8 a.m.–3 p.m.) is equally good. Credit cards: A, CB, DC, D, MC, V.

Monte Carlo's Buffet $
3770 Las Vegas Boulevard South, Las Vegas, ☎ *(702) 730-7777.*
Located on the Strip.
Buffet cuisine.

WHERE TO EAT

Lunch: 11 a.m.–4 p.m., prix fixe $7.
Dinner: 4–10 p.m., prix fixe $9.
Many items are prepared exhibition style at this Moroccan-themed spot. Sunday champagne brunch is served from 7 a.m. to 3 p.m. and costs $7.49.

Palace Station's The Feast   **$**   ★★★
2411 West Sahara Avenue, Las Vegas, 89102, (702) 367-2411.
Buffet cuisine.
Lunch: 11 a.m.–2:30 p.m., prix fixe $6.
Dinner: 4:30–10 p.m., prix fixe $8.
Meals are prepared right before your wondering eyes, with dishes such as grilled chicken, broiled steak and stir fry. Credit cards: A, CB, DC, D, MC, V.

Rio's Carnival World Buffet   **$**   ★★★★★
3700 West Flamingo Road, Las Vegas, 89103, (702) 252-7777.
Buffet cuisine.
Lunch: 11 a.m.–3:30 p.m., prix fixe $7.
Dinner: 3:30–11 p.m., prix fixe $9.
The best brunch in town, as far as I'm concerned, though the lines are always *tremendously* long and the dining room is short on ambience. Locals just love this place, and with good reason: There are nine separate stations serving food from around the globe, including Brazil, Italy, Mexico and Asia, and it's all delicious. Well worth the wait, if you're the patient type (and you'll need to be; count on at least 45 minutes). Once inside, though, you'll zip right through the food selection. Be sure to carefully note where your table is, or you'll never find it again. A few bucks more lets you nosh on fresh-grilled seafood. Saturday and Sunday brunch, from 7 a.m.–3:30 p.m., is $8.99. Credit cards: A, CB, DC, MC, V.

Riviera's World's Fare   **$**   ★★★★
2901 Las Vegas Boulevard South, Las Vegas, 89109, (702) 734-5110.
Buffet cuisine.
Brunch: 10 a.m.–3 p.m., prix fixe $7.
Dinner: 4:30-10:30 p.m., prix fixe $9.
"Lunch" is actually a champagne brunch each day. Each evening features a different cuisine from around the world. Mondays are Mexican, Tuesdays Italian, Wednesdays Oriental, Thursdays German. Saturdays are prime rib night, while Sundays are given over to a western barbecue. Credit cards: A, CB, DC, MC, V.

Sahara Buffet   **$**   ★★★
2535 Las Vegas Boulevard South, Las Vegas, 89109, (702) 737-2111.
Buffet cuisine.
Lunch: 11 a.m.–2:30 p.m., prix fixe $4.
Dinner: 4-10:30 p.m., prix fixe $6.
Lots of variety at all meals, and a carving station at dinner in the Moroccan-style dining room. Credit cards: A, CB, DC, D, MC, V.

Stardust's Warehouse All-You-Can-Eat $ ★★★
3000 Las Vegas Boulevard South, Las Vegas, 89109, (702) 732-6111.
Buffet cuisine.
Lunch: 11 a.m.–3 p.m., prix fixe $6.
Dinner: 4–10 p.m., prix fixe $8.
Lots of variety and top-quality items. Sunday champagne brunch runs from 7 a.m.–3 p.m. and costs $6.95. Credit cards: A, CB, DC, D, MC, V.

WHERE TO EAT

Stratosphere Buffet   **$**

> *2000 Las Vegas Boulevard South, Las Vegas,* ☎ *(702) 380-7777.*
> *Located on the Strip.*
> *Buffet cuisine.*
> *Lunch: 11 a.m.–4 p.m., prix fixe $7.*
> *Dinner: 4-9 p.m., prix fixe $9.*
>
> The theme is World's Fair at this brightly colored buffet, which features a carving station, Asian wok station and a rotisserie. Open until 11 p.m. on Saturday.

WHERE TO EAT

Many buffet-goers time their meal at Treasure Island to include the pirate battle.

Treasure Island Buffet   **$**   ★★★★

> *3300 Las Vegas Boulevard South, Las Vegas, 89109,* ☎ *(702) 894-7111.*
> *Buffet cuisine.*
> *Lunch: 11 a.m.–3:45 p.m., prix fixe $7.*
> *Dinner: 4–11 p.m., prix fixe $9.*
>
> Dinner features three buffets with American, Italian and Chinese themes. Sunday brunch runs from 7:30 a.m.–3:30 p.m., and costs

$8.99 for adults, $4.50 for kids. Plan your meal so you can catch the free pirate show out front. Credit cards: A, CB, DC, D, MC, V.

Tropicana's Island Buffet $$

3801 Las Vegas Boulevard South, Las Vegas, ☎ *(702) 739-2222.*
Located at the Tropicana's Island Tower.
Buffet cuisine.
Dinner: 5–11 p.m., prix fixe $11.

All the usual offerings at the Trop's pleasant buffet. The Saturday and Sunday champagne brunch, served from 7:30 a.m.–2:30 p.m. for only $9.95, is especially fine.

Vacation Village Buffet $ ★★★

6711 Las Vegas Boulevard South, Las Vegas, 89119, ☎ *(702) 897-1700.*
Located a few miles south of the Strip.
Buffet cuisine.
Lunch: 11 a.m.–3 p.m., prix fixe $5.
Dinner: 5–9:30 p.m., entrées $7.

Items change daily at this reasonably priced buffet, but the accent is always on Chinese food. Credit cards: A, MC, V.

Elsewhere

Boomtown's Blue Diamond Buffet $ ★★★

3333 Blue Diamond Road, Las Vegas, ☎ *(702) 263-7777.*
Located a few miles south of the Strip at I-15.
Buffet cuisine.
Lunch: 11:30 a.m.–3:30 p.m., prix fixe $5.
Dinner: 4–10 p.m., prix fixe $7.

This fun casino is a bit off the beaten track but well worth a visit. The buffet includes omelettes cooked to order, a salad bar, seafood, Chinese dishes, barbecue chicken and ribs and a chili and soup bar. Saturday and Sunday brunch is served 7 a.m.–3 p.m. for $5.99. Credit cards: A, CB, DC, D, MC, V.

Lone Mountain Buffet $ ★★★★

4949 North Rancho Drive, Las Vegas, ☎ *(702) 658-4900.*
Located 10 miles from the Strip.
American cuisine.
Lunch: 11:30 a.m.–2:30 p.m., prix fixe $5.
Dinner: 4–9 p.m., prix fixe $7.

A real locals' favorite with display cooking and lots of variety. Kids eat for half price. Sunday brunch is 7:30 a.m.–2:30 p.m. and costs $7.95.
Credit cards: A, CB, DC, D, MC, V.

Sam's Town Great Buffet $ ★★★★

5111 Boulder Highway, Las Vegas, 89122, ☎ *(702) 456-7777.*
Buffet cuisine.
Lunch: 11 a.m.–3 p.m., prix fixe $7.
Dinner: 4–9 p.m., prix fixe $9.

Like the casino, the buffet at Sam's Town is popular with locals. The Sunday champagne brunch costs $7.99 and runs from 8 a.m.–2:30 p.m. Credit cards: A, CB, DC, D, MC, V.

Cheap Eats

Cheap eats can be found at all hours in the coffeeshops and at the buffets. Here are a few other ideas.

Downtown

Big Dogs Cafe & Casino $$ ★★★★

6390 West Sahara Avenue, Las Vegas, ☎ *(702) 876-3647.*
Located a few blocks off the Strip.
American cuisine.
Lunch: entrées $4–$6.
Dinner: entrées $8–$14.

You can't miss this dog-themed restaurant as you're driving down
Sahara—the facade is covered with huge murals of man's best friend.
This trendy hangout is for locals in their 20s and 30s and stays abso-
lutely shoulder-to-shoulder on Friday and Saturday nights. The menu
was recently redone to get away from a bar food emphasis, and now
offers prime rib, steak, pastas, salads and seafood. Credit cards: MC, V.

Leilani's Island Cafe $ ★★★

202 East Fremont Street, Las Vegas, 89101, ☎ *(702) 385-4011.*
Hawaiian cuisine.
Lunch: from 11 a.m., entrées $3–$7.
Dinner: to 11 p.m., entrées $3–$7.

Lots of aloha spirit at this very reasonably priced Hawaiian cafe that
includes an animated three-minute rotating show to boot. A bowl of
beef or chicken teriyaki is just $1.49, and ice cream is only 95 cents a
scoop. Open until midnight on Friday and Saturday. Credit cards: A, CB,
DC, D, MC, V.

Tony Roma's $$ ★★★★

200 East Fremont Street, Las Vegas, 89101, ☎ *(702) 385-3232.*
American cuisine. Specialties: ribs; seafood; onion rings.
Lunch: 11 a.m.–2 p.m., entrées $8–$15.
Dinner: 5–11 p.m., entrées $10–$20.

Baby back ribs star, along with chicken, steak and seafood. Don't go
if you're concerned about cholesterol levels. Another location in the
Stardust Hotel. Features: full bar, non-smoking area, late dining. Reservations not accepted. Credit cards: A, CB, DC, MC, V.

The Strip

Country Star American Music Grille $$ ★★★★

3724 Las Vegas Boulevard South, Las Vegas, ☎ *(702) 740-8400.*
Located on the Strip next to New York-New York.
American cuisine.
Lunch: from 11 a.m., entrées $6–$18.
Dinner: to 10 p.m., entrées $6–$18.

County music fans get their own version of the Hard Rock Cafe at
this large eatery, owned by Reba McEntire and Vince Gill. The place
hops with music videos—country only, of course—listening posts,
interactive displays and lots of memorabilia. The cuisine is western,
with buffalo steaks and burgers, hickory-smoked barbecue ribs and
chicken and angus beef. Open until 11 p.m. on Friday and Saturday.
Credit cards: A, CB, DC, D, MC, V.

Dive! $$ ★★★

3200 Las Vegas Boulevard South, Las Vegas, ☎ *(702) 369-3483.*
Located in the Fashion Show Mall.
American cuisine.
Lunch: from 11:30 a.m., entrées $7–$14.
Dinner: to 10 p.m., entrées $7–$14.

The two wonder Steves (Spielberg and Wynn) teamed up to open this
trendy spot in 1995. The decor—portholes, waterfalls—makes you
think you're in a submarine far beneath the water's surface. The
extensive menu offers up such appetizers as wood oven-roasted mushrooms and grilled garlic toast; entrées consist of pizzas, salads, burgers
and fries with seven different dipping sauces. There's also chargrilled
salmon, pasta and wood-oven roasted chicken dishes. Save room for
the "to dive for" desserts. Open until 11:00 p.m. on Friday and Saturday. Credit cards: A, DC, D, MC, V.

Guadalajara Bar and Grille $$ ★★★
4111 Boulder Highway, Las Vegas, ☎ *(702) 432-7777.*
Mexican cuisine.
Lunch: 11 a.m.–5 p.m., entrées $5–$9.
Dinner: 5 –11 p.m., entrées $7–$15.
Perfect for those craving Mexican food but watching their waistlines,
as they offer low-fat sour cream and beans and chips that are baked
instead of deep-fried. Of course, there's also a full range of fat-rich
dishes, too. The salsa, guacamole and flour tortillas are made fresh
daily. Credit cards: A, DC, D, MC, V.

HIPPO & the Wild Bunch $ ★★★
4503 Paradise Road, Las Vegas, 89109, ☎ *(702) 731-5446.*
American cuisine. Specialties: gourmet pizza.
This spot, opened in April 1995, has a tropical decor and a gift shop
whose proceeds benefit the Save the Wildlife Foundation. It's a hip
combination restaurant/nightclub, with food that runs the gamut
from gourmet pizzas to fruit and vegetable juices to clams, ribs and
tacos. D.J.s blast out music most nights. Features: own baking, late
dining. Reservations recommended. Credit cards: A, CB, DC, D, MC, V.

Hard Rock Cafe $$ ★★★★
4475 Paradise Road, Las Vegas, 89109, ☎ *(702) 733-8400.*
American cuisine. Specialties: watermelon ribs; lime barbecued chicken.
Lunch: from 11:30 a.m., entrées $5–$15.
Dinner: to midnight, entrées $5–$15.
Look for the 72-foot neon guitar that marks this branch of these hip
international restaurants/nightclubs. The solidly American cuisine is
pretty good, but the real fun is simply being there, amid a huge collection of rock memorabilia and crowds of trendy diners. The casino
is especially hip. Features: own baking, full bar, non-smoking area,
late dining.

Holy Cow! $$ ★★★
2423 Las Vegas Boulevard South, Las Vegas, ☎ *(702) 732-2697.*
Located across from the Sahara.
American cuisine.
Dinner: entrées $4–$15.
You can't miss this place from the outside—it's all done up in cow
decor Las Vegas style. It's fun inside, too, with the cow theme extend-
ing all the way down to the Megabucks slot machine. This micro-
brewery opened in late 1992 and the next year won a gold medal at
the Great American Beer Festival for its "Amber Gambler." Holy
Cow! brews three other beers as well, and offers free tours of the process each day at 11 a.m., 1, 3, and 5 p.m. It serves breakfast all day, as
well as ribs, chicken, fish and chips, burgers and the like, and some

unique items such as armadillo eggs (fried jalapenos stuffed with cream cheese and breaded). The gift shop is a bovine-lovers delight. Fun and loud, tourists sit elbow-to-elbow with locals playing video poker at the bar. Features: late dining. Credit cards: A, CB, DC, D, MC, V.

Lance-a-Lotta Pasta $ ★

3850 Las Vegas Boulevard South, Las Vegas, ☎ *(702) 597-7777.*
Italian cuisine.
Dinner: 5–10 p.m., entrées $6–$12.
It's hard to expect much with a dorky name like Lance-a-Lotta Pasta, but this spot on the Excalibur's second floor is actually quite good for the price. The menu features chicken and shrimp dishes, but is mainly dominated by, you guessed it, pasta—you can choose from five shapes and 12 sauces. It's open for lunch only on Saturday and Sunday from 11:30 a.m.–2 p.m. (entrées run from $5–$6), and serves dinner until midnight on the weekends. The dining room is comfortable, but I could live without the strolling musicians. Reservations not accepted. Credit cards: A, CB, DC, D, MC, V.

Mama Ilardo's Pizzeria $ ★★★★★

3799 Las Vegas Boulevard South, Las Vegas, 89109, ☎ *(702) 736-2022.*
Italian cuisine.
This cafe located inside the MGM Grand Adventures theme park has some of the best pizza I've ever tasted. You can get a cheese slice for $1.95 (thin crust) or $2.15 (thick crust); toppings cost an extra 30 cents or so. Pies start at $9.75 and go up to $15.80. There's also a location in the MGM Grand's food court *(☎ 736-2550)*, which serves breakfast daily from 7–11 a.m. It charges just $1.59 for an egg and cheese, sausage or bacon "omwich." Hotel guests can order ahead by dialing 3018. Credit cards: A, CB, DC, D, MC, V.

Motown Cafe $$ ★★★

3155 West Harmon Avenue, Las Vegas, ☎ *(702) 740-6969.*
Located on the Strip.
American cuisine.
Lunch: from 11 a.m., entrées $7–$18.
Dinner: to 11 p.m., entrées $7–$18.
You can burn off calories between courses by dancing to the continuous live music at this brightly lit and colored spot in New York-New York. There's lots of Motown memorabilia from the likes of the Supremes, Jackson Five and the Commodores. The menu has it all: burgers, salads, grilled chicken and meats, seafood, pasta and southern specialties like "Smokey's Ribs." Credit cards: A, CB, DC, D, MC, V.

Official All-Star Cafe $$ ★★★

3785 Las Vegas Blvd. South, Las Vegas, 89109, ☎ *(702) 795-8326.*
Located in the Showcase Mall across from New York-New York.
American cuisine.
Lunch: 11 a.m.–4 p.m., entrées $7–$25
Dinner: 4 p.m.–1 a.m., entrées $7–$25
Designed as a larger than life tribute to sports, the Official All Star Cafe seats 600 people over three levels. Patrons are surrounded by video monitors, scoreboards and booths shaped like huge baseball mitts. The walls are covered with memorabilia and equipment once owned by sports stars like Shaquille O'Neal, Emmett Smith and Michael Jordan as well as funky items like Jack Nicholson's L.A. Lak-

ers chair from The Forum. The ballpark menu includes 11 types of burgers, Philly cheesesteaks, hot dogs, Buffalo chicken wings, and special recipes including Andre Agassi's spaghetti, Joe Montana's ravioli, Monica Seles' chicken Caesar salad and Wayne Gretsky's T-Bone steak.

Planet Hollywood $$ ★★★

3570 Las Vegas Boulevard South, Las Vegas, 89109, ☎ *(702) 791-7827.*
Located in the Forum Shops.
American cuisine.
Dinner: to 1 a.m., entrées $6–$18.
Prepare to have your senses assaulted at this latest incarnation of the fast-growing and hip chain. Once you pass by the hand- and foot-prints of some of Hollywood's finest—everyone from Bob Hope to Geena Davis—your ears are blasted with rock music while your eyes feast on the huge collection of movie memorabilia, leopard and zebra print carpeting and large 3-D mural of the stars. Even the restrooms are way cool. The extensive menu offers up everything from blackened shrimp to gourmet pizzas to grilled ribs, chicken and pork. Only for the young who don't mind crowds and shouting all through dinner. The bar stays open until 2 a.m. Naturally, there's also a store where you can stock up on Planet Hollywood logoed items. Reservations not accepted. Credit cards: A, DC, MC, V.

Sfuzzi $$ ★★★★

3200 Las Vegas Boulevard South, Las Vegas, ☎ *(702) 699-5777.*
Located in the Fashion Show Mall.
Italian cuisine.
Lunch: 11:30 a.m.–4 p.m., entrées $9–$13.
Dinner: 4–10 p.m., entrées $9–$13.
The prices are quite reasonable for the upscale setting at this fine Italian restaurant, which has a pretty, classically decorated dining room and a large outdoor patio right on the Strip—a real rarity. Start with flash-fried mushrooms or white bean soup, then move onto pasta dishes, skillet-roasted sea bass or pizzas from the wood-burning oven. Open until 11 p.m. Friday and Saturday. Credit cards: A, DC, D, MC, V.

Wolfgang Puck Cafe $$ ★★★

3799 Las Vegas Boulevard South, Las Vegas, ☎ *(702) 891-3019.*
Continental cuisine. Specialties: gourmet pizzas.
Lunch: from 11 a.m., entrées $9–$14.
Dinner: to 11 p.m., entrées $9–$14.
Puck continues to expand his empire with this casual cafe that offers his most successful dishes at reasonable prices. Since it's in the MGM Grand's mega-casino, it gets pretty noisy. Features: own baking. Reservations not accepted. Credit cards: A, CB, DC, D, MC, V.

Elsewhere

Vineyard $$ ★★★

3630 Maryland Parkway South, Las Vegas, 89109, ☎ *(702) 731-1606.*
Italian cuisine.
Lunch: from 11 a.m., entrées $5–$10.
Dinner: to 11 p.m., entrées $8–$15.
A great value, this casual Italian restaurant features a huge, all-you-can-eat antipasto salad bar, homemade bread, and large portions of decent Italian food. Located in the Boulevard Mall. Features: own

WHERE TO EAT

baking, full bar, non-smoking area, late dining. Credit cards: A, CB, DC, MC, V.

Gourmet Cuisine

Every large casino-hotel has at least one gourmet room; the mega-resorts each have several. There are also a number of independent restaurants that offer a good range of fine dining. You'll pay prices similar to other cities—no 99-cent specials here!

Downtown

Binion's Steak House   **$$$**   ★★★
128 Fremont Street, Las Vegas, 89101, ☎ (702) 382-1600.
American cuisine. Specialties: steak; prime rib.
Dinner: 5–10:30 p.m., entrées $20–$35.
If you're hankering for a big chunk of red meat with all the trimmings, this is the place to go. A 20-ounce porterhouse steak and prime rib roasted in rock salt are favorites. Dress is strictly cowboy chic. Features: full bar, rated wine cellar. Reservations recommended. Credit cards: A, CB, DC, MC, V.

Burgundy Room   **$$$**   ★★★
206 North 3rd Street, Las Vegas, 89101, ☎ (702) 477-3000.
American cuisine. Specialties: beef Wellington; Maine lobster.
Dinner: 5–11 p.m., entrées $13–$25.
The plush atmosphere features extra-large booths and the artwork of Salvador Dali and Max Le Verrier, and the wines are well chosen to match the gourmet American/Continental specialties at this pleasant hotel restaurant. Specialties include black angus chateaubriand, veal valdostana and seafood kabobs. Features: full bar, rated wine cellar. Reservations recommended. Credit cards: A, MC, V.

Center Stage Restaurant   **$$**   ★★★
1 Main Street, Las Vegas, ☎ (702) 386-2110.
American cuisine. Specialties: roast prime rib of beef.
Dinner: 5–11 p.m., entrées $9–$15.
The best reason to come to this steakhouse on the second floor of Jackie Gaughan's Plaza is the dazzling display of lights along Fremont Street, also known as Glitter Gulch. The menu features the usual assortment of steaks, chicken and fish, and the portions are huge. Open only to adults over 18. Features: rated wine cellar. Reservations recommended. Credit cards: A, CB, DC, D, MC, V.

Hugo's Cellar   **$$$**   ★★★★
202 East Fremont Street, Las Vegas, 89101, ☎ (702) 385-4011.
American cuisine. Specialties: red snapper, prawns.
Dinner: 5–11 p.m., entrées $20–$38.
Fancy New Orleans-style ambience and special service (including a fresh rose presented to each lady) combine with homemade breads and excellent American/Continental fare to make this one of the favorite gourmet rooms downtown. Good wines, fine seafood and an intriguing salad cart that's rolled to your table; you choose from 10–15 items, and the salad is mixed tableside. Features: full bar, rated wine cellar. Jacket requested. Reservations recommended. Credit cards: A, CB, DC, D, MC, V.

Lilly Langtry's   **$$$**   ★★★★
129 East Fremont Street, Las Vegas, 89101, ☎ *(702) 386-8181.*
Chinese cuisine.
Dinner: 6–11 p.m., entrées $9–$27.
Traditional Cantonese specialties are served in a pretty dining room
where Lilly herself oversees things from a stained-glass portrait. Din-
ers sit on a number of levels; lovers can draw the curtains at the
booths for a private tête-à-tête. Extra-special choices include lobster
Cantonese, Mongolian beef and almond duck. Reservations recom-
mended. Credit cards: A, CB, DC, D, MC, V.

Pasta Pirate   **$$**   ★★★
12 Ogden Street, Las Vegas, 89101, ☎ *(702) 385-1222.*
Italian cuisine. Specialties: seafood.
Dinner: 5:30–10:30 p.m., entrées $8–$22.
The name seems to indicate that this is a low-end spaghetti-and-meat-
balls sort of place, but the menu is actually quite sophisticated, with
specials such as mesquite-grilled seafood and filet mignon. The homemade pasta is good, too. The reasonable prices include a good dinner
salad with bay shrimp, mushrooms and tomatoes. Try the house special, two baby lobster tails with filet mignon, for just $10.95. Fea-
tures: own baking, full bar. Reservations recommended. Credit cards: A,
CB, DC, D, MC, V.

Redwood Bar and Grill   **$$$**   ★★★
12 Ogden Avenue, Las Vegas, 89101, ☎ *(702) 385-1222.*
American cuisine. Specialties: steak; seafood.
Dinner: 5:30–10 p.m., entrées $13–$29.
This California-style grill is a cozy meat-and-potatoes spot where the
porterhouse steak special ($12.95 for an 18-ounce steak, soup or
salad, potatoes, vegetable and dessert) is a local favorite. There's also
chicken and seafood for those who shun the high-cholesterol fare, and
decent wines to match. Features: full bar, rated wine cellar. Reserva-
tions recommended. Credit cards: A, CB, DC, D, MC, V.

Stefano's   **$$$**   ★★★★
129 East Fremont Street, Las Vegas, 89101, ☎ *(702) 385-7111.*
Italian cuisine. Specialties: agnoloti; piccata al limone.
Dinner: 6–11 p.m., entrées $12–$35.
Hand-painted Italian murals, Venetian glass chandeliers and a charming country cottage setting provide the backdrop for authentic
Northern Italian dishes. Fresh seafood is a specialty, and singing, costumed waiters add to the ambience. Open on Friday and Saturday
from 5:30–11:30 p.m. Features: own baking, full bar, rated wine cel-
lar, late dining. Jacket requested. Reservations required. Credit cards: A,
CB, DC, D, MC, V.

The Strip

Ah-So   **$$$**   ★★★★
3570 Las Vegas Boulevard South, Las Vegas, 89109, ☎ *(702) 731-7110.*
Japanese cuisine. Specialties: sushi.
Dinner: 6–11 p.m., prix fixe $55. Closed: Mon.
A Japanese garden atmosphere, complete with waterfall, a tiny stream
that flows under bridges and kimono-clad waitresses, prevails at this
upscale restaurant. The six-course prix-fixe menu features a variety of

Teppan-Yaki specialties; you can also order fresh sushi, sashimi and zensai. Reservations recommended. Credit cards: A, CB, DC, D, MC, V.

Alpine Village Inn $$ ★★★★

3003 Paradise Road, Las Vegas, 89109, ☎ *(702) 734-6888.*
Located near the Convention Center.
German cuisine.
Dinner: 5 p.m.–midnight, entrées $10–$20.

This venerable German-Swiss restaurant, located across from the Las Vegas Hilton, is in its 43rd year, an amazing achievement in this young town. It offers both traditional and modern cuisine, a nice selection of wines and beers and friendly service in a Swiss chalet-style ambience. There's also a rathskeller and sing-along piano bar on the premises. Features: own baking, full bar, rated wine cellar, late dining. Reservations recommended. Credit cards: A, CB, DC, D, MC, V.

Alta Villa $$ ★★★★

3555 Las Vegas Boulevard South, Las Vegas, 89109, ☎ *(702) 733-3111.*
Italian cuisine. Specialties: minestrone soup; filet mignon alta villa; pizza.
Dinner: 5:30–11 p.m., entrées $10–$20. Closed: Thur., Fri.

Italian village ambience provides the backdrop for solid cooking that features appetizer and main dish pizzas and garlic bread baked on-site. Recent reviews suggest the food is slipping and the service needs work. Features: own baking, full bar, rated wine cellar, non-smoking area, late dining. Reservations recommended. Credit cards: A, CB, DC, D, MC, V.

Andre's $$$ ★★★★★

401 South Sixth Street, Las Vegas, 89101, ☎ *(702) 385-5016.*
Located a block east of the Strip.
French cuisine. Specialties: fresh fish; marget of duck with port-wine sauce; roast rack of lamb.
Dinner: 6–10 p.m., entrées $20–$40.

A converted home in the downtown area serves as a backdrop for chef-owner Andre Rochat's innovative cooking. Lace curtains and cut-glass lamps add a romantic atmosphere; lovers can be tucked away in a private room. They have a fabulous wine cellar housing more than 500 varieties, some more than 150 years old. Locals consider this the best French restaurant in town, as well as a great place to impress a date. Closing times vary, so call ahead. Features: own baking, full bar, rated wine cellar. Reservations required. Credit cards: A, CB, DC, MC, V.

Antonio's $$$ ★★★★

3700 West Flamingo Road, Las Vegas, 89103, ☎ *(702) 252-7777.*
Located a few blocks off the Strip.
Italian cuisine. Specialties: Vitello al Marsala.
Dinner: 5–11 p.m., entrées $11–$27.

A lovely romantic atmosphere complete with fresh flowers provides a pleasant backdrop for traditional Italian fare prepared with some interesting touches. The locals say the breadsticks, which can be used to sop up the aromatic olive oil, are one of the best reasons to come. Features: own baking, full bar. Reservations recommended. Credit cards: A, CB, DC, D, MC, V.

Bacchanal $$$ ★★★★★

3570 Las Vegas Boulevard South, Las Vegas, ☎ *(702) 731-7731.*
Continental cuisine.

Dinner: 6 and 9 p.m., prix fixe $70.

Go back in time to the age of Antony and Cleopatra (who made an appearance) at this Roman banquet-themed restaurant where "goddesses" pour wine, costumed waitpersons are at your beck and call, and you hear the voices of Zeus and Venus along with simulated thunder and lightning. They even massage your shoulders with exotic balm! The prix fixe dinner takes about two hours and includes three wines and dessert. For anyone who has time to notice, the food is good, too. It's quite an experience! Jacket and tie requested. Reservations required. Credit cards: A, CB, DC, D, MC, V.

Bally's Steakhouse   **$$$**   ★★★★

3645 Las Vegas Boulevard South, Las Vegas, 89109, ☎ *(702) 739-4661.*
American cuisine. Specialties: steak; seafood.
Dinner: 6–11 p.m., entrées $20–$40. Closed: Mon., Sun.

This New York club-style restaurant offers standard American/Continental fare. Formerly Barrymore's. Features: own baking, full bar, rated wine cellar, non-smoking area, late dining. Reservations recommended.

Barronshire   **$$$**   ★★★

3000 Paradise Road, Las Vegas, 89109, ☎ *(702) 732-5859.*
English cuisine. Specialties: prime rib.
Dinner: 6–11 p.m., entrées $18–$23. Closed: Wed.

An English country-like setting is the motif at this eatery best known for its prime rib carved tableside. The menu also features salads, fish and chicken dishes. Reservations recommended. Credit cards: A, CB, D, MC, V.

Beijing   **$$**   ★★★★

3900 Paradise Road, Las Vegas, 89109, ☎ *(702) 737-9618.*
Located a block off the Strip.
Chinese cuisine. Specialties: Peking duck.
Lunch: 11 a.m.–2:30 p.m., entrées $5–$8.
Dinner: to 3 a.m., entrées $8–$15.

A nice atmosphere—lots of Oriental crafts and artwork—complements the gourmet Beijing dishes at this reasonably priced restaurant. Provincial specialties include pine nut shrimp, luscious lobster creations and Mongolian Hot Pot. During large conventions, you can wait as long as an hour for a table, so call ahead. Open 5–11 p.m. on Sunday. Features: full bar. Reservations recommended. Credit cards: A, CB, DC, D, MC, V.

Benihana Village   **$$$**   ★★★★

3000 Paradise Road, Las Vegas, 89109, ☎ *(702) 732-5111.*
Located one block off the Strip, next to the Convention Center.
Japanese cuisine.
Dinner: 5–11 p.m., entrées $15–$30.

Benihana gets high marks for its stunning surroundings, which practically ooze tranquility. The setting is a Japanese village with lush gardens, koi ponds, exotic statues and a small steam flowing throughout. Thanks to some nifty special effects, there's even periodic fireworks and thunder showers. The complex consists of a cocktail lounge that serves Oriental hors d'oeuvres; the Seafood Grille; the Garden of the Dragon, a gourmet Chinese restaurant; and Hibachi, where they slice and dice right at your table. The latter is out of view of the village and while the teppan cuisine is good, it's better at Mizuno's at the Tropicana. Reservations recommended. Credit cards: A, CB, DC, D, MC, V.

Bertolini's   **$$**   ★★★★★

3500 Las Vegas Boulevard South, Las Vegas, ☎ *(702) 735-4663.*
Located at the Forum Shops.
Italian cuisine.
Lunch: from 11:30 a.m., entrées $8–$19.
Dinner: to midnight, prix fixe $8–$19.

This is one of my favorite restaurants in Las Vegas, although it is a bit overpriced and portions are small. It's worth it, though, for the splendid setting right at the foot of the massive Fountain of the Gods in the Forum Shops. You can dine "outside" beneath the changing "sky" right next to the gushing water (my choice, but it's a bit noisy) or inside in the more sedate dining room. There are five kinds of pizza for $9.95, as well as pasta and chicken dishes with a Northern Italian flair. Open until midnight on Friday and Saturday. Features: rated wine cellar. Reservations recommended. Credit cards: A, MC, V.

Bistro Le Montrachet   **$$$**   ★★★★★

3000 Paradise Road, Las Vegas, 89114, ☎ *(702) 732-5111.*
French cuisine. Specialties: New Zealand venison; Long Island scallops.
Dinner: 6–11 p.m., entrées $20–$40. Closed: Tue.

This elegant gourmet room features dramatic flower arrangements, original oils on the walls, fine china and crystal and forward-looking French cuisine both well-conceived and beautifully presented. Dressy and expensive. Excellent wine list and irresistible desserts, too. Features: own baking, full bar, rated wine cellar, late dining. Jacket requested. Reservations required. Credit cards: A, CB, DC, D, MC, V.

Bistro, The   **$$$**   ★★★★

3400 Las Vegas Boulevard South, Las Vegas, 89109, ☎ *(702) 791-7111.*
French cuisine.
Dinner: 6–11:30 p.m., entrées $21–$40. Closed: Tue., Wed.

This richly decorated room gives you the feeling of being in grand old Paris during the impressionistic craze. Choices include lamb, fresh seafood, lobster, game and breast of duck. Save room for the sinful traditional French desserts. Jacket requested. Reservations recommended. Credit cards: A, CB, DC, D, MC, V.

Brown Derby   **$$$**   ★★★★

3799 Las Vegas Boulevard South, Las Vegas, ☎ *(702) 891-7777.*
Located on the Strip.
American cuisine.
Dinner: 5:30–11 p.m., entrées $38–$45.

The famed Hollywood restaurant, which dates to the 1920s, has been faithfully recreated at the MGM. Oversized portions of steak and beef, poultry, lamb, pork and seafood—named for Hollywood legends—grace the menu, as well as the signature Cobb salad and grapefruit cake made famous by the original. Despite the high prices, the atmosphere is casual. Sunday brunch, served from 9 a.m.–2 p.m., is a feast with a seafood station, sushi, eggs Benedict, rack of lamb, omelettes cooked to order and unlimited champagne. $28.95, adults, $10.95 kids 6–12, under five free. Reservations recommended. Credit cards: A, CB, DC, D, MC, V.

WHERE TO EAT

Buccaneer Bay Club   **$$$**   ★★★★

3300 Las Vegas Boulevard South, Las Vegas, 89109, ☎ (702) 894-7111.
Continental cuisine.
Dinner: 5–10:30 p.m., entrées $18–$30.

Probably the best place to view the Treasure Island's live pirate bat-
tles—if you're lucky enough to get a table that overlooks the lagoon.
You can't reserve these in advance, so you may want to slip the maître
d' a few bucks if your heart is set on seeing the show during dinner.
Classic Continental cuisine, with the huge prime rib and mushroom
chicken among the standouts. Reservations recommended. Credit
cards: A, CB, DC, D, MC, V.

Camelot   **$$$**   ★★★★

3850 Las Vegas Boulevard South, Las Vegas, 89109, ☎ (702) 597-7777.
Continental cuisine.
Dinner: 6–11 p.m., entrées $13–$19.
The magical King Arthur's castle theme of the hotel extends into this
moderately priced restaurant where specialties range from "Filet King
Arthur" to pastas and seafood. Good value for the money, and a nice
surprise in this decidedly middle-market hotel. Features: full bar,
rated wine cellar. Reservations recommended. Credit cards: A, CB, DC, D,
MC, V.

Chin's   **$$$**   ★★★★

3200 Las Vegas Boulevard South, Las Vegas, ☎ (702) 733-8899.
Located in the Fashion Show Mall.
Chinese cuisine. Specialties: dim sum; strawberry chicken.
Lunch: from 11:30 a.m., entrées $9–$13.
Dinner: to 9:30 p.m., entrées $14–$30.
Excellent Cantonese fare prepared by chef-owner Tola Chin, who will
whip up special dishes that are not on the menu if you ask. The inno-
vative cooking—which, by the way, not everyone likes—is accompa-
nied by a nice wine list; the set-price meals can be a good value. The
restaurant started as a small storefront and was successful enough to
move to this modern and impressive location in the Fashion Show
Mall, which is next to Treasure Island. Try the raspberry or strawberry
shrimp, lemon chicken or ruby pork. Reservations recommended.
Credit cards: A, CB, DC, D, MC, V.

Cipriani   **$$$**   ★★★★

2790 East Flamingo Road, Las Vegas, ☎ (702) 369-6711.
Italian cuisine. Specialties: fettuccine with caviar and salmon; calamari.
Lunch: 11:30 a.m.–2 p.m., entrées $9–$14.
Dinner: 5:30–10 p.m., entrées $14–$28.
Watching the lively open kitchen is half the fun at this very good con-
temporary Italian restaurant. When you tire of that, turn to the eclectic food and fine wines, and enjoy the exceptional service. The dining
room is lovely, with crystal chandeliers, French doors, and hanging
plants, with a three-story lighthouse and small pond out front. Jacket
requested. Reservations recommended. Credit cards: A, CB, DC, MC, V.

Claudine's   **$$$**   ★★★★

3475 Las Vegas Boulevard South, Las Vegas, 89109, ☎ (702) 369-5000.
American cuisine. Specialties: steak; seafood.
Dinner: 5:30–10:30 p.m., entrées $14–$21.

Basic Continental/American fare and an excellent wine list make this turn-of-the-century theme dining room a favorite with both tourists and locals. Salads are prepared table-side and compliment the high-quality cuts of beef and fresh seafood. Good service and show tunes at the piano bar add to the ambience and solid cooking. Features: full bar, rated wine cellar. Reservations recommended. Credit cards: A, CB, DC, D, MC, V.

Coyote Cafe $$ ★★★

3799 Las Vegas Boulevard South, Las Vegas, 89109, ☎ *(702) 891-7349.*
Southwestern cuisine.
Lunch: 11 a.m.–4 p.m., entrées $7–$13.
Dinner: 4–10 p.m., entrées $7–$13.

Mark Miller, who is behind the trendy Coyote Cafe in Santa Fe and Red Sage in Washington, D.C., proves that quality restaurants without a gimmick can actually make it in Las Vegas with his Coyote Cafe in the MGM Grand. Great food with lots of spices and innovative touches. You can dine in the casual cafe, whose hours and prices are quoted above, or in the formal grill room, which is open for dinner only from 6–10 p.m. Entrées range from $26-$34, and reservations are required. Features: own baking, full bar, rated wine cellar, non-smoking area. Credit cards: A, CB, DC, D, MC, V.

Embers $$$ ★★★★

3535 Las Vegas Boulevard South, Las Vegas, 89109, ☎ *(702) 731-3311.*
Continental cuisine.
Dinner: 5–11 p.m., entrées $16–$28. Closed: Mon., Tue.

Flickering candles and paintings of Europe set the mood at this cozy gourmet room where men can go without the oft-required jacket and tie. You can munch on a complimentary basket of fresh vegetables and fresh-baked bread while perusing the menu, which includes wonderful French onion soup, Australian lobster tail, orange roughy sauteed with macadamia nuts and roast Long Island duck. All entrées come with a vegetable and a choice of potato, rice or pasta. Desserts are prepared tableside; at $6, the cherries jubilee is a steal. Excellent value. Reservations recommended. Credit cards: A, CB, DC, MC, V.

Emeril's New Orleans Fish House $$$ ★★★★★

3799 Las Vegas Boulevard South, Las Vegas, ☎ *(702) 891-7777.*
Located on the Strip.
Seafood cuisine.
Lunch: 11 a.m.–2:30 p.m., entrées $16–$40.
Dinner: 5:30–10:30 p.m., entrées $16–$40.

Well-known chef Emeril Lagasse, winner of numerous awards for his innovative cuisine, offers up his signature barbecued shrimp as well as lobster, fresh seafood, steaks and double-cut pork chops. Save room for his famed desserts such as banana cream pie with banana crust and caramel. With its pretty dining room and atmospheric courtyard, this spot is a real tribute to the Big Easy. Reservations required. Credit cards: A, CB, DC, D, MC, V.

Empress Court $$$ ★★★★★

3570 Las Vegas Boulevard South, Las Vegas, 89109, ☎ *(702) 731-7110.*
Chinese cuisine. Specialties: shark's fin soup; Peking duck.
Dinner: 6–11 p.m., entrées $25–$55. Closed: Tue., Wed.

WHERE TO EAT

If you're used to tacky storefront Chinese restaurants, you will be awed by the sight (and tastes!) of Empress Court, where Cantonese cuisine reaches gourmet levels in a dramatic setting. Everything costs a bundle, but most believe the regional specialties, imported teas and spices, and first-class service are worth it. If you're torn over several entrées, you can order from a prix-fixe menu that includes appetizer, soup and several main dishes for $40 and $55. No jeans or sneakers. Features: own baking, full bar, rated wine cellar. Jacket requested. Reservations recommended. Credit cards: A, CB, DC, D, MC, V.

Fisherman's Broiler $$$ ★★★

2411 West Sahara Avenue, Las Vegas, ☎ *(702) 367-2411.*
Seafood cuisine. Specialties: seafood; clam chowders.
Lunch: from 11 a.m., entrées $4–$13.
Dinner: to 11 p.m., entrées $12–$27.

Save your money for the gaming tables and stop in here for a refreshingly inexpensive lunch buffet or light dinner. The food isn't always perfect, but it's a nice change of pace, and most of it is grilled over mesquite to cut the calories. The restaurant has the feel of a New England eatery with a quaint nautical theme. At $6.95, the lunchtime soup and salad bar is an especially good deal. Features: rated wine cellar. Reservations recommended. Credit cards: A, CB, DC, MC, V.

Garden of the Dragon $$$ ★★★

3000 Paradise Road, Las Vegas, 89109, ☎ *(702) 732-5111.*
Chinese cuisine. Specialties: Peking duck; lobster.
Dinner: 5–11 p.m., entrées $12–$36.

The eclectic menu encompasses food from all of China's districts, with authentic dishes from Beijing and Northern Mongolia, as well as spicy Szechuan and Cantonese fare. The pretty dining room overlooks the Japanese gardens of Benihana Village; for a real Asian experience, come early for a cocktail in the lovely Benihana Cocktail Lounge. Features: splendid view, full bar, rated wine cellar. Reservations recommended. Credit cards: A, CB, DC, D, MC, V.

Ginza $$$ ★★★

1000 East Sahara Avenue, Las Vegas, 89104, ☎ *(702) 732-3080.*
Located a few blocks east of the Sahara.
Japanese cuisine. Specialties: sushi bar; yosenabe; sukiyaki.
Dinner: 5-2 p.m., entrées $11–$20. Closed: Mon.

This neighborhood favorite has been around for nearly 20 years. The service by kimono-clad waitresses is warm, the setting is attractive, the food is good and the price is right. The sushi bar offers a great selection of both raw fish and Japanese beers and wines. Features: wine and beer only, nonsmoking area, late dining. Reservations recommended. Credit cards: A, CB, DC, MC, V.

Golden Steer Steak House $$$ ★★★

308 West Sahara Avenue, Las Vegas, ☎ *(702) 384-4470.*
Located about five minutes from the Strip.
American cuisine. Specialties: prime rib, steak, seafood.
Dinner: 5-11:45 p.m., entrées $20–$43.

Conventioneers are sometimes packed like cattle into the various dining rooms of this establishment with an Old West theme. Huge portions of prime rib and steak appeal to the ravenous appetite, with some seafood and game dishes added for variety. It's been around 30 years, so you know they're doing something right. Features: rated wine cellar. Reservations recommended. Credit cards: A, CB, DC, D, MC, V.

Hamada Sushi Bar $$$ ★★★★

3555 Las Vegas Boulevard South, Las Vegas, 89109, ☎ *(702) 733-3111.*
Japanese cuisine.
Dinner: 5 p.m.–12:30 a.m., entrées $8–$26.
Tucked off on its own on the Flamingo Hilton's lower level (take the escalators near the lobby), this tiny spot offers authentic, tasty sushi. Combinations cost $24. There's also a fine selection of Japanese beer, wine and sake. Credit cards: A, CB, DC, D, MC, V.

Ho-Wan $$$ ★★★★

3145 Las Vegas Boulevard South, Las Vegas, 89109, ☎ *(702) 733-4547.*
Chinese cuisine. Specialties: Peking duck; shark's fin soup.
Dinner: 6–11 p.m., entrées $25–$42.
Walk past a tank full of live seafood into a dramatic dining room featuring Oriental tapestries, art, and artifacts. Cuisine includes Mandarin, Szechuan and Cantonese influences very attractively presented. Specialties include Hong Kong-style seafood, Peking beef, Mongolian lamb and Macao braised squab. Features: own baking, full bar, rated wine cellar. Reservations recommended. Credit cards: A, CB, DC, D, MC, V.

House of Lords $$$ ★★★★

2535 Las Vegas Boulevard South, Las Vegas, 89109, ☎ *(702) 737-2111.*
American cuisine. Specialties: lobster; Beef Wellington; prime rib.
Dinner: 6-10:30 p.m., entrées $21–$55. Closed: Tue., Wed.
An English club atmosphere prevails at this sophisticated restaurant, where the menu features American, Mediterranean and Continental fare, mostly consisting of various cuts of well-prepared red meat, veal, and lamb. Features: own baking. Jacket requested. Reservations required.

Isis $$$ ★★★★

3900 Las Vegas Boulevard South, Las Vegas, 89119, ☎ *(702) 262-4773.*
Continental cuisine.
Dinner: 5–11 p.m., entrées $35–$45.
This wonderfully dramatic dining room carries out the Luxor's Egyptian theme to the nth degree with lots of authentic antiques and artifacts, and full-sized replicas of Pharaoh's tomb statues. The menu features classic Continental fare. Jacket requested. Reservations required. Credit cards: A, CB, DC, D, MC, V.

Isis $$$ ★★★★★

3900 Las Vegas Boulevard South, Las Vegas, ☎ *(702) 262-4773.*
Located on the Strip.
Continental cuisine.
Dinner: 5–11 p.m., prix fixe $18–$30.
After passing the full-size replicas of pharaohs' tomb statues and through the glass doors with gold-embossed "wings of Isis," it's not surprising to find this elegant dining room graced with fine reproductions of Egyptian artifacts. The splendid surroundings set the stage for a wonderfully prepared meal of beef, seafood, chicken or lobster. Flaming desserts are prepared tableside. Reservations are recommended. Continue the theme by a walk through Luxor's excellent

King Tut's Tomb Museum (see "Attractions"). Credit cards: A, CB, DC, D, MC, V.

Kokomo's $$$ ★★★★

3400 Las Vegas Boulevard South, Las Vegas, 89109, ☎ (702) 791-7111.
American cuisine.
Lunch: 11 a.m.–2:30 p.m., entrées $12–$18.
Dinner: 5:30–11 p.m., entrées $27–$35.
Great steaks and seafood, but what really sets this place apart is its tropical location in the Mirage's exotic rainforest. Breakfast is served from Thursday to Sunday 8–11 a.m. Reservations recommended. Credit cards: A, CB, DC, D, MC, V.

Marrakech $$$ ★★★★

3900 Paradise Road, Las Vegas, ☎ (702) 737-5611.
Located a few blocks east of the Strip in the Citibank Plaza.
African cuisine. Specialties: lamb.
Dinner: 5:30–11 p.m., prix fixe $26.
Lounge around on fluffy floor pillows, watch belly dancers do their thing, and eat great Moroccan food at this lively restaurant done up in "Arab chic." One price buys a six-course dinner and the floor show. Pretty cool. Reservations recommended. Credit cards: A, D, MC, V.

Michael's $$$ ★★★★★

3595 Las Vegas Boulevard South, Las Vegas, 89109, ☎ (702) 737-7111.
American cuisine. Specialties: steak; seafood; rack of lamb.
Dinner: 6–11 p.m., entrées $22–$40.
Reservations are hard to get at this elegant, small rococo-style dining room. If you can get in, you'll enjoy a quiet, romantic atmosphere, wonderful service and American/Continental cuisine that is well-prepared and served with flair. The excellent wine list is well matched to the food. Features: own baking, full bar, rated wine cellar, late dining. Jacket requested. Reservations required. Credit cards: A, CB, DC, MC, V.

Mizuno's Teppan Dining $$$ ★★★★★

3801 Las Vegas Boulevard South, Las Vegas, ☎ (702) 739-2713.
Japanese cuisine.
Dinner: 5-10:30 p.m., entrées $14–$41.
My sister and I have made eating here a tradition each time we visit Las Vegas, and it's always just as good as we remembered. Your chef whips up teppan goodies right at the table—the shrimp is to die for—with a lot of good-natured theatrics. Dinner comes with a zesty salad, soup, white rice and green tea. The sedate dining room and gracious service complement the food nicely, though the entire experience depends a lot on whether or not you like (or even acknowledge) your table mates. Better than the similar Benihana at the Las Vegas Hilton. Reservations recommended. Credit cards: A, MC, V.

Monte Carlo $$$ ★★★★★

3145 Las Vegas Boulevard South, Las Vegas, 89109, ☎ (702) 733-4437.
Continental cuisine. Specialties: hobo steak; Nevada quail.
Dinner: 6–11 p.m., entrées $25–$55. Closed: Tue., Wed.
This lovely dining room, accented with crystal chandeliers and hand-painted murals, overlooks the Desert Inn's gardens and pool area. The menu offers veal and game specialties, as well as fine traditional dishes. Large selection of French and California wines. Seatings are

every half-hour. Jacket requested. Reservations required. Credit cards:
A, CB, DC, D, MC, V.

Morton's of Chicago $$$ ★★★★

3200 Las Vegas Boulevard South, Las Vegas, ☎ (702) 893-0703.
Located in the Fashion Show Mall.
American cuisine. Specialties: steak; chops.
Dinner: 5:30–11 p.m., entrées $19–$32.

The Morton's of Chicago steakhouse chain continues its move west
with this restaurant in the Fashion Show Mall. The 24-ounce porterhouse and New York strip steaks are legendary. If you're not in the
mood for red meat, the enormous salads are a meal in themselves.
Bring lots of money, because everything is served à la carte. Features:
full bar, rated wine cellar. Reservations recommended. Credit cards: A,
MC, V.

Nippon $$ ★★★

101 Convention Center Drive, Las Vegas, 89109, ☎ (702) 735-5565.
Japanese cuisine. Specialties: sushi.
Lunch: 11:30 a.m.–2 p.m., entrées $8–$17.
Dinner: 5:30–11 p.m., entrées $8–$17. Closed: Sun.

Sushi is the standout at this casual Japanese restaurant in the Valley
Bank Center. Features: wine and beer only, late dining. Reservations
recommended. Credit cards: A, CB, DC, MC, V.

Palace Court $$$ ★★★★★

3570 Las Vegas Boulevard South, Las Vegas, 89109, ☎ (702) 731-7731.
French cuisine. Specialties: rack of lamb; breast of roast duck; steamed
Maine lobster.
Dinner: 6–11 p.m., entrées $30–$55.

One of the most romantic spots in town, the restaurant is nestled
amid displays of art, statuary, dramatic flower arrangements, live trees
and flawless table settings. Excellent haute cuisine and fabulous wines.
There's a dramatic stained-glass dome overhead, and the windows
look onto the pretty pool area. Nice! Seatings are at 6 and 9:30 p.m.
daily. Features: own baking, rated wine cellar. Jacket requested. Reservations required. Credit cards: A, CB, DC, D, MC, V.

Palm, The $$$ ★★★★

3500 Las Vegas Boulevard South, Las Vegas, ☎ (702) 732-7256.
Located at the Forum Shops.
American cuisine.
Lunch: from 11:30 a.m., entrées $22–$30.
Dinner: to 11 p.m., entrées $22–$30.

This classic American steakhouse often draws local and international
celebrities who come to nosh on their jumbo lobster, prime aged beef
or tasty crab cakes. This is one of the successful chain's 12 restaurants.
Credit cards: A, CB, DC, D, MC, V.

Pamplemousse $$$ ★★★★★

400 East Sahara Avenue, Las Vegas, 89104, ☎ (702) 733-2066.
Located three blocks off the Strip.
French cuisine. Specialties: fresh fish.
Dinner: 6–10 p.m., entrées $19–$40. Closed: Mon.

One of the most charming dining experiences in the city—especially
if you're tired of the elaborate theme rooms at the Strip hotels. Begin
with a wonderful basket of fresh vegetables and count on your waiter

to steer you right from there. Good selection of fine-sauced dishes and wines to match. Features: rated wine cellar. Reservations required. Credit cards: A, CB, DC, MC.

Pegasus $$$ ★★★★★

375 East Harmon Avenue, Las Vegas, 89109, *(702) 796-3300. Located a block off the Strip, across form the Hard Rock Cafe. Continental cuisine. Specialties: seafood; beef Wellington. Dinner: 6–10:30 p.m., entrées $15–$35.*

Bask in the light from chandeliers of imported, hand-blown Italian glass, listen to the soothing music of a piano and prepare to be pampered. The sophisticated Continental cuisine is elegantly prepared and presented, and large picture windows overlook a cascading waterfall. Very romantic! Jacket requested. Reservations required. Credit cards: A, CB, DC, D, MC, V.

Philips Supper House $$$ ★★★

4545 West Sahara Avenue, Las Vegas, 89102, *(702) 873-5222. American cuisine. Specialties: black angus beef; seafood. Dinner: 5–11 p.m., entrées $17–$32.*

This off-the-Strip restaurant, housed in an old Victorian home, serves large portions of American/Continental fare, including steak, lamb chops, prime rib and seafood. Early evening prix-fixe menu, $10–$15, is a good buy. Features: own baking, full bar, non-smoking area, late dining. Reservations recommended. Credit cards: A, CB, DC, MC, V.

Piero's $$$ ★★★★

355 Convention Center Drive, Las Vegas, 89109, ☎ *(702) 369-2305. Located near the Convention Center. Italian cuisine. Dinner: 5:30–11 p.m., entrées $18–$35.*

The Northern Italian cuisine and fresh seafood at Piero's is fine, the service excellent and the wine list very good, but is all this worth the high prices? Lots of the locals apparently think so, so you'd better have a reservation if you want to dine here. Osso Buco is a house specialty. Features: own baking, full bar, rated wine cellar, non-smoking area, late dining. Reservations required. Credit cards: A, CB, DC, MC, V.

Plank, The $$$ ★★★★★

3300 Las Vegas Boulevard South, Las Vegas, ☎ *(702) 894-7111. American cuisine. Dinner: 5:30–11 p.m., entrées $16–$30.*

This elegant dining room is just off the Treasure Island casino, but worlds away in ambience with its dark woods and decor meant to resemble a pirate's library—assuming, of course, that pirates really had libraries. Appetizers, which range from $6 to $14, include whole chilled or baked artichokes and salmon cakes; entrées run the gamut from steak, lamb and mesquite-broiled beef to chicken and seafood (great salmon). Service is attentive and caring. A winner! Features: rated wine cellar. Jacket requested. Reservations recommended. Credit cards: A, CB, DC, D, MC, V.

Portofino $$$ ★★★★

3145 Las Vegas Boulevard South, Las Vegas, 89109, *(702) 733-4444. Italian cuisine. Specialties: osso buco. Dinner: 6–11 p.m., entrées $12–$35. Closed: Mon., Sun.*

Northern Italian cuisine served à la carte gets an elegant backdrop at this posh restaurant with oak and marble floors, velvet booths and candlelight. Wonderful sauces! Two can splurge on the rack of lamb or roast beef tenderloin for $60. Features: rated wine cellar. Jacket requested. Reservations recommended. Credit cards: A, CB, DC, D, MC, V.

Rosewood Grille $$$ ★★★★

3339 Las Vegas Boulevard South, Las Vegas, 89109, ☎ *(702) 792-9249.*
Located across from the Mirage.
American cuisine. Specialties: steak; lobster.
Dinner: 4:30-11:30 p.m., entrées $17–$40.

This restaurant probably sells more live Maine lobster than any other restaurant in town, and there are many other seafood specialties as well as beef and chicken. You pay for your lobster by the pound ($22), and some of them are huge, so watch your wallet. A nice alternative to the casino restaurants. A great wine list, and 38 types of single malt scotch. Features: own baking, full bar, rated wine cellar. Jacket requested. Reservations recommended. Credit cards: A, CB, DC, MC, V.

Ruth's Chris Steakhouse $$$ ★★★★

3900 Paradise Road, Las Vegas, 89109, ☎ *(702) 791-7011.*
American cuisine. Specialties: steak; seafood.
Lunch: 11 a.m.–4:30 p.m., entrées $7–$20.
Dinner: 11-10:30 p.m., entrées $18–$35.

Plan to spend a bundle, but the beef is fabulous and the ambience pleasing at this upscale steakhouse chain. Everything is à la carte and the wines can be pricey, too, but the portions are big enough to share. Locals love this spot, and many casino dealers getting off the late shift head for a bite at Ruth's second location, *4561 W. Flamingo Road* (☎ *(702) 248-7011*), which is open until 3 a.m. It offers a special late-night menu (as well as the usual fare), with dishes such as grilled chicken and filet mignon sandwiches going for $10–$15. There's also live jazz. Features: full bar, rated wine cellar, late dining. Reservations recommended. Credit cards: A, CB, DC, D, MC, V.

Seasons $$$ ★★★★

3645 Las Vegas Boulevard South, Las Vegas, 89109, ☎ *(702) 739-4111.*
American cuisine. Specialties: Chilean sea bass; creme brulée.
Dinner: 6–10 p.m., entrées $25–$33. Closed: Mon., Sun.

Fancy decor with American/Continental cooking and wines to match are the hallmark of Seasons, where, appropriately, the menu and decor change to reflect the season. Request a curtained booth for a romantic tête-a-tête. Typical dishes include baked chicken, imported Dover sole and fresh Maine lobster. Features: own baking, full bar, rated wine cellar. Jacket requested. Reservations required. Credit cards: A, CB, DC, D, MC, V.

Shalimar $$ ★★★★

3900 Paradise Road, Las Vegas, 89109, ☎ *(702) 796-0302.*
Indian cuisine. Specialties: Buriani; Vinderlo.
Lunch: 11 a.m.–2 p.m., entrées $6–$10.
Dinner: 5:30–10 p.m., entrées $8–$15.

Another location at *2605 S. Decatur* (☎ *(702) 252-8320*). The tandoori oven turns out spicy and delectable breads and meats at this casual restaurant. The prix fixe lunch buffet is an especially good value. Features: own baking, full bar, non-smoking area, late dining. Reservations recommended. Credit cards: A, CB, DC, MC, V.

Sir Galahad's $$ ★★★

3850 Las Vegas Boulevard South, Las Vegas, 89109, ☎ *(702) 597-7448.*
English cuisine. Specialties: prime rib.
Dinner: 5–11 p.m., entrées $11–$15.

The Excalibur's theme continues into this Tudor-style dining room, where servers in King Arthur-era garb carve huge portions of prime rib from tableside carts. Most of the menu also reflects Merry Old England, with Yorkshire pudding and English trifle making an appearance. Entrées are served with soup, salad, potatoes and creamed spinach. Features: own baking, full bar, rated wine cellar. Reservations recommended. Credit cards: A, CB, DC, D, MC, V.

Spago $$$ ★★★★★

3500 Las Vegas Boulevard South, Las Vegas, 89109, ☎ *(702) 369-6300.*
Located in the Forum Shops.
American cuisine.
Lunch: 11 a.m.–10:30 p.m., entrées $10–$20.
Dinner: 6-9 p.m., entrées $20–$35.

Spago has all the upscale sophistication of the Los Angeles original, plus a little Las Vegas glitz. The Adam Tihany-designed dining room serves dinner only, while the less-expensive "patio" cafe serves gourmet pizzas and sandwiches from 11 a.m. to 10:30 p.m. I prefer the latter, which overlooks the Forum Shops with its impressive statuary and constantly changing "sky." (It's also a lot cheaper.) If you're lucky, you may get to schmooze with Wolfgang Puck himself. Features: own baking. Reservations recommended. Credit cards: A, CB, DC, D, MC, V.

Steak House at Circus Circus $$$ ★★★★

2880 Las Vegas Boulevard South, Las Vegas, 89114, ☎ *(702) 734-0410.*
American cuisine. Specialties: steak, seafood.
Dinner: 5- midnight, entrées $14–$32.

Need a red meat fix? The Steak House's claim to fame is aging the huge selection of beef 21 days. Steaks are cooked to order in four styles: top sirloin, New York strip, porterhouse, and filet mignon. The casual dining room has a comfortable, turn-of-the-century look with lots of oak and brass. Reservations required. Credit cards: A, CB, DC, D, MC, V.

Tokyo $$ ★★★★

953 East Sahara Avenue, Las Vegas, 89104, ☎ *(702) 735-7070.*
Japanese cuisine. Specialties: sushi; steamed clams with sake.
Dinner: 5–10 p.m., entrées $7–$13.

This pleasant restaurant and sushi bar serves reasonably priced Japanese specialties such as teriyaki, tempura and sushi. You can cook your own meat at your table on a hibachi if you so desire. Nice Oriental decor, and friendly service by waitresses in kimonos. Features: own baking, full bar. Reservations recommended. Credit cards: A, CB, DC, D, MC, V.

Top of the World $$$ ★★★★

2000 Las Vegas Boulevard South, Las Vegas, ☎ *(702) 380-7711.*
Located on the Strip.
Continental cuisine.

Dinner: 5–11 p.m., entrées $21–$29.

The food is decent enough, but it's the view you'll be writing home about. Perched up on the 106th floor of the Stratosphere tower, some 800 feet above the Strip, the restaurant slowly revolves so you can drink in all the sights; it's especially spellbinding at night. The dining room is one of the few in town that prohibits smoking (you can duck upstairs to the bar to light up). The atmosphere is quite romantic with small brass table-top lamps. The menu offers up lobster, pan-seared pepper steak, rack of lamb and the like; the bruchetta appetizer is large enough for two. Don't let the occasional slight rumble give you the willies—it's from the roller coaster up above. Open until midnight on Friday and Saturday. Reservations required. Credit cards: A, CB, DC, D, MC, V.

William B's $$$ ★ ★ ★ ★

3000 Las Vegas Boulevard South, Las Vegas, 89109, ☎ (702) 732-6111.
American cuisine.
Dinner: 5–11 p.m., entrées $15–$50.

The room has a late-1800s period theme, and the food is solidly American, featuring such specialties as rib eye steak, whole Dover sole, prime rib and oysters Rockefeller. A quiet, relaxed atmosphere. Open until midnight on Friday and Saturday. Features: full bar, rated wine cellar, late dining. Reservations recommended. Credit cards: A, CB, DC, D, MC, V.

Elsewhere

Aristocrat, The $$$ ★ ★ ★ ★

850 South Rancho Drive, Las Vegas, ☎ (702) 870-1977.
Continental cuisine. Specialties: mussels in vinaigrette sauce, duck à l'orange.
Lunch: 11:30 a.m.–2 p.m., entrées $9–$14.
Dinner: 6–10 p.m., entrées $18–$30.

This small—and some say too dark—dining room is loaded with English charm all the way down to the imported crystal candlesticks and fine china. The Aristocrat serves an interesting selection of French/Continental specialties along with excellent wines. Friendly service, too. If you're feeling adventurous, try the pheasant. Be sure to save room for the yummy peach melba. Closed for lunch on Saturday and Sunday. Jacket requested. Reservations recommended. Credit cards: A, CB, DC, MC, V.

Billy Bob's Steakhouse $$$ ★ ★ ★

5111 Boulder Highway, Las Vegas, 89122, ☎ (702) 456-7777.
Located a few miles off the Strip.
American cuisine. Specialties: 28-ounce ribeye steak.
Dinner: 4:30–10 p.m., entrées $11–$37.

Vegetarians will run screaming from the room, but carnivores are kept happy with top-grade meats. The large restaurant is long on western atmosphere, with a silver dollar bar top, working water wheel and (since this is Las Vegas) a talking buffalo head. Reservations recommended. Credit cards: A, CB, DC, D, MC, V.

Boison's $$$ ★ ★ ★

4508 South Paradise Road, Las Vegas, 89103, ☎ (702) 368-2257.
Located across from the Hard Rock Cafe.
French cuisine.

WHERE TO EAT

Dinner: 5–11 p.m., entrées $11–$26.
This is a great place for consistently good Continental and French cuisine. House specialties include steaks, chops and pasta dishes, and the wine selection is extensive. Features: own baking, full bar, rated wine cellar. Reservations recommended. Credit cards: A, CB, DC, D, MC, V.

Bootlegger   **$$**   ★★★

5025 South Eastern Avenue, Las Vegas, 89119, ☎ (702) 736-4939.
Located near the Liberace Museum.
Italian cuisine. Specialties: veal piccata; homemade pasta.
Lunch: from 11:30 a.m., entrées $5–$7.
Dinner: to 10:30 p.m., entrées $10–$19.
As they like to say, the Bootlegger is "everything you'd expect from an Italian woman's kitchen." There are lots of good seafood dishes to admire at this popular family-owned restaurant, and everything is made fresh by "Mama" Maria Perri and her family. There's lots for vegetarians, as well as a pasta diet menu for those watching their calories. Open until 11 p.m. on Friday and Saturday. Closed Monday. Features: own baking, full bar, rated wine cellar. Reservations recommended. Credit cards: A, CB, DC, MC, V.

Garlic Cafe   **$$$**   ★★★★★

3650 South Decatur Boulevard, Las Vegas, ☎ (702) 221-0266.
Located about a mile off the Strip.
International cuisine.
Lunch: from noon, entrées $4–$15.
Dinner: to 10:30 p.m., entrées $9–$31.
If dishes with names such as "Mo & Todd's Passionate Peppery Poetic Pasta with Lobsta" and "New England Eat with Your Eyes See Shore Dinner" intrigue you and you live, love and eat garlic, this is your kind of place. The extensive menu has an international flair, and you get to choose how many cloves of garlic (1–5) you'd like in every made-to-order dish. Everything from the decor to the menu to the drinks is a bit quirky, but the Garlic Cafe delivers. A gourmet experience! Features: full bar. Reservations recommended. Credit cards: A, CB, DC, D, MC, V.

Tillerman   **$$$**   ★★★

2245 East Flamingo Road, Las Vegas, 89109, ☎ (702) 731-4036.
Located three miles east of the Strip.
Seafood cuisine. Specialties: salmon; grouper; steaks.
Dinner: 5–11 p.m., entrées $16–$37.
This attractive restaurant is pretty pricey, but fans say the seafood is about the best in Las Vegas and it serves full dinners. The open, airy dining room has atrium-like decor, with lots of live plants and trees. The excellent wine list has won a Wine Spectator award, and everyone loves the all-you-can-eat salad bar, which is included in the price of an entrée. Features: full bar, rated wine cellar, non-smoking area, late dining. Reservations not accepted. Credit cards: A, CB, DC, D, MC, V.

Jean

Steak House, The   **$$**   ★★★★

1 Main Street, Jean, 89019, ☎ (702) 477-5000.
Located 34 miles south of Las Vegas, near the border.
American cuisine.
Dinner: 5–10 p.m., entrées $7–$20. Closed: Mon., Tue.

WHERE TO EAT

What a happy surprise! I came in expecting the worst—the Gold Strike is a very low-market joint—and left singing the praises of this tiny gourmet restaurant. It's not necessarily worth driving all the way out from Las Vegas, but definitely a must if you're staying in Jean or Primm. The dining room is cozy and intimate, with large red booths, a wood-paneled ceiling and lots of candlelight. Max, the maître d', is the consummate professional, all the way down to his European accent. The menu features steaks, seafood, lobster and chicken dishes; chateaubriand bouquetière for two, the house specialty, is carved right at the table and costs $22. I had a wonderful meal of the house salad, yummy bread and salmon—for $12.79, including tax! Hotel guests get a free glass of wine with dinner. Reservations recommended. Credit cards: A, DC, MC, V.

Local Hangouts

While you may find some locals hanging out at the casino-hotels, most stay as far from vacationers as possible. Who can blame them? Las Vegas' building boom has meant nightmarish traffic for its residents, and, since most are forced to be cheerful for the tourists while at work, the last thing they want is to share a meal with a bunch of Midwesterners.

Downtown

Swiss Cafe   **$**   ★ ★ ★

1431 East Charleston Avenue, Las Vegas, ☎ *(702) 382-6444.*
Scandinavian cuisine.
Lunch: 11:30 a.m.–2 p.m., entrées $7–$9.
Dinner: 5–10 p.m., entrées $7–$9. Closed: Sun.
This Scandinavian-style chalet just oozes old-world charm. The menu features hardy Swiss and German cuisine. Try the jumbo sea scallops, fillet of beef au poivre and, of course, schnitzel. A good selection of wines by the glass. No lunch Saturday. Credit cards: MC, V.

Tricia's Teas   **$**   ★ ★ ★ ★

1109 Western, Las Vegas, ☎ *(702) 876-0682.*
Located inside the Red Rooster Antique Mall.
English cuisine.
Here's just about the last thing you would expect to find in Las Vegas: an old-fashioned tea room where patrons don vintage hats, gloves and jewels and sit down to a few civilized hours of gracious living. Proprietor Patricia Snell, a registered nurse faced with empty-nest syndrome, started the business a few years ago and is herself astounded by its success. She envisioned the project as appealing to little girls, but adults actually make up most of the tea drinkers in her quaint, antique-filled room. Tea is served with all the formal trappings—genteel music; fine china, silver and linens; fresh-baked scones and jam—while Snell explains all the long-lost idiosyncrasies of proper tea etiquette. It's all veddy proper—and lots of fun. The tea room is open by reservation only; parties can be booked daily from 11 a.m.–4 p.m. Prices start at $15; you can reserve the entire room for a cozy tea for two for $60. Reservations required.

The Strip

All American Bar & Grille $$$ ★★★★

3700 West Flamingo Road, Las Vegas, 89103, ☎ *(702) 252-7600.*
Located a few blocks off the Strip.
American cuisine.
Lunch: 11 a.m.–5 p.m., entrées $13–$24.
Dinner: 5–11 p.m., entrées $13–$24.
Located right in the middle of the Rio's hip and happening casino, this cafe serves up mesquite-grilled steaks and seafood prepared in an exhibition kitchen. Sit on the "patio" and watch the world pass by, or choose the inner dining room, nicely done with high ceilings, large booths, dark woods, a fireplace and lots of American flags. The house specialty is New Zealand Lamb Rack basted in Dijon, basil and honey marinade and roasted ($24). Reservations recommended. Credit cards: A, CB, DC, D, MC, V.

Big Dogs Cafe & Casino $$ ★★★★

6390 West Sahara Avenue, Las Vegas, ☎ *(702) 876-3647.*
Located a few blocks off the Strip.
American cuisine.
Lunch: entrées $4–$6.
Dinner: entrées $8–$14.
You can't miss this dog-themed restaurant as you're driving down Sahara—the facade is covered with huge murals of man's best friend. This trendy hangout is for locals in their 20s and 30s and stays absolutely shoulder-to-shoulder on Friday and Saturday nights. The menu was recently redone to get away from a bar food emphasis, and now offers prime rib, steak, pastas, salads and seafood, including walleye. The walls are adorned with photographs of doggies, and the theme extends all the way down to the pretzels served in a dog food dish. Don't come to escape the slots—they have 35 machines here. Credit cards: MC, V.

Cafe Michelle $$$ ★★★

1350 East Flamingo, Las Vegas, ☎ *(702) 735-8686.*
Located in Mission Center, six blocks from the Strip.
Continental cuisine.
Lunch: 11 a.m.–5 p.m., entrées $7–$13.
Dinner: 5–11 p.m., entrées $14–$25.
Cafe Michelle is one of Las Vegas' rare sidewalk cafes. The menu offers up an eclectic mix of French, Greek, Italian and American dishes, with fresh seafood a dinner specialty. Besides the standard sandwiches and salads, lunch options include eggs benedict and a variety of omelettes. There's live piano music in the lounge, which stays open until 4 a.m.; after 11 p.m., you can order late-night munchies from a special menu. Michelle opened a second cafe in 1995 at 2800 W. Sahara; 873-5400. Credit cards: A, D, MC, V.

Venetian Ristorante $$ ★★★

3713 West Sahara Avenue, Las Vegas, ☎ *(702) 876-4190.*
Located five minutes west of the Strip.
Italian cuisine.
Dinner: 4–11 p.m., entrées $6–$18.
This atmospheric restaurant is practically an antique by Las Vegas standards, going all the way back to the olden days of 1955. The early-bird specials, served from 4-6 p.m., are an especially good deal,

with complete dinners starting at $7.95. After 6 p.m., the menu features veal, home-made pasta and scampi either a la carte or as a full dinner with beverage. Features: rated wine cellar. Reservations recommended. Credit cards: A, CB, DC, MC, V.

Wild Bill's $$ ★★★

3850 Las Vegas Boulevard South, Las Vegas, 89109, ☎ *(702) 597-7777.*
American cuisine.
Dinner: 5–10 p.m., entrées $9–$20.

A nice respite from the medieval theme that dominates the Excalibur, Wild Bill's is a western-style steakhouse and saloon with live music. You can burn off the calories between courses by joining the ever-present line dancers (they give free lessons Monday–Wednesday from 7–8 p.m. so you too can join in the fun). The menu features mostly beef, with catfish and chicken dishes throw in for good measure. Open until 11 on Friday and Saturday. Credit cards: A, CB, DC, D, MC, V.

Elsewhere

Brittany's $$ ★★

7770 West Ann Road, North Las Vegas, ☎ *(702) 658-8998.*
American cuisine. Specialties: steak, seafood.
Lunch: from 11 a.m., entrées $4–$18.
Dinner: to 10 p.m., entrées $4–$18.

This out-of-the-way restaurant in North Las Vegas scores big with locals for its charming art-deco decor and moderate prices. Choices run the gamut—from burgers to boiled seafood—and quality can vary though it's usually dependable. Credit cards: A, CB, DC, D, MC, V.

Great Moments $$$ ★★★★

18 East Fremont Street, Las Vegas, ☎ *(702) 385-1664.*
Located downtown in the Las Vegas Club.
Continental cuisine.
Dinner: 5–11 p.m., entrées $11–$24.

Tucked away in a corner of the Las Vegas Club, this gourmet room is very atmospheric with dark wood furnishings, leather circular booths and a dark paneled ceiling. With its plush armchairs and couches, the entranceway is especially appealing. Stuffed filet mignon is the house specialty; there are also steaks and seafood. Vegetarian choices are limited to pasta primavera or the ubiquitous steamed vegetable platter. Credit cards: A, CB, DC, D, MC, V.

TGI Fridays $$ ★★★

1800 East Flamingo Road, Las Vegas, ☎ *(702) 732-9905.*
Located 2.5 miles east of the Strip at Spencer.
American cuisine.
Lunch: from 11 a.m., entrées $5–$9.
Dinner: to 1:30 a.m., entrées $8–$14.

This casual spot assaults the senses with its red and white stripes and walls jammed with antiques and artwork. The menu is huge and features everything from seafood and steaks to Mexican to Italian dishes. The daily happy hour, from 4 -7 p.m., brings out the locals in droves, especially on Fridays. The kitchen stays open until midnight on weekdays, 1 a.m. on weekends. The sit-down Sunday brunch, from 11 a.m.–3 p.m., is also popular and runs about $6-$9. Credit cards: A, CB, DC, D, MC, V.

WHAT TO
SEE AND DO
IN LAS VEGAS

Coca-Cola Oasis, Sega Gameworks and the All Star Cafe are attracting crowds to the new Showcase complex.

If you are trying to escape from the casinos to see a little daylight or just trying to keep the kids entertained, Las Vegas has countless attractions and other daytime events to keep you occupied, in or out of the sun. These include everything from the exotic to the usual, from the $595 dogfight in the air to a free circus.

Fun for Free

It's an interesting paradox that a city so devoted to taking away your money offers such a wealth of fun things to do for free.

LAS VEGAS

THE STRIP (SOUTH)

Three new European-themed properties are under construction: Bellagio, Paris and Grand Venetian. Project Paradise is slated to be open by 1999.

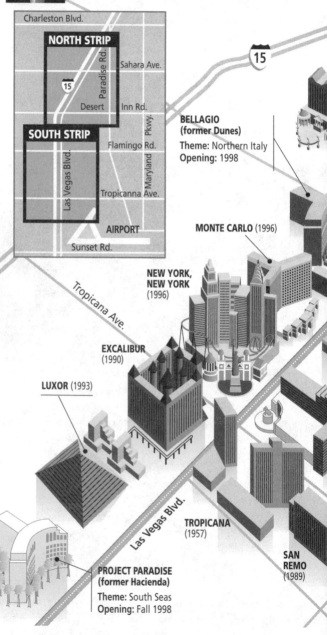

Charleston Blvd.

NORTH STRIP

Paradise Rd.

Sahara Ave.

Desert   Inn Rd.

SOUTH STRIP

Flamingo Rd.

Maryland Pkwy.

Las Vegas Blvd.

Tropicanna Ave.

AIRPORT

Sunset Rd.

**BELLAGIO
(former Dunes)**
Theme: Northern Italy
Opening: 1998

MONTE CARLO (1996)

NEW YORK, NEW YORK
(1996)

Tropicana Ave.

EXCALIBUR
(1990)

LUXOR (1993)

TROPICANA
(1957)

Las Vegas Blvd.

SAN REMO
(1989)

**PROJECT PARADISE
(former Hacienda)**
Theme: South Seas
Opening: Fall 1998

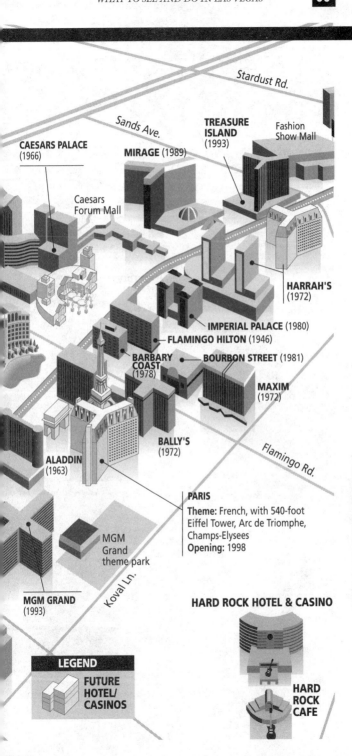

Stardust Rd.

Sands Ave.

TREASURE ISLAND (1993)

Fashion Show Mall

CAESARS PALACE (1966)

MIRAGE (1989)

Caesars Forum Mall

HARRAH'S (1972)

IMPERIAL PALACE (1980)

FLAMINGO HILTON (1946)

BARBARY COAST (1978)

BOURBON STREET (1981)

MAXIM (1972)

BALLY'S (1972)

Flamingo Rd.

ALADDIN (1963)

PARIS
Theme: French, with 540-foot Eiffel Tower, Arc de Triomphe, Champs-Elysees
Opening: 1998

MGM Grand theme park

Koval Ln.

MGM GRAND (1993)

HARD ROCK HOTEL & CASINO

LEGEND

FUTURE HOTEL/ CASINOS

HARD ROCK CAFE

WHAT TO SEE AND DO IN LAS VEGAS

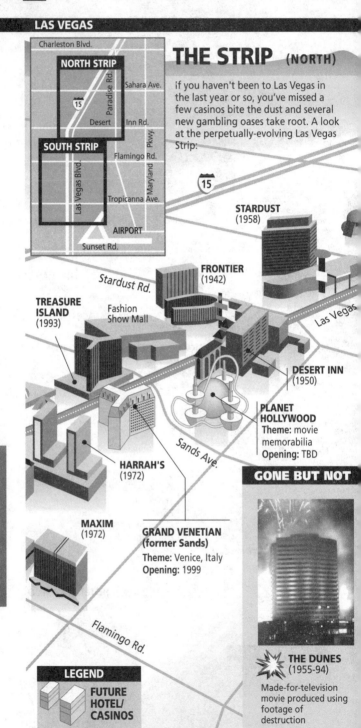

LAS VEGAS

THE STRIP (NORTH)

If you haven't been to Las Vegas in the last year or so, you've missed a few casinos bite the dust and several new gambling oases take root. A look at the perpetually-evolving Las Vegas Strip:

NORTH STRIP

SOUTH STRIP

AIRPORT

Charleston Blvd.
Sahara Ave.
Paradise Rd.
Desert Inn Rd.
Flamingo Rd.
Maryland Pkwy.
Tropicanna Ave.
Sunset Rd.
Las Vegas Blvd.

STARDUST (1958)

FRONTIER (1942)

Stardust Rd.

Las Vegas

TREASURE ISLAND (1993)

Fashion Show Mall

DESERT INN (1950)

PLANET HOLLYWOOD
Theme: movie memorabilia
Opening: TBD

Sands Ave.

HARRAH'S (1972)

MAXIM (1972)

GRAND VENETIAN (former Sands)
Theme: Venice, Italy
Opening: 1999

GONE BUT NOT

THE DUNES (1955-94)

Made-for-television movie produced using footage of destruction

Flamingo Rd.

LEGEND

FUTURE HOTEL/ CASINOS

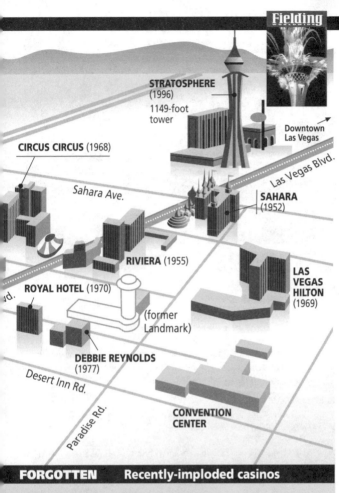

STRATOSPHERE (1996)
1149-foot tower

Downtown Las Vegas

Las Vegas Blvd.

CIRCUS CIRCUS (1968)

Sahara Ave.

SAHARA (1952)

RIVIERA (1955)

LAS VEGAS HILTON (1969)

ROYAL HOTEL (1970)

(former Landmark)

DEBBIE REYNOLDS (1977)

Desert Inn Rd.

Paradise Rd.

CONVENTION CENTER

FORGOTTEN **Recently-imploded casinos**

 LANDMARK (1969-95)

Closed for several years prior to implosion, cleared to make room for convention parking

 SANDS (1952-96)

Former playground of "Rat Pack" – Frank Sinatra, Dean Martin, Sammy Davis Jr.

 HACIENDA (1956-96)

Reduced to rubble with 1,000 explosives on New Year's Eve television special

Don't miss the Mirage volcano, pirate battle at Treasure Island and light show at the Fremont Experience.

Kids have a great time at the Circus Circus, where they can play Skee Ball and watch trapeze artists.

Circus Circus   ★★★

2880 Las Vegas Boulevard South, Las Vegas, 89114, ☎ (702) 734-0410. Located across from the Riviera.

You don't have to gamble to enjoy the free circus acts under the cement "big top" in the casino each day from 11 a.m. to midnight. In fact, gamblers routinely ignore the trapeze artists doing daring deeds right over their heads. The hotel also has a carnival-like midway area where kids can try to win stuffed animals and play Skee Ball.

Cranberry World West   ★★★

5975 American Pacific Drive, Henderson, 89014, ☎ (702) 566-7160. Located half an hour from Las Vegas.
Hours open: 9 a.m.–5 p.m.

More than you probably ever wanted to know about the cranberry is detailed at this new Ocean Spray facility. You can watch a brief film on the history and cultivation of cranberries, tour the juice packaging and processing plant and ooh and ahh over multi-media exhibits and the demonstration kitchen. Of course, you get to taste the little buggers, too. To get there, take I-95 south to the Sunset Road exit. Go right. At the second light, go left onto Stephanie Street. You'll see it on the left about a mile down the road.

Don Pablo Cigar Company   ★★

3025 Las Vegas Boulevard South, Las Vegas, ☎ (702) 369-1818. Located across from the Stardust.
Hours open: 9 a.m.–5:30 p.m. Special Hours: Sunday, 10 a.m.–4 p.m.
Ever wonder how they roll those cigars so neat and tight? At Don Pablo, you can watch Cuban masters hand-roll the stogies with tobacco from five countries. Naturally, there's a store on the premises, too.

Ethel M Chocolate Factory Tour   ★★★

One Sunset Way, Henderson, 89014, ☎ (702) 458-8864. Located on the way to Hoover Dam.
Hours open: 8:30 a.m.–7 p.m.

This is a paradise for chocolate lovers, and it's free! Run by the Mars company (Ethel headed the company in the early days) who also make Snickers and Milky Ways, the factory is located in Nevada because it's one of the only places in the country where liquor-filled chocolates can be produced and sold. More than a thousand people a day take the self-guided tour and sample the adult bon-bons. There's also a nice cactus garden to stroll. Not necessarily worth a special trip, but do stop in if you're on your way to Hoover Dam. To get there, take Tropicana Avenue east 5.5 miles, then go right on Mount Vista. Two miles later, go left on Sunset Way, then left onto Cactus Garden Drive.

Forum Shops at Caesars ★★★★★

3570 Las Vegas Boulevard South, Las Vegas, ☎ (702) 731-7110.
Hours open: 10 a.m.–11 p.m.

It's hard to believe a shopping mall could be so exciting, but the Forum Shops, located next to Caesars on the Strip, is really not to be missed. It is designed to resemble an ancient Roman streetscape and succeeds admirably, with immense columns and arches, ornate fountains, sidewalk cafes, large piazzas and lots of classic statuary. Overhead is a painted sky that changes throughout the day from puffy clouds to dramatic sunsets to starry nights. It might sound like too much, but it's really quite beautiful. If you enter from the street (as opposed to the casino), you'll run smack into the Festival Fountain, which every hour on the hour features robotic statues of Bacchus, Pluto, Venus and Apollo in the midst of a party. Most of the shops are tremendously expensive, with the likes of Louis Vuitton, Gucci and Armani well represented. But there are also a number of affordable shops, including one that sells nothing but refrigerator magnets. There's also a fair sprinkling of restaurants, including Wolfgang Puck's Spago and the recently opened Planet Hollywood. My favorite is Bertolini's, where you can people-watch from the "outdoor" patio next to the towering Fountain of the Gods. My only complaint about the Forum Shops—and it's a big one—is that you can only exit through Caesars' casino, for obvious reasons. This is truly annoying, but can be avoided if you take advantage of the mall's free valet parking.

Fremont Street Experience ★★★★★

Fremont Street's Glitter Gulch, Las Vegas, ☎ (702) 678-5777.
Located at the Downtown Casino Center.

Fremont Street has a new look, and downtown hotels are hoping the revamp of the area will bring a much-needed shot in the arm. Fremont Street, the main thoroughfare through the casino area known as Glitter Gulch, is now closed to cars and has been transformed into one giant attraction. The entire street is a pedestrian walkway with a 90-foot-high Space Frame overhead. Beneath that high-tech awning is the "Sky Parade," a light show incorporating 2.1 million lights for some dazzling special effects. Each six-minute show is operated by 31 computers with sound churning out of 208 speakers. It's really quite amazing and definitely worth a trip downtown to see. Hint: Be on the lookout for pickpockets—with everyone looking up, the climate is ripe for rip-offs. Shows are nightly on the hour from 8 p.m. to midnight.

Holy Cow! Brewery Tours ★★★★
2423 Las Vegas Boulevard South, Las Vegas, *(702) 732-2697.*
Located across from the Riviera.
Special Hours: 24 hours.

This cow-themed restaurant, bar and microbrewery is a fun place to forget about life for a while. Four house beers, brewed right on the premises, can help in that process. The aptly named "Amber Gambler" won the gold medal in the 1993 Great American Beer Festival. You can tour the brewery for free each day at 11 a.m., and at 1, 3 and 5 p.m. Don't miss the "moo-velous" gift shop filled with all things bovine.

Kidd Marshmallow Factory Tour ★★★
8203 Gibson Road, Henderson, 89015, *(702) 564-5400.*
Located on the way to Hoover Dam.
Hours open: 9 a.m.–4:30 p.m. Special Hours: Weekends, 9:30 a.m.–4:30 p.m.

This is a self-guided tour through marshmallow land where gooey white nuggets abound. You'll get a free packet at the end of the tour, and you can stock up on more in the souvenir shop. Call before you go because production occasionally shuts down without notice. To get there, take Highway 95 south to the Sunset Road exit. Go east. Make a right onto Gibson, then 2.5 miles later, a right onto Marycrest.

Masquerade Show in the Sky ★★★★★
3700 West Flamingo Road, Las Vegas, *(702) 252-7777.*
Located at the Rio.

A bit of Mardi Gras comes to Las Vegas daily (except Wednesdays) in this new $25-million show. The show consists of three complete parades—Mardi Gras, Rio/South of the Border and Venice—each with its own floats, elaborate costumes and music. Most of the fun takes place 13 feet over the casino floor, and guests can ride along on one of the floats in complete costume. Showtimes are every hour on the hour from noon to 10 p.m. Sunday through Tuesday, 1 p.m. to 11 p.m. Thursday through Saturday. Dark Wednesday. The show lasts about 12 minutes.

Mirage Volcano ★★★★
3400 Las Vegas Boulevard South, Las Vegas, *(702) 791-7111.*

The Mirage made a big splash when it opened with its 54-foot-high volcano, and rightfully so. It's a pretty spectacular sight when it erupts in a spectacular blaze, spewing smoke and fire 100 feet into the air. Since it happens every 30 minutes from dusk until midnight, it's easy to catch at least one or two eruptions while you're in town. If you're not staying in the area, plan to see the volcano before or after viewing the pirate battle next door at Treasure Island. You'll find lots of viewing areas right along the Strip, so you don't have to make the effort to arrive early.

Sunset Stampede ★★★★
5111 Boulder Highway, Las Vegas, *(702) 456-7777.*
Located at Sam's Town Hotel & Gambling Hall.

Sam's Town, long a local's favorite, is going after the visitor market with its original laser-light and waterfall show. Choreographed to a symphonic score, Sunset Stampede is a "musical journey" through the Western Frontier, with special effects, laser animation, synchronized fountains and computerized lighting taking you on a race across the great plains, over the Rockies, through the desert and into a gold rush camp. The show takes place in the hotel's Mystic Falls Park, a lush, indoor "forest" complete with babbling brooks and animal sounds. Well worth a visit, and Sam's Town—which, after 15 expansions in six years has become Las Vegas' second-largest casino—is a fun place to try your luck. Sunset Stampede runs daily at 2, 6, 8 and 10 p.m. Admission is free.

Treasure Island Pirate Battle ★ ★ ★ ★ ★

3300 Las Vegas Boulevard South, Las Vegas, ☎ *(702) 894-7111.*

This free show is a hoot, and I highly recommend you take it in at least once. It takes place in Buccaneer Bay in front of the Treasure Island daily at 4, 5:30, 7, 8:30 and 10 p.m., weather permitting (they can't do it in the rain or high winds). A life-size pirate ship, the Hispaniola, does battle with a life-size British frigate. There's lots of corny dialogue as the Brits try to convince the pirates to surrender their stolen booty. The pirates are not about to give in—they're pirates, after all—and a full-scale battle ensues, with lots of explosions, snapping masts and sailors flying into the water. The pirates emerge victorious, destroying the frigate in the process. It really sinks! This show is perfect for kids, but one can't help getting caught up in the drama and fiery spectacle. Come EARLY—at least a full half-hour before showtime—to ensure a good view. Afterward, stroll over to the Mirage to catch the volcano eruption (every 30 minutes until midnight). Insider's tip: One of the best places to view the battle is from the second floor of the Tam O'Shanter Motel across the street. Management probably doesn't appreciate this, so park elsewhere and just nonchalantly walk up the stairs. And if you're staying at the Vagabond Inn next door, request a room whose balcony overlooks the battle.

Don't miss Treasure Island's pirate battle with explosions, lots of men overboard and even the sinking of a ship!

WHAT TO SEE AND DO IN LAS VEGAS

White Tiger Habitat   ★★★

3400 Las Vegas Boulevard South, Las Vegas, ☎ *(702) 791-7111.*
Located in the Mirage.

Royal Siberian white tigers, in a large water-accented habitat, can be
viewed daily at the Mirage. The rare cats are owned by Siegfried &
Roy, who breed them and use them in their show. If you're really cap-
tivated, you can buy stuffed versions of the critters at the S&R gift
shop just across the hall. While you're in the Mirage, wander over to
the hotel lobby to check out the 20,000-gallon saltwater aquarium
behind the front desk, home to small sharks and other creatures of the
sea.

*If you fall in love with The Mirage's white Siberian tigers, you can
take home a stuffed version at Siegfried and Roy's gift shop.*

Wildlife Walk   ★★

3801 Las Vegas Boulevard South, Las Vegas, ☎ *(702) 739-2222.*
Located in the Tropicana.

The Tropicana's two hotel towers are connected via a long walkway,
which they recently christened the Wildlife Walk. If you're already
familiar with the Tropicana's extensive collection of Amazon parrots,
toucans and other large birds, you can skip this. Worth a look,
though, if you've never been here and like exotic birds. There are also
pygmy marmosets (small monkeys), butterflies and other small caged
creatures. "Wings of the World," a free show with Joe Krathwohl, is
presented Wednesday-Monday at 11 a.m., 3 and 5 p.m. The walkway
gives a nice view of the Tropicana's very impressive pool—but they've
started giving wristbands out to hotel guests to keep pool-crashers
out.

Theme/Amusement Parks

MGM Grand Adventures is the biggest and the best, but there are still several other venues where kids of all ages can while away the hours.

Grand Slam Canyon   ★ ★ ★ ★

2880 Las Vegas Boulevard South, Las Vegas, 89114, ☎ *(702) 734-0410. Located behind Circus Circus.*

Grand Slam Canyon is a small amusement park housed inside a really cool pink glass dome some 15 stories high. It's supposedly not doing so hot, and that's because the moron who picked the site placed it behind Circus Circus—you would never even know it's there. If they had located it right on the Strip, it would be a runaway hit. Everything here is really nicely done, from the "Grand Slam" waterfalls when you first enter to the simulated cliffs that really look like the Grand Canyon, to the "Parent's Relaxation Center" where adults can chill out while watching their kids work their way through a maze or paw through a fossil dig sandbox. The park's showpiece is the Canyon Blaster, the only indoor double-loop, double-corkscrew roller coaster in the United States. There are lots of spots where you can stand and watch the roller coaster whiz just a few feet from your face. There's also a neat water flume ride, a high-tech laser tag game, bumper cars, lots of rides for wee tots, animatronic dinosaurs, an amusement midway and several food outlets. I like this place a lot, but it's much more geared to kids than the MGM Grand, which has a wider range of activities. Since it's inside and air-conditioned, Grand Slam Canyon is the perfect place to take the little ones during the often-unbearable heat of summer. Open 11 a.m.–7 p.m., until 11 p.m. Friday and Saturday. Open till 10 p.m. weekdays and midnight weekends during the summer. General admission is free. An unlimited ride pass costs $15.95, $11.95 for kids 3–9. Each ride costs from $2 to $5.

MGM Grand Adventures   ★ ★ ★ ★ ★

3799 Las Vegas Boulevard South, Las Vegas, 89109, ☎ *(702) 891-7979. Located behind the MGM Grand.*
Hours open: 10 a.m.–6 p.m. Special Hours: Until 10 p.m. during Daylight Savings Time.

Las Vegas' only theme park is really worth a trip, with or without kids. MGM Grand Adventures—which, naturally, can only be entered after walking through the MGM Grand's enormous casino—encompasses 33 acres and has 14 major attractions. It's not Disneyland, but it's still a lot of fun, especially now that admission is free. (It used to cost about $25 to get in, but sluggish demand took care of that.) There are nine themed areas, including an old-fashioned New York, an Asian Village, a waterfront at Salem and streets depicting France, New Orleans and Olde England. Street performers such as Betty Boop,

Dixieland bands and swashbucklers put on impromptu shows throughout the day—one minute you're walking along, the next you're in the middle of a song-and-dance routine. There are eight major rides. My favorites are Grand Canyon Rapids, where you swirl along white-water rapids in an inner tube without tracks (it's a blast!) and Over the Edge, a water flume ride that leaves you soaking wet, especially if you sit up front. I also like the Backlot River Tour, which takes you on a boat ride through simulated movie sets, despite its very corny and grating live narration. There's also a Haunted Mine; the Lightning Bolt indoor roller coaster; Deep Space Exploration, a futuristic motion-based simulator; Parisian Taxis, French-style bumper cars; and the new Sky Screamer, which costs $22.50. Four theaters feature acts that range from dueling pirates to cliff divers to The Three Stooges. "You're in the Movies" is very entertaining, especially if you're one of the lucky audience members who get to don a costume and act in a scene that's electronically combined with an existing film. There's also a wedding chapel, some incredibly expensive gift shops and a variety of more reasonable food outlets—Mamma Ilardo's Pizzeria has the best slices west of the Mississippi. Adults over 21 can play the slots and guzzle beer at the riverboat-style Cotton Blossom. You can buy a wristband for $14 ($12 under age 12) that gets you into everything, but unless you plan to spend hours here, you're better off paying the $1 to $3 charge per ride or show. Try to come on a weekday to avoid the crowds.

Old Nevada ★★★★

Red Rock Canyon, Black Diamond, ☎ *(702) 875-4191.*
Located half an hour from Las Vegas.
Hours open: 10:30 a.m.–5 p.m. Special Hours: until 6 p.m. in the summer.

I've been to many recreated old mining towns—Old Nevada is the best, and the surrounding scenery is awesome. Nestled beneath the towering peaks of Red Rock Canyon, it is quite authentic and stops just short of being too cute. Attractions include a wax museum of western trail blazers and scoundrels, heroes and whores—the figures won't win any awards, but are nicely displayed with witty explanatory signs. There's also a cactus garden, Boot Hill Cemetery, blacksmith display, gunfights and hangings in the street, a train ride, petting zoo and lots of old buildings into which to peer. Best of all are the 1880 melodramas in the old saloon in which the audience is encouraged—via cue cards—to boo and hiss the villain and cheer the spunky heroine. It's fun! Trail rides on horseback and hayrides are available at the adjacent Bonnie Springs Ranch. $5.50 for seniors, $4 kids 5–11. General Admission: $6.50.

Secrets of the Luxor Pyramid ★★★★★

3900 Las Vegas Boulevard South, Las Vegas, ☎ *(702) 262-4000.*
Located at the Luxor.
Hours open: 9 a.m.–11 p.m.

This Indiana Jones-type attraction carries a mystery of the pyramid theme over three rides. The first, "In Search of the Obelisk" ($5) is the most impressive by far. It starts with a hairy ride on a runaway elevator followed by about 10 frantic minutes in a motion-based simulator theater. The special effects are dazzling, so much so that I nearly threw up in all the swooping about as the good guys fight the bad guys for an ancient obelisk. The next two rides ($5 each) are much more sedate (and a little dull after the excitement of the first). "Luxor Live" is a 3-D movie that continues the story line in a talk-show format, while the "Theater of Time" is a pretty, but too long, movie shown on a 70-foot screen. Unless you're really into it, you can do just the first ride and forget the rest.

Star Trek: The Experience ★★★★★

3000 Paradise Road, Las Vegas, ☎ *(702) 732-5111.*
At the Las Vegas Hilton.
Hours open: 10 a.m.–10 p.m. Special Hours: later on weekends.

This new attraction, just opened in the summer of 1997, boldly takes tourists where they have never gone before. A joint venture between Hilton and Paramount Parks, the facility is reached by walking through Hilton's new Spacequest Casino with its "24th-century" table games, futuristic slot machines and space windows that create the illusion of gambling high up among the heavenly bodies. (The theme even extends to the men's room, where those who use the urinal get an instant analysis of their specimen.) Once inside the attraction proper, groups of 27 are taken on a three-part, 22-minute interactive adventure based on the newer edition of the TV show. Knowing how seriously Trekkers take their show, Paramount has painstakingly recreated the famed sets. Once the "experience" ends, guests can stay as long as they like in the bar, restaurant and gift shop, or mingle among the costumed characters. Admission is a reasonable $9.95.

Stratosphere Tower ★★★★

2000 Las Vegas Boulevard South, Las Vegas, ☎ *(702) 380-7777.*
Located at the Stratosphere Hotel.

You won't be in Las Vegas long before noticing the Stratosphere, the new 1149-foot tower that dominates the skyline. It's well worth a ride to the top—via one of four high-speed double-deck elevators moving at 1800 feet per second—to check out the awesome views. If just being that high isn't daring enough, try the two daredevil rides. Let It Ride is the world's highest roller coaster, while Big Shot offers a sensation similar to bungee jumping. It shoots passengers at 45 miles per hour from the 921-foot-level of the tower to the top, then lets them "free fall" back to the launching pad. Both rides operate from 10 a.m. to midnight Sunday through Thursday, and 10 a.m. to 1 a.m. on Friday, Saturday and holidays. Tower admission is $5 ($4 for locals and kids under 12); while each ride costs $5. (You can also buy a tower admission and one ride for $8.)

WHAT TO SEE AND DO IN LAS VEGAS

For the Kids

Buffalo Bill's   ★★★★★

I-15 & the California border, Primm, ☎ *(702) 679-RIDE.*
Located 45 minutes south of Las Vegas.

There's tons to do at the new Buffalo Bill's Hotel & Casino, a great
place for kids of all ages. The top attraction is the Desperado ($4), the
world's fastest roller coaster. I planned to ride it until I actually saw it,
but I wimped out after seeing the bright-yellow contraption's amazing vertical drops. Braver souls report that it's the best roller coaster
they've ever tried. The Adventure Canyon water flume ride ($4) is
thrilling too, but not as hair-raising. It crisscrosses the casino and has
some heart-stopping plunges. New is the Turbo Drop, in which riders
are lifted 200 feet off the ground, then plunge down at speeds of 45
miles per hour. Rides operate Monday–Thursday from 10 a.m.–6
p.m., Friday and Saturday from 10 a.m.–11 p.m., and Sunday from 10
a.m.–8 p.m. Kids have to be at least 42 inches tall to ride them. Buffalo Bill's also has the kind of motion-simulator theaters ($3) made
popular by the Excalibur. They run from 10 a.m.–10 p.m. (Winter
hours vary, so call first.) Monday–Thursday, and 10 a.m.–11 p.m. Friday–Sunday. The hotel also offers a kids' arcade, fast-food outlets and
an ice cream parlour.

Buffalo Bill's has the world's tallest and fastest roller coaster.

Cinema Ride   ★★★★

3570 Las Vegas Boulevard South, Las Vegas, ☎ *(702) 369-4008.*
Located in the Forum Shops.
Hours open: 11 a.m.–11 p.m.

This ride in the Forum Shops' Cyberstation is a step above Las Vegas'
many motion-simulator rides. It uses lots of 3-D effects to transport
riders on various adventures such as a futuristic submarine race, a wild

roller coaster ride and a seek-and-destroy mission in outer space. Each ride lasts about 10 minutes and costs $7; "double features" take 15 minutes and cost $10.

Excalibur's Fantasy Faire ★★★★★

3850 Las Vegas Boulevard South, Las Vegas, 89119, ☎ *(702) 597-7777.* This entire hotel is an amusing attraction for children, with towers, turrets, battlements, drawbridges, a moat, serfs, pages, squires and ladies-in-waiting. Kids can test their aim with a crossbow or fire William Tell darts in Sherwood Forest, practice archery, watch stunning visual effects in a theater with Merlin's Magic Motion Machines ($3), see the world-famous Royal Lipizzaner stallions perform or watch a medieval jousting tournament while eating dinner with their bare hands. The only problem parents have is keeping an eye on the little tykes among the ever-present crowds.

IMAX Theatre ★★★★★

39000 Las Vegas Boulevard South, Las Vegas, ☎ *(702) 262-4555.* *At the Luxor.*
Las Vegas' first IMAX theater has a screen that measures 68 feet by 84 feet, with a film frame more than 10 times the size of conventional 35mm film. The 312-seat theater, located on Luxor's attractions level, has a six-channel, 15,000 watt sound system to complement the seven-story-high screen. At presstime, the theater was showing "L5: First City in Space in 3-D" and "Special Effects," but be sure to call ahead as shows constantly change. Shows generally run from 9 a.m. to 10:20 p.m., but again, call ahead. Tickets are $7 to $8.50.

The Lied Discovery Children's Museum features educational interactive exhibits.

Lied Discovery Children's Museum ★★★★

833 Las Vegas Boulevard North, Las Vegas, 89101, *(702) 382-3445. Located next to the Las Vegas Library.*
Hours open: 10 a.m.–5 p.m. Special Hours: Wednesday 10 a.m.–7 p.m., Sunday noon–5 p.m. Closed: Mon., Tue.

Lots of interactive exhibits in this 22,000-square-foot facility offer youngsters hands-on fun and learning about the arts, sciences and humanities. Opening a savings account and writing checks, inflating a hot air balloon and how to choose a career are some of the more practical activities available here. Not exactly the carnival atmosphere at Excalibur, but then it's a lot more educational. $4 for seniors and children 12 and older, $3 for kids 2–11. General Admission: $5.

Manhattan Express ★★★★

3155 West Harmon Avenue, Las Vegas, *(702) 740-6969. Located at New York-New York.*

Designed to call to mind "the kind of roller coaster that made Coney Island famous," Manhattan Express zips around the outside and inside of the new New York-New York Hotel & Casino. It's the world's first to feature a "heartline" twist and dive maneuver, in which the train rolls 180 degrees, suspending riders at 86 feet above the casino roof before diving directly under itself. (A heartline roll is similar to what a pilot feels during a barrel-roll in an airplane, when the center of rotation becomes the same as the passenger's center of gravity.) The coaster reaches speeds of 67 miles per hour and has a maximum height of 203 feet. The ride costs $5, operates from 10:30 a.m. to 10:30 p.m. daily (and until midnight on weekends), and is open only to those at least 42 inches tall.

Omnimax Theatre ★★★★

2570 Las Vegas Boulevard South, Las Vegas, 89109, *(702) 731-7901. Located at Caesars Palace.*
Hours open: 2–10 p.m.

Moviegoers recline in tilt-back chairs and watch a 70mm curved screen like the one at the Smithsonian. You'll really feel like you're surfing in Hawaii, rafting in the Grand Canyon or exploring space in this theater. $5 for seniors, kids under 12, military personnel, physically challenged and Caesars hotel guests. General Admission: $7.

Scandia Family Fun Center ★★★

2900 Sirius Avenue, Las Vegas, 89102, *(702) 364-0070. Hours open: 10 a.m.–10:30 p.m. Special Hours: Friday and Saturday 10 a.m.–midnight. Closed: Sun.*

A mini-Indy raceway, video games, bumper boats, batting ranges (one that pitches at 125 miles per hour; $1.25 for 25 pitches) and three 18-hole miniature golf courses will keep the kids busy. A wrist band for $15.95 lets you try everything. Miniature golf costs $5.95, while most other rides are $3.95. Everything is a dollar less on Monday nights.

Showcase Mall

3785 Las Vegas Blvd. South., Las Vegas, 89109, *(702) 597-3122. Located on the Strip next to the MGM Grand Hotel and across from New York, New York.*

One of the star attractions of the new Showcase complex is the Coca-Cola Oasis, (including a towering 100 ft. glass bottle encasing a pair of elevators) plus Everything Coca-Cola, a store featuring all Coke merchandise. The complex, which opened in June 1997, also features Sega Gameworks, one of the largest video arcades in the world, a United Artists cinema with eight theaters, and the Official All-Star Cafe, an upscale sports-themed restaurant. Ethel M/M&M World offers a fascinating look at how chocolate is made and gives the kiddies a chance to be hugged by a giant walking M&M. Other retail shops and restaurants are scheduled to open in the complex soon.

Wet 'n Wild Water Park   ★★★★

2601 Las Vegas Boulevard South, Las Vegas, 89109, ☎ *(702) 737-3819. Special Hours: early May to late September.*

This 15-acre water park is just the thing for those dog days of summer. There are various pools for surfing, swimming and rafting, and lots of water slides for plummeting wildly into the wet stuff. The hairiest is Bomb Bay, a 76-foot-high slide with lots of twists and turns. More sedate types can laze on lounge chairs on the large sunbathing deck. The park is open from 10 a.m.–6 p.m. from April 1 to June 3 and Sept. 5 to Oct. 3, when it closes until spring. Summer hours (June 4–Sept. 4) are 10 a.m.–11 p.m. General admission is $21.95 for those 10 and older, $15.95 for senior citizens and kids 3–9 and free for kids under 3.

Tours

Fly over the Grand Canyon, take in the sunset on Lake Mead, soar above the city in a hot-air balloon. For more ideas on exploring the area, see "Day Trips."

Grand Canyon Tours   ★★★★

Various locations, Las Vegas.

The Grand Canyon is a 300-mile, six-hour drive from Las Vegas. Several tour companies will take you there, including **Gray Line** (☎ *(702) 384-1234*), **SilverLine** (☎ *(702) 733-8283*), **Ray & Ross Transport** (☎ *(702) 646-4661*), **Interstate Tours** (☎ *(702) 293-2268*), and **America's Travel Company** (☎ *(702) 456-1355*). Motor tours can usually be had for about $100. Numerous firms will fly you over the canyon; some also land there and give you the chance to hike around. It's worth noting that there have been several fatal crashes over the years. Prices vary by company—shop around and be on the lookout for discount coupons in the tourist magazines—but plan on shelling out at least $129 per person. These airlines all offer tours: **Grand Canyon Specialists** (☎ *(702) 383-8592*), **Eagle Canyon Airlines** (☎ *(702) 736-3333 and (800) 446-4584*), **Scenic Airways** (☎ *(702) 739-1900 and (800) 634-6801*), **Adventure Airlines** (☎ *(702) 293-3446*), **Air Nevada** (☎ *(702) 736-8900 and (800) 634-6377*), **Canyon Fliers** (☎ *(702) 293-3446*) and **Helicop Tours**

WHAT TO SEE AND DO IN LAS VEGAS

(☎ *(702) 736-0606)*. For something really special, take **Scenic Airways'** $199 tour, which includes a flight to the Grand Canyon, a grand tour there, and then dinner at Las Vegas' Planet Hollywood. Call ☎ *(702) 739-1900* for information. For more on the Grand Canyon, see "Day Trips."

Hoover Dam   ★ ★ ★ ★

P.O. Box 60400, Boulder City, 89006, ☎ (702) 294-3523.
Located about a 40-minute drive from the Strip.
Hours open: 8:30 a.m.–5:30 p.m.

Built during the Depression, this is one of the largest public works projects in history. A 35-minute guided tour takes visitors inside the 727-foot-high structure, which used enough concrete to build a highway from New York to San Francisco. It's pretty interesting, especially for engineering types. To get there, take U.S. 93 south through Henderson and Boulder City to the Nevada/Arizona border. For more details, see "Day Trips." $5 for seniors, $2 for kids under 16. General Admission: $6.

Hoover Dam is one of the largest public works projects in history.

Lake Mead Recreation Area   ★ ★ ★ ★ ★

Near Boulder City, Boulder City, ☎ (702) 293-4041.
Located 30 miles southwest of Las Vegas.

Lake Mead is huge—27,000 square miles with 550 miles of shoreline—and beautiful, the perfect respite from Las Vegas' concrete and neon. Created during the construction of Hoover Dam, it is a much-visited national recreation area. Numerous tour companies offer all sorts of ways to enjoy Lake Mead; **SilverLine** *(☎ (702) 733-8283)*, for example, offers a three-hour sunset cruise on a triple-deck steam-wheeler that includes dinner, dancing and round-trip transportation from your hotel for $55; while **America's Travel Company** *(☎ (702) 456-1355)* offers an all-day tour of Hoover Dam and a 1.5-hour cruise on Lake Mead for $33. **Ray & Ross Transport** *(☎ (702) 646-4661)* has a similar tour for $31.90. Check the tourist magazines for other options and two-for-one coupons. For more on Lake Mead, see "Day Trips."

The waters of Lake Mead's Recreation Area offer a wonderful change of pace, whether you ride a jet ski or take a sunset cruise.

Las Vegas Helicopters ★★★★★

3712 Las Vegas Boulevard South, Las Vegas, 89109, ☎ *(702) 736-0013.*
Located across from the Aladdin.
Hours open: 7:30 p.m.–midnight. Special Hours: until 1 a.m. Friday–Sunday.

Here's a neat idea for those too jaded to get excited by the Mirage volcano: a helicopter ride over the Strip. Lots of oohing and ahhing as you hover and dip above all the bright lights. The price is $45. Bring a camera!

Mount Charleston ★★★★

Kyle Canyon exit off U.South Highway 95, Las Vegas, ☎ *(702) 873-8800.*
Located 35 miles northwest of Las Vegas.

When the oppressive heat of summer gets you down (and it will), head for Mount Charleston, a 11,918-foot-high peak in the Spring Mountain Range. You can ski here in the winter (see Lee Canyon under "Sports and Recreation") and spend the rest of the year hiking, picnicking, bike riding and camping among the Joshua trees, wildflowers, pines and sage. You can trek to the summit (11 miles round trip) from Lee Canyon; less hardy types can enjoy a number of shorter and easier trails. **Downhill Bicycle Tours** (☎ *897-8287*) offers bike tours that drop you off at the top of Lee Canyon and let you cruise on down 18 miles without ever having to pedal. The trips are offered every day except Monday; hours vary by season. The fee is about $65, which includes transportation from the Strip. For more on Mount Charleston, see "Day Trips."

Parks

Parks and gardens in Las Vegas? It's true, and your visit will be well enhanced by checking out some of the area's natural respites.

Floyd Lamb State Park   ★★★

9200 Tule Springs Road, Las Vegas, 89131, ☎ *(702) 486-5413.*
Hours open: 8 a.m.–dusk. Special Hours: Closed Christmas and New Year's.

This is a cool oasis in the desert 20 minutes outside Las Vegas. It is also one of the oldest confirmed sights of the presence of humans dating back 11,000 years, and important fossil remains of mammoths have been found here. There are many daytime activities available, such as barbecue grills for picnicking, fishing in the four small lakes and a trapshooting range. Lots of nice walking tours, such as the arboretum, are also available. To get there, take I-15 north to Highway 95 north (toward Reno) about 15 miles to the State Park exit—it's not marked as the Floyd Lamb because this former senator became unpopular after being busted (but later exonerated) in an Abscam-type sting. Admission is $5 per car.

Red Rock Canyon   ★★★★★

Off Highway 159, Blue Diamond.
Located half an hour from Las Vegas.

This is a gorgeous natural canyon formed by a thrust fault—a fracture in the earth's crust where one rock plate is thrust horizontally over another. Now home to wild horses and burros as well as bighorn sheep and antelope, it has a lovely scenic drive and hiking trails. Well worth a visit, and a real surprise. To get there, take I-15 south to Route 160 north to Route 159. For more details, see "Day Trips."
City Street Bike Tours of Red Rock Canyon *(* ☎ *(702) 596-2953)* and **Downhill Bicycle Tours** *(* ☎ *(702) 897-8287)* both offer bicycle trips through the canyon. While you're in the area, stop by Old Nevada, a cute recreated old mining town.

Fortunate visitors to dramatic Red Rock Canyon may catch a glimpse of bighorn sheep or wild horses and burros.

Southern Nevada Zoological Park   ★★★

1775 North Rancho Drive, Las Vegas, 89106, ☎ *(702) 648-5955.*
Hours open: 9 a.m.–4:30 p.m.

Don't expect a large, modern zoo with lots of exotic animals, and you won't be disappointed. There are more than 50 species of reptiles and small animals of the southwestern desert, as well as monkeys, a lion and a tiger. $3 for senior citizens and children 2–12. General Admission: $5.

Valley of Fire State Park   ★ ★ ★ ★

Highway 176, Overton, ☎ *(702) 397-2088.*
Located 52 miles northwest of Las Vegas.
Hours open: 8:30 a.m.–4:30 p.m. Special Hours: until 5:30 p.m. during daylight savings time.

This beautiful desert park is well worth the 52-mile drive to see its exotically shaped red sandstone rock formations. Come at sunset for an especially dramatic view. Lots of petroglyphs carved by Native Americans can be viewed. too. The visitor's center is open daily from 8:30 a.m.–4:30 p.m., and until 5:30 p.m. during Daylight Savings Time. It's generally too hot to enjoy this spot in the summer unless you come early, early in the morning. To get there, take I-15 north to 176 east. For further details, see "Day Trips." General Admission: $4 per car.

Golf

Golf is almost as popular as gambling in Las Vegas. Though winter may see some unseasonably cold days, courses are open year-round. Summer hours are generally 6 a.m. to 7:30 p.m., while winter goes from 7:30 a.m. to dark. Keep in mind that summer daytime temperatures can frequently top 100 degrees, so plan ahead for a morning tee time.

Several reservation systems offer tee times: **Stand By Golf** (☎ *(907) 597-2665),* **Las Vegas Golf Reservations** (☎ *(702) 382-4653)* and **Las Vegas Golf Systems** (☎ *(702) 220-9225 and (800) 777-5698).*

Angel Park Golf Club

100 South Rampart Boulevard, Las Vegas, 89128, ☎ *(702) 254-4653.*
Located off Summerlin Parkway.
There are three courses totaling 36 holes designed by Arnold Palmer, and a highly regarded 18-hole putting course at this locals' favorite. The course features re-creations of 12 of the most famous par-3s in the world, including ones at St. Andrews and Royal Troon. Other facilities include a lighted driving range and clubhouse. Greens fees are $22 for the par-3 course and $110 for the others. Reservations accepted 60 days out.

Black Mountain Country Club

500 Greenway Road, Henderson, 89005, ☎ *(702) 565-7933.*
Located half an hour from Las Vegas.
This 18-hole course has a par 72. Facilities include a driving range, cocktail lounge and coffee shop. Greens fees are $55 on weekdays,

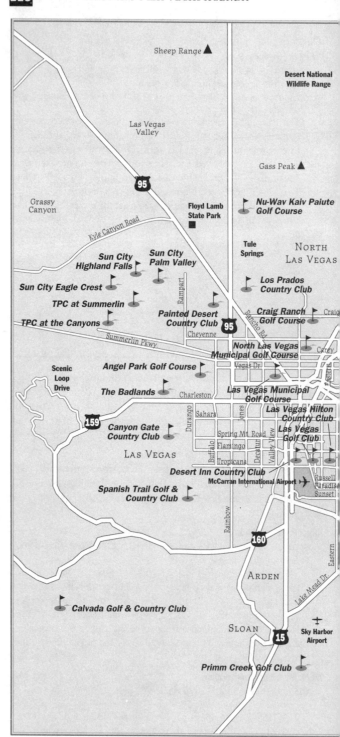

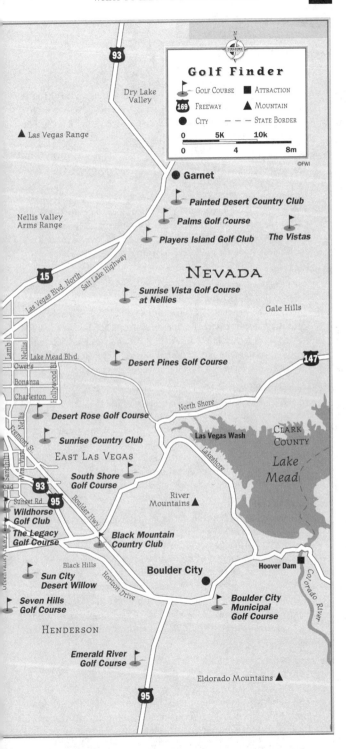

Golf Finder

🏌 GOLF COURSE	■ ATTRACTION
🛣 169 FREEWAY	▲ MOUNTAIN
● CITY	– – STATE BORDER

0	5K	10k
0	4	8m

©FWI

Dry Lake Valley

▲ Las Vegas Range

● **Garnet**

🏌 **Painted Desert Country Club**

🏌 **Palms Golf Course**

🏌 **Players Island Golf Club**

🏌 **The Vistas**

Nellis Valley Arms Range

NEVADA

🏌 **Sunrise Vista Golf Course at Nellies**

Gale Hills

Las Vegas Blvd. North

Salt Lake Highway

🏌 **Desert Pines Golf Course**

Lake Mead Blvd.

147

Lamb
Nellis
Owens
Bonanza
Charleston

Hollywood Blvd.

🏌 **Desert Rose Golf Course**

North Shore

🏌 **Sunrise Country Club**

Las Vegas Wash

CLARK COUNTY

Lakeshore

Lake Mead

EAST LAS VEGAS

Fremont St.
N. Vista St.
Nellis
Sandhill

🏌 **South Shore Golf Course**

Boulder Hwy.

River Mountains ▲

93
95

Sunset Rd.

🏌 **Wildhorse Golf Club**

🏌 **The Legacy Golf Course**

🏌 **Black Mountain Country Club**

Black Hills

Boulder City ●

Hoover Dam ■

Colorado River

🏌 **Sun City Desert Willow**

🏌 **Seven Hills Golf Course**

Horizon Drive

🏌 **Boulder City Municipal Golf Course**

Greenway Pkwy.

HENDERSON

🏌 **Emerald River Golf Course**

Eldorado Mountains ▲

95

WHAT TO SEE AND DO IN LAS VEGAS

$55 on weekends, including cart. Reservations are accepted four days out.

Boulder City Municipal Golf Course

1 Clubhouse Drive, Boulder City, 89005, ☎ *(702) 293-9236.*
Located near Hoover Dam.

It's a bit of a drive, but the greens fees are reasonable for this 18-hole, par-72 course. There's also a driving range, clubhouse and snack bar. Fees are $25 with cart for nine holes; $36 with cart for 18 holes. Reservations are taken a week ahead.

Craig Ranch Golf Club

628 West Craig Road, Las Vegas, 89115, ☎ *(702) 642-9700.*
Located near North Las Vegas.
Hours open: 6 a.m.–dusk

This club is a great bargain and a favorite with locals. More than 6000 trees make you forget you're in the desert, and the green fees ($15 or $23 with a cart), are within everyone's means. Clubs rent for only $8, and you can book tee times seven days in advance.

Desert Rose Golf Club

5483 Clubhouse Drive, Las Vegas, 89122, ☎ *(702) 431-4653.*
Located off of Nellis Blvd.

This is a well-maintained course with a good layout covering 6511 yards. Cart and greens fees for non-residents are $65 on weekdays and $75 on weekends. Clubs rent for $15. There's also a driving range, pro shop, restaurant and a cocktail lounge. Reservations are taken seven days out for weekdays, three days out for weekends.

Highland Falls Golf Club

10201 Sun City Boulevard, Las Vegas, ☎ *(702) 254-7010.*
Located northwest of the city, in Summerlin.

The public is welcome at this newer (1992) semi-private course, which has a par of 72 (no one broke it until it was open for six months). Facilities include a driving range, putting and chipping greens, restaurant, bar and pro shop. Greens fees are $95 with cart. Reservations are taken one week out, after 3 p.m.

Las Vegas Golf Club

4349 Vegas Drive, Las Vegas, 89108, ☎ *(702) 646-3003.*
Located near the I-95.
Hours open: 6 a.m.–dusk

This course is a bargain with green fees at $25.75 (with a cart) and $16.95 without. Nine holes are just $10 to walk, $15 to ride. It's an 18-hole, par 72 course, and the greens have been recently remodeled. A lighted driving range, pro shop, coffee shop and a cocktail lounge add to the enjoyment. Clubs rent for $14 for 18 holes, $9 for nine. Reservations taken a week out, and with rates like this, sell out quickly.

Las Vegas Hilton Country Club

1911 East Desert Inn Road, Las Vegas, ☎ *(702) 796-0013.*
Located just off the Strip.

This public, championship course has been the site of many prestigious tournaments; it's not recommended for novices. Par is 71. Facilities include a driving range (lit at night), putting green, pro shop and snack bar. Greens fees are $130 weekdays, $145 Friday-Sunday, including cart. Reservations are taken 60 days out.

Legacy Golf Club

130 Par Excellence Drive, Las Vegas, ☎ *(702) 897-2187.*
Located near the airport.
This 18-hole, par-72 links-type course is well bunkered and creatively spread out over a natural desert terrain. Greens fees are $115 daily, $125 weekends, with cart and range balls. There's also a driving range, golf shop, lounge, restaurant and snack bar on the premises. Reservations are taken 60 days out.

Los Padres Country Club

5150 Los Padres Circle, Las Vegas, ☎ *(702) 645-5696.*
Located north of the Strip.
This 18-hole, par-70 course is semi-private, so you'll have to make reservations 10 days in advance. It's located in a residential area and is quite narrow with small greens. There's a clubhouse with bar and restaurant, locker room and putting green, but no driving range. Fees, including cart, are $40 weekdays, $45 Saturday, Sunday and holidays, and $30 at twilight. Like other country clubs, Los Padres enforces a dress code that forbids cutoffs and tank tops. No credit cards accepted.

North Las Vegas Community Course

324 East Brooks Avenue, North Las Vegas, 89030, ☎ *(702) 633-1833.*
With greens fees as low as this, don't expect Pebble Beach. The nine-hole course has a par of 27, and is best suited to beginners. There's a snack bar on the premises. Fees: $5 Monday–Friday, $6.50 weekends and holidays. Add $1 for nightly play; the last tee time is 10 p.m. Reservations are taken seven days in advance.

Painted Desert Country Club

5555 Painted Mirage Way, Las Vegas, 89129, ☎ *(702) 645-2568.*
Located near North Las Vegas.
Locals and tourists alike love this course because the scenery is breath-taking. Tee boxes come right out of the desert floor, and if your ball misses the fairway, it might hit a coyote. Greens fees (including cart) are $99 Monday–Thursday, $117 Friday-Sunday and cheaper in the summer. Reservations are taken eight to 60 days in advance.

Sheraton Desert Inn Golf Course

3145 South Las Vegas Boulevard, Las Vegas, 89109, ☎ *(702) 733-4290.*
Located at the Desert Inn.
Hotel guests have priority, but the public is welcome if all the tee times have not been reserved. Greens fees are steep—$120 Monday–Thursday, including a cart, and $145 on weekends. And that's for hotel guests! Non-guests pay $195 every day. Clubs rent for a hefty $25. This is a championship course, though, and the site of many professional golf tournaments. Lots of celebrities and political figures play here, and the location, right behind the Strip, is convenient. Hotel guests can reserve a tee time a year in advance; non-guests can book weekdays 90 days out, but just two days out for weekends.

Wildhorse Golf Club

1 Showboat Country Club Drive, Las Vegas, 89119, ☎ *(702) 434-9009.*
Located near the airport.

Hours open: 5:30 a.m.–dusk

Previously called the Royal Kenfield, this is an 18-hole, par 72, championship course that has been the site of the Seniors Open. Amenities here include a pro shop, putting green, driving range and a clubhouse with a coffee shop and cocktail lounge. Greens fees, including cart, are $99 weekdays and $135 weekends. Reservations accepted 60 days out.

Other Sports

Golf is to the day what neon is to the night: *de rigeur* in Las Vegas. There's also tennis, bowling, ice skating—even bungee jumping.

Ballooning

Dream Flights Company   ★★★★

Pickup at your hotel, Las Vegas, ☎ *(800) 223-4373.*

Would you like to fly in their beautiful balloon? Way up in the air in their beautiful balloon? The 15-passenger, 10-story-high hot-air balloon soars over the Strip and surrounding desert—it's especially picturesque at night. Ten-minute tethered flights (which don't exceed 150 feet) cost $25, while the more elaborate (and higher soaring) half-hour and hour flights cost $85 and $149, respectively. The price includes round-trip transportation from your hotel.

Baseball

Las Vegas Stars-Baseball

850 North Las Vegas Boulevard, Las Vegas, 89109, ☎ *(702) 386-7200.*

This is a triple-A farm club for the San Diego Padres, playing at Cashman Field each April to September. Baseball fanatics give this stadium high marks—and best of all, they never strike! Tickets are $12.50.

Bicycling

Bikes USA

1539 North Eastern Avenue, Las Vegas, 89101, ☎ *(702) 642-2453.*

Bicycles are available for rental here but, because of the summer heat, you won't find very many shady riding trails. There is one interesting ride via Charleston Boulevard that takes you out of the city to Red Rock Canyon. Rates are $25 for the first day, $15 for the next day(s), or $80 a week.

Bowling

Showboat Hotel-Bowling

2800 East Fremont Street, Las Vegas, 89104, ☎ *(702) 385-9153.*

One hundred and six of the most modern and best-equipped lanes are located in the Showboat Hotel, making it the world's largest bowling alley. There's also a pro shop, snack bar and a kids' playroom with an attendant on duty at all times. Each game costs $2.25 for adults and

$1.55 for seniors and kids. Shoes rent for $1.75. It's open 24 hours, but call first because the facility is often booked solid with tournaments, especially on the weekends. Bowling is also available at the Gold Coast *(4000 W. Flamingo, ☎ 367-7111, 72 lanes)*, **Sam's Town** *(5111 Boulder Highway, ☎ 454-8022, 56 lanes)* and **Santa Fe** *(4949 Rancho Drive North, ☎ 658-4995, 60 lanes)*.

Bungee Jumping

A.J. Hackett Bungee

810 Circus Circus Drive, Las Vegas, ☎ (702) 385-4321.
Located just off the Strip, behind Circus Circus.
Hours open: 11 a.m.–7 p.m. Special Hours: Saturdays, 10 a.m.–10 p.m.; call for summer hours.
If you're crazy enough to bungee jump, they're happy enough to help you out. Doubles jump from a 175-foot platform, North America's highest. Jump at sunset for a really spectacular sight. Couples can even arrange a bungee wedding! Jumps cost $51, which includes a T-shirt and certificate. If you can talk three others into the experience, you'll pay just $41 each.

Horseback Riding

Bonnie Springs Ranch

1 Gunfighter Lane, Old Nevada, 89004, ☎ (702) 875-4400.
Located a half-hour southwest of town.
Besides year-round horseback riding ($20 per hour for a guided ride), there's a petting zoo with pigs, goats, buffalo, coyotes and turkeys here. Ask about the all-day horseback tours. Stagecoach rides are also offered on weekends and holidays for $5 adults, $3 kids. A good restaurant and bar make it worth the 30-minute drive from Las Vegas, and the scenery is fantastic. While you're at it, visit the adjacent Old Nevada western town (see separate listing for details).

Ice Skating

Santa Fe Ice Arena

4949 North Rancho Drive, Las Vegas, ☎ (702) 658-4900.
Located off U.S. 95 north, 20 minutes from the Strip.
The Santa Fe Hotel and Casino is home to a professional ice arena. DJs spin tunes to put skaters in the mood. It costs $5 per two-hour session for adults, $4 for kids. Skate rentals are $1.50. The hours vary like crazy, so call first.

Racing

Las Vegas Motor Speedway

7000 Las Vegas Boulevard North, Las Vegas, ☎ (702) 644-4444.
Located at I-15 and Las Vegas Boulevard North.
This new 107,000-seat speedway opened in late 1996. The $200-million speedway features 24 racing venues, a 4000-foot drag strip and facilities for legends cars, go-karts and junior dragsters. Call for a schedule of events while you're in town.

Racquetball

Las Vegas Racquetball Club

3333 West Raven Avenue, Las Vegas, 89118, ☎ (702) 361-2202.
Hours open: 10 a.m.–10 p.m.
There are two outdoor courts lit for night play, at a cost of $10 per hour.

Rafting

Black Canyon Raft Tours

1297 Nevada Highway, Boulder City, 89005, ☎ (702) 293-3776.
Located near Hoover Dam.

Float down the Colorado River in large rafts that seat 45. The scenery is fantastic, and the start, right at the base of Hoover Dam, is awesome! Plan on getting wet, although there's more lazy floating than white-water action—and definitely bring a camera. The cost is $64.95 for adults, $35 for kids 5–12. Lunch at Willow Beach Resort at the ride's conclusion is included. The entire trip takes three hours. Tack on $10 if you need transportation from your hotel. Open Feb. 1–Nov. 30. Highly recommended!

A raft trip down the Colorado River at Black Canyon provides a wet and wonderful excursion.

Skiing

Lee Canyon Ski Area

State Highway 156, Mt. Charleston, ☎ (702) 872-5462.
Located an hour's drive from the Strip.

Skiing in Las Vegas? Strange but true, and the locals say the slopes are quite decent and wonderfully empty on weekdays. This scenic area in the Spring Mountain Range of Toiyabe National Forest has a base elevation of 8510 feet. They get about 80 inches of the white stuff per season, and supplement that with extensive snowmaking. There are three double chairlifts servicing 40 acres of maintained slopes surrounded by forested terrain. Runs have appropriate names such as Highroller, Blackjack, Slot Alley, The Strip and Bimbo. The season generally runs Thanksgiving to Easter. There's also a coffee shop, cocktail lounge, ski shop and rentals, a ski school and Ski Wee for kids 4 to 12. It's not Aspen, but then again, lift tickets are only $27.

Tennis

Tennis at the Hotels

Various locations, Las Vegas.

Non-guests can play tennis at one of the following hotels (though guests generally have priority): **Aladdin** (☎ 736-0330, three lighted courts), **Alexis Park** (☎ 796-3300, two lighted courts), **Bally's** (☎ 739-4598, 10 outdoor courts, five lighted), **Frontier** (☎ 734-

0110, two outdoor lighted courts), **Riviera** (☎ *734-5110*, two lighted courts) and the **Sheraton Desert Inn** (☎ *733-4577*, five lighted courts).

University of Nevada, Las Vegas-Tennis

4505 South Maryland Parkway, Las Vegas, 89119, ☎ *(702) 895-3150.* The university courts are available to the public, but students and faculty have priority, so call before you go. There are eight racquetball courts, which cost $2 per person per hour. There are also 12 tennis courts; call ☎ *(702) 895-3009* for information.

Health Clubs

Nearly every large casino-hotel has at least an exercise room; some, like Bally's, the Golden Nugget and the Las Vegas Hilton, have state-of-the-art spas with men's and women's locker rooms, aerobics classes, weight rooms and whirlpools. Obnoxiously enough, hotel guests must pay a daily fee (about $10 or $15) for the privilege of working up a sweat. Or, try one of these independent facilities.

24-Hour Fitness Centers

Three locations, Las Vegas.
These three health clubs are each open 24 hours, and offer all the usual weight and toning machines, extensive aerobics classes, juice and snack bars, and baby-sitting for an extra fee. Non-members pay $10 a day or $25 a week. Locations: *2605 S. Eastern Avenue* (☎ *(702) 641-2222*), *3055 S. Valley View Boulevard.* (☎ *(702) 368-1111*), and *3141 N. Rainbow Boulevard.* (☎ *(702) 656-7777*).

Gold's Gym

2610 Decatur, Las Vegas, 89102, ☎ *(702) 877-6966.*
Located four miles west of the Strip.
Special Hours: 24 hours.
Want to sweat next to David Copperfield? (What woman wouldn't?) Then head for this upscale Gold's, where all the usual toning equipment awaits. It's the health club of the stars! General admission: $10 or $35 for a week.

Las Vegas Athletic Clubs

Four locations, Las Vegas, 89104.
These four health clubs all offer exercise machines (stairmasters, lifecycles, etc.), weight rooms, aerobics classes, locker rooms and spa facilities, and child care, which requires a 24-hour advance reservation. All are open on weekdays from 5 a.m. to 11 p.m., 8 a.m. to 8 p.m. Saturday and Sunday, unless otherwise noted. Fees are $10 per day or $25 per week. Locations: *1070 E. Sahara,* ☎ *(702) 733-1919* (open 24 hours); *3315 Spring Mountain Road,* ☎ *(702) 362-3720*

WHAT TO SEE AND DO IN LAS VEGAS

(also has an outdoor lap pool); *5090 S. Maryland Parkway,* ☎ *(702) 795-2582* (also has indoor lap pools); and *3830 Flamingo Road,* ☎ *(702) 451-2526* (also has an indoor pool).

Las Vegas Sporting House

3025 Industrial Road, Las Vegas, ☎ *(702) 733-8999.*
Located behind the Stardust Hotel.
This large facility—65,000 square feet—supplements its exercise equipment and aerobics classes with racquetball, squash and tennis courts. There are also swimming pools indoor and out, an indoor/outdoor track and a restaurant and bar. Fees are $15 per day or $50 per week.

World Gym

4754 South Eastern Avenue, Las Vegas, ☎ *(702) 435-5646.*
Located at the corner of Tropiana.
This 24-hour gym is close to the Strip and includes all the latest fitness and cardiovascular equipment, as well as aerobics classes, saunas, a nutrition cafe, child care and a boxing fitness center. Fees are $10 per day or $30 per week.

Museums

Yes, it is true Las Vegas has museums—these are sometimes unnoticed for all the bright lights of the big city. But these museums offer a good history lesson on Vegas, its people and its money maker (gambling).

Boulder City/Hoover Dam Museum ★★★

444 Hotel Plaza, Boulder City, ☎ *(702) 294-1988.*
Located near Hoover Dam.
Hours open: 10 a.m.–4 p.m.
Exhibits focus on the workers and construction of Hoover Dam, with a free film detailing the hardships overcome to complete the mammoth project. General Admission: $1.

Clark County Heritage Museum ★★★

1830 South Boulder Highway, Henderson, 89015, ☎ *(702) 455-7955.*
Located 18 miles from the Strip.
Hours open: 9 a.m.–4:30 p.m.
Besides exhibits on gambling (which, of course, has made Nevada famous), there are five restored houses from 1904 to the 1940s, a 19th-century print shop, a historic railroad diesel engine, Native American artifacts, and an authentic ghost town exactly as it looked in its original northern Nevada location. $1 for those over 55 and between 3–15. General Admission: $1.50.

Debbie Reynolds' Movie Museum ★★★★

305 Convention Center Drive, Las Vegas, 89109, ☎ *(702) 734-0711.*
Located at the Debbie Reynolds Hotel and Casino.

Hours open: 10 a.m.–10 p.m.

This spot, which just opened in 1995, showcases actress Debbie Reynolds' extensive collection of Hollywood memorabilia. Patrons are ushered into a plush 80-seat theater and watch a multimedia presentation complete with revolving stages, thousands of movie costumes, props and set furniture and reminiscences from Debbie herself (on tape). Shows are every hour on the hour. General Admission: $7.95.

Guinness World of Records Museum ★★★

2780 Las Vegas Boulevard South, Las Vegas, 89109, ☎ (702) 792-3766. Located next to Circus-Circus.
Hours open: 9 a.m.–6 p.m.

If you're curious about the world's largest plastic pig, you can find it here, along with a life-sized version of the world's tallest man (8 feet, 11.1 inches) and the most tattooed woman (more than 95 percent of her body is tattooed) and all sorts of other oddities. Kids love it. Lots of statistical information is available: Did you know that Oreos are the world's top-selling cookies (100 billion)? That the world's heaviest man weighed in at 1069 pounds? There's also a "World of Las Vegas" exhibit saluting all that is goofy in this decidedly goofy town. $3.95 for seniors and students, $2.95 for kids 5–12, under 5 free. General Admission: $4.95.

Imperial Palace Automobile Museum ★★★

3535 Las Vegas Boulevard South, Las Vegas, 89109, ☎ (702) 731-3311. Located at the Imperial Palace.
Hours open: 9:30 a.m.–11:30 p.m.

More than 200 vintage cars are on display, including a 1936 Mercedes once owned by Adolf Hitler, Jack Benny's famous Maxwell, Mussolini's 1939 Alfa Romeo and cars owned by presidents from Kennedy to Nixon. You can also see autos owned by Elvis, Liberace, W.C. Fields, Howard Hughes, Marilyn Monroe and Gypsy Rose Lee. Great for car buffs—a yawn for everyone else. General admission is $6.75, but it's worth a trip to the casino's redemption booth to try and score a free ticket.

King Tut's Tomb and Museum ★★★★★

3900 Las Vegas Boulevard South, Las Vegas, ☎ (702) 262-4000. Located at the Luxor.
Hours open: 10 a.m.–10:30 p.m.

This museum is absolutely fantastic from start to finish. It's a complete recreation of King Tut's tomb as Howard Carter found it in 1922. Upon entering, you're given a Walkman; the tape contains a 20-minute audio tour with "Carter" detailing exactly what you're looking at and why it was placed there. Included is the vestibule, passage, antechamber, annex, burial chamber and treasury. You can turn the tape on and off at will to really absorb the incredible riches and works of art that sent this young and not particularly popular king off to his next life. Fascinating! You exit the museum directly into "The Source" gift shop, which has a dazzling array of all things Egyptian. Among the items for sale are a seven-foot-tall Pharaonic throne chair ($3000) and a lapis-lazuli obelisk ($33,750), plus tons of engravings, artworks and antiques from ancient Egypt priced into the high, high thousands. There's also a good assortment of reasonably priced recreations and curios, and some excellent books on the days when pharaohs ruled and cats were considered sacred. General Admission: $3.

Las Vegas Art Museum   ★★★★

3333 West Washington Avenue, Las Vegas, 89207, ☎ *(702) 647-4300. Located in Lorenzi Park.*
Hours open: 10 a.m.–3 p.m. Special Hours: Sunday, noon–3 p.m. Closed: Mon.

Don't expect the Metropolitan, but Las Vegans are trying to add some culture to their city with this art museum built in 1935 from railroad ties. There are displays of western art, and changing exhibits of local and national artists. The gift shop features original art by locals. To get there, drive north of Las Vegas Blvd. and turn left on Washington Avenue, which runs past the park.

Las Vegas Mormon Temple   ★★★

827 Temple View Drive, Las Vegas, 89110, ☎ *(702) 452-5011.*
Hours open: 5:30 a.m.–3:30 p.m. Special Hours: Saturday, 5:30 a.m.–3 p.m. Closed: Mon., Sun.

You must have a pass and be a member of the Mormon religion to enter this imposing, granite temple, but the public can stroll among the grounds and enjoy the view of Las Vegas from Sunrise Mountain. At night, the church is bathed in white light.

Las Vegas Natural History Museum   ★★★

900 Las Vegas Boulevard North, Las Vegas, 89119, ☎ *(702) 384-3466.*
Hours open: 9 a.m.–4 p.m.

Exhibits range from wood sculptures to an extensive wildlife art gallery to a 300-gallon aquarium that houses small sharks. There's also more than 300 exhibits on birds and animals, a hands-on area for children and an animated dinosaur exhibit. $4 for students, seniors, and military personnel; $2.50 kids 4–12. General Admission: $5.

Liberace Museum   ★★★

1775 East Tropicana Avenue, Las Vegas, 89119, ☎ *(702) 798-5595.*
Located a few miles east of the Strip.
Hours open: 10 a.m.–5 p.m. Special Hours: Sunday 1-5 p.m.

Believe it or not, this is one of Nevada's biggest tourist attractions, with more than 200,000 visitors a year who come to see Liberace's stage costumes, automobiles (including a rhinestone-covered roadster and a mirror-tiled Rolls-Royce) and the biggest rhinestone in existence, a 115,000-karat gem the size of a grapefruit. One of the highlights of the exhibit is a nine-foot Baldwin Grand Piano once played by Chopin at Versailles. There's so much stuff, in fact, that it takes three buildings to hold it all. Most of the money generated by admission fees is donated to the Liberace Foundation for the Performing and Creative Arts, which supports scholarships for struggling music students. Admission for senior citizens is $4.50; kids (6–12), $2. General Admission: $6.50.

Lost City Museum   ★★★

721 South Moapa Valley Boulevard, Overton, 89040, ☎ *(702) 397-2193.*
Located 60 miles north of Las Vegas.
Hours open: 8:30 a.m.–4:30 p.m.

The Lost City Musuem has one of the most complete collections of the early Pueblo Indians in the Southwest. The display starts with the

Desert Culture of 10,000 years ago and continues through the Ancient Basketmaker I, II and III cultures, which existed until about 500 A.D. Other exhibits highlight the Mormon pilgrims who first settled the valley in 1865. Those under 18 are admitted free. Many petroglyphs are found carved into the rocks around the area, and nearby is the gorgeous Valley of Fire State Park (see "Day Trips"). Great gift shop. General Admission: $2.

Magic and Movie Hall of Fame   ★★★★
3555 Las Vegas Boulevard South, Las Vegas, 89109, ☎ *(702) 737-1343.*
Located at O'Shea's Hilton Casino.
Hours open: 10 a.m.–6 p.m. Closed: Mon., Sun.
This new and large exhibit on the second floor of O'Sheas celebrates everything magical, with some terrific items such as the Water Torture Cell made famous by Houdini and famous ventriloquists' dummies among the 5000 exhibits. A roving magician wows the crowd with slight-of-hand illusions, and everyone loves the life-sized robot band. There's also a good collection of movie memorabilia, but the emphasis is on magic. General admission: $9.95, $3 for kids 12 and under.

Mirage Dolphin Habitat & Secret Garden   ★★
3400 Las Vegas Boulevard South, Las Vegas, 89109, ☎ *(702) 791-7111.*
Hours open: 11 a.m.–5:30 p.m. Special Hours: Weekends and holidays, 10 a.m.–5:30 p.m.
Steve Wynn spent $14 million on this outdoor habitat that houses seven Atlantic bottleneck dolphins in four pools. Dolphins in Las Vegas? At least these were already in captivity, not caught in the open seas. And, at least, the creatures don't have to jump through hoops—just swim around in (very) relative freedom while handlers give talks. New is the Secret Garden, a self-guided tour past tigers, an elephant, lions and other creatures. It's open every day but Wednesday; you can still see the dolphins then for $5. General admission is $10. Kids under 10 are free. If you're into captive animals, check out the tiger habitat inside the Mirage where rare white Himalayan tigers belonging to Siegfried and Roy prance about. It's free and open 24 hours.

Nevada Banking Museum   ★★
3800 Howard Hughes Parkway, Las Vegas, 89109, *(702) 791-6373.*
Located in the First Interstate building.
Hours open: 9 a.m.–4 p.m.
If you lose all your money at the tables, at least you can look at a bunch here. The history of banking is chronicled through displays of old currency, coins, gambling tokens, gold scales and a turn-of-the-century loan processing calculator.

Nevada State Museum & Historical Society   ★★★
700 Twin Lakes Drive, Las Vegas, 89107, ☎ *(702) 486-5205.*
Located in Lorenzi Park.
Hours open: 9 a.m.–5 p.m.
The history of gambling, the building of Hoover Dam and the days of atomic testing can all be studied here through artifacts, graphics and historic photos. There are also exhibits on anthropology and Nevada's natural history, and a display—appropriately enough—on how neon has been used in Las Vegas. Those under 18 are admitted free. To get there, drive north of Las Vegas Boulevard and turn left onto Washington Avenue, which runs past the park. General Admission: $2.

WHAT TO SEE AND DO IN LAS VEGAS

Sports Hall of Fame   ★★★★

18 East Fremont Street, Las Vegas, 89101, ☎ *(702) 385-1664.*
Located at the Las Vegas Club Hotel and Casino.
Special Hours: 24 hours.
The world's only collection of World Series bats from 1946 through
1958 and Maury Willis' bronzed base-stealing shoes are the main
events here. There's also a nod to basketball and boxing greats, but
the emphasis is primarily on the boys of summer.

Music

Performing Arts at UNLV   ★★★★

4505 Maryland Parkway, Las Vegas, 89154, ☎ *(702) 895-3801.*
The University of Nevada, Las Vegas, is a great spot to catch a variety
of performing arts. The Charles Vanda Master Series features
acclaimed international classical musicians and orchestras; tickets
range from $27.50 to $150. The more affordable Chamber Music
Series costs just $8. There's also opera, dance and theatrical events.
Call the box office for details. UNLV also offers a host of free music
and arts events. Call ☎ *895-3332* for a schedule.

City Celebrations

National Finals of Rodeo   ★★★

4505 South Maryland Parkway, Las Vegas, 89154, ☎ *(702) 731-2115.*
Located at the Thomas and Mack Center.
Western gear and country-western stars performing in the showrooms
are the order of the day when the National Finals Rodeo comes to
town each December. Rodeos may be shamefully cruel to the animals,
but don't try telling these folks that—this annual event sells out more
than six months in advance. This is the Super Bowl of the professional
rodeo circuit, offering more than $2 million in prize money. General
Admission: $24.

HOW TO PLAY

Gambling is a 24-hour activity in the glittering casinos.

No matter how many pirate battles or volcanoes they add, Las Vegas will always be first and foremost a gambler's haven. The wide array of slot machines and growing variations of table games help keep it all interesting. I used to limit my play to video poker and craps, but on the past few trips, tried out virtually everything. It didn't pay off in terms of dollars, but it was more fun.

Many casinos offer classes in how to play blackjack, craps, roulette, poker and baccarat. I highly recommend taking advantage of these—they're free, fun and informative. Some, such as those at the Tropicana and the Las Vegas Hilton, follow the class with an hour of slow play with $1 minimums. This is the best way to learn. After years of trying to figure out craps on my own, I finally took a class at the Tropicana, and it all instantly became clear.

The following casinos all offer lessons, usually on weekdays. Call for a schedule.

Aladdin (☎ *736-0111*) all table games; **Bally's** (☎ *739-4111*) craps, roulette, blackjack, baccarat; **Caesars Palace** (☎ *731-7110*) blackjack, craps, paid go poker, mini baccarat, roulette, race and sports wagering; **Sheraton Desert Inn** (☎ *733-4444*) poker; **Excalibur** (☎ *597-7777*) craps, blackjack, roulette; **Fremont** (☎ *385-3232*) poker; **Flamingo Hilton** (☎ *733-3111*) blackjack, Caribbean stud poker, craps, roulette, let it ride; **Harrah's** (☎ *369-5000*) roulette, blackjack, craps, baccarat, pai gow poker; **Imperial Palace** (☎ *731-3311*) blackjack, craps; **Lady Luck** (☎ *477-3000*) all table games; **Las Vegas Hilton** (☎ *732-5111*) craps, roulette, super pan nine, pai gow poker, blackjack; **MGM Grand** (☎ *891-1111*) all table games; **Riviera** (☎ *734-5110*) craps, blackjack, roulette, baccarat, poker; **Sahara** (☎ *737-2111*) craps, blackjack, roulette; **Stardust** (☎ *732-6111*) all table games; **Tropicana** (☎ *739-2222*) craps, roulette, blackjack. In addition, the **San Remo** (☎ *739-9000*) teaches all table games—but only in Japanese.

Here are a few tips to help you keep sane during your gambling junket:

Set a daily limit—and stick to it. If you're going to Las Vegas for three days, break your gambling bankroll into thirds. When you tap out the first night, drown your sorrows in the lounge or check out a show—but don't keep gambling.

Watch what you drink. The drinks flow freely (literally), and it's easy to get carried away. The casinos don't give you free drinks because they are so nice, they do it because alcohol impairs your judgment. This is especially true at the table games, where some modicum of skill is necessary. If you really feel like getting bombed and gambling, stick to five-cent or quarter slot machines. And don't forget to tip the cocktail waitress, usually $1 per round.

Stay away from the ATMs and Visa machines. They are dangerous! You'll be charged at least $1 for each transaction on an ATM machine, above whatever your bank already charges. The Comchek machines especially rip you off—it costs $11.99 just to get $100 on your credit card. And you'll hate yourself in the morning.

Don't even think about cheating. In the old days when the Mafia ran the casinos, they'd take cheaters out back and whack them. Today you get to live, but you'll have a felony on your record. The "eye in the sky" has likewise progressed from a crude system of catwalks to sophisticated electronic surveillance—these guys watch EVERYTHING. They sit up in a little room with tons of TV monitors and look out for suspicious players. They can zoom in on the wart on your nose or push a button, get an instant picture of you, then fax it to other casinos in town to see what THEY make of you.

If you are going to cheat, at least be sophisticated about it. If you're counting cards at blackjack, bet consistently—jumping from $5 to $100 when you're sure of the count tips the dealer off. This is called a "tell," and you can be sure he'll "tell" the pit boss. Placing a bet when the winning number has been determined, as in roulette or craps, is called "past posting." You may get away with it once or twice, but remember, they're not only watching you up there, they're taping it, too.

Tip the dealers. This is optional, of course, but if you get a great dealer who helps explain the rules and is patient with your dumb moves, it's good form to tip. Either give a chip or, more common, make a bet for the dealer next to your own. These "tokes" are greatly appreciated, and besides, it's good karma.

Blackjack

If you can count to 21, you'll want to play Blackjack, the most popular of all casino games.

Blackjack, also called 21, is the most popular casino table game, probably because it is one of the easiest to learn. If you play correctly, you have decent odds of winning.

The house used to keep 22 percent, but players have become savvy enough to lower that edge to 16 percent.

The object is simple: have your cards total up closer to 21 than the dealer, without going over (busting). All players play against the house (dealer), not each other.

The game begins when the dealer deals each person two cards. The dealer deals herself two cards, one face up and one face down. Cards are counted at their face value; all picture cards equal 10, while an ace equals one or 11, your choice. If the first two cards dealt equal 21, you have a blackjack and are paid one and a half times your bet. If the dealer also has a blackjack, you push, or tie. If you go over 21, you immediately lose.

When it's your turn, indicate your wish to draw by scratching your cards on the table toward you. When you want to stand, make a flat wave with your hand parallel to the table or slide your cards under your bet money.

You want your hand closer to 21 than the dealers, but whether you decide to draw another card depends almost completely on the dealer's face up card. If she has 16 or less, she must draw; she must stand on 17 or more. The assumption is always that the next card dealt will equal 10. In fact, 10-value cards show up four times more often than any other card.

Numerous books are devoted completely to blackjack strategy, but as a general rule, stand on 17 or more and hit, double down or split on 11 or less. When the dealer shows a seven, eight, nine, 10 or ace, hit all hard (no ace) totals of 16 or less. When the dealer shows a two, three, four, five or six, stand on a hard total of 12 or more in assumption that the dealer will bust—unless you have 12 and the dealer shows a two or three.

The dealer has no options, but the player has several:

Splitting pairs: If you're dealt two cards of equal value, you can match your original bet and split them into two hands. This is always done with aces and eights. You can take as many hits (draws) as you like with each hand, except in the case of aces, when you draw on each hand only once.

Doubling down: After receiving your first two cards, you can increase your bet up to the amount of the original bet. You receive only one extra card. This is generally done if your cards equal 10 or 11, or you're dealt an ace with a two–seven, depending on what the dealer has.

Insurance: If the dealer's up card is an ace, you can take insurance by wagering up to half the amount of your original bet. The assumption is that the dealer's hidden card has a 10 value, equaling a blackjack. If the dealer's hidden card is indeed a 10, you win and are paid two to one of your insurance bet. If not, you lose that bet, but keep playing your regular hand. Insurance is considered a sucker's bet and is never recommended.

Craps

Craps is, in my opinion, by far the most fun and social casino game. There is nothing in the world like a hot craps table that erupts into cheers and high-fives when the right number comes up. It also has one of the best odds for players—if you bet correctly and stay away from the proposition bets.

Craps is difficult to grasp without the benefit of hands-on learning. For that reason, I highly recommend taking advantage of the free craps classes offered at many casinos. Once you're shown how to play it's pretty simple, but just watching or reading about it is generally not enough to understand the game. Here's a brief rundown of the rules just the same. Whatever you do, DON'T come up to the table and ask the person next to you to explain what's going on. It's obnoxious!

Players have the option of betting on the "pass" or "don't pass" line. One player, known as the shooter, rolls two dice. This is called the "coming out" roll. If the dice total seven or 11, those on the pass line automatically win. If he rolls a two, three, or twelve, those on the pass line lose. Any other number rolled is the "point." If the player rolls that number again before he rolls a seven, those on the pass line win. If he rolls a seven, they lose, and the dice is passed to the next player. If you're on the don't pass line, the exact opposite holds true.

Most players play the pass line. It's frankly obnoxious when someone plays the don't pass line, because his win is everyone else's loss.

Usually, the shooter will throw other numbers before either the point or a seven comes up. To keep the game interesting (and you betting) in the meantime, there are lots of options:

Odds: You can match your bet on the pass or don't pass line once the point is established. To do this, put another chip of equal value behind your original bet. Most casinos offer at least double odds and a few go all the way up to 12 times odds. Taking at least even odds is a good bet and should always be done. Watch out for 12-times odds though—it gets mighty expensive if sevens keep coming up.

Come: You can make a come bet anytime after the point has been established. This is exactly the same as playing the pass line, except that the next number to come up becomes your own point. If you're playing the pass line and also make a come bet, you're now rooting for both numbers to come up before a seven. You can (and should) also take odds on your come bet.

Place: Once the point is established, you can make a bet on the numbers four, five, six, eight, nine and 10. If the shooter throws that number before a seven, you win the following payoffs: nine-to-five on four and 10, seven-to-five on five and nine, and seven-to-six on six and eight.

Field: This is a one-roll bet that pays even money on a three, four, nine, 10, and 11; two-to-one on a two and three-to-one on a 12. You lose on a five, six, seven or eight. Generally considered a stupid bet.

Hardways: You can bet on double twos, three, fours or fives. You win nicely if it comes up before a seven or that number the "easy way" (six and four instead of double fives, for instance). Not the smartest bet in the world, but because it's fun, many do it anyway—and the payoffs are nice.

Propositions: These are one-roll bets. Two or 12 pays 31 to one, "any craps" (two, three or 12) pays eight-to-one. Three or 11 pays 16-for-one. The payoffs are so good because the odds are well against you.

Don't come to a craps table with absolutely no knowledge of how the game is played, but on the other hard, don't be intimidated, either. Craps dealers are generally quite friendly and happy to explain the intricacies if the table is not too busy. And don't be embarrassed if you make a mistake; rules on taking odds can get confusing and everyone messes up sometimes.

Seasoned players look for a table that's hot—signified by excited shouts, lots of chips piled on the numbers and elbow-to-elbow people. It can be hard to squeeze in, so try at the edges near the pit. Many don't realize you can stand back there, but as long as that little rim that holds your chips is in front of you, it's okay.

Some casinos advertise "crapless craps," in which dice totals of two, three, 11 and 12 count as point numbers.

A word of caution: Craps is extremely exciting and fast-paced. It's very easy to get carried away and have bets all over the table, only to see them disappear when a seven comes up. One way to keep from going overboard is to take some of your winnings, put them in your pocket and try to forget they exist.

Roulette

Few can resist the urge to play their lucky numbers at roulette.

Roulette—called the "wheel" by dealers—is one of the easiest games to master. The house advantage isn't the greatest for players—it keeps from 5.26 to seven percent—but that doesn't seem to stop many people from playing their lucky numbers at least a few times.

The roulette wheel is marked with numbers one through 36 and the symbols 0 and 00. The numbers are alternatively colored red and black, while the 0 and 00 are green. You can bet on red or black, odd or even, on an individual number or a group of numbers. The dealer spins the ball into the wheel; as it slows down she says "no more bets," and you wait for your number to (hopefully) come up.

Roulette chips are purchased in stacks of 20. You decide the value—for instance, if you'd like your bets to be worth $1 each, you purchase a sack for $20. Every player has their own color chips to keep things from getting too confusing.

If your number comes up, you win 35-to-one. Double numbers pay 17-to-one, triple numbers 11-to-one, and so on. Red or black and odd or even pay even money. Everyone loses on 0 and 00 unless they've bet those numbers. In European casinos, the wheel has only one 0, making roulette there a better bet.

Caribbean Stud Poker

I just love this game, although casino executives tell me it is one of the highest-paying games for the house—in other words, a sucker's bet. Still, it's fun. The basic rules are similar to stud poker, and you need at least a pair of anything to win.

Each player makes an ante bet. If you want to be in the progressive jackpot as well (definitely recommended), you wager another $1. All players receive five cards face down. The dealer also gets five cards, with the last one face up. If you feel your hand will beat the dealer's, you place another bet exactly twice your original ante. If your hand sucks, you fold.

The catch—and it's a big one—is that the dealer must have an ace or a king or at least a pair to "qualify." If she doesn't qualify, you only get your ante bet back—even if you're holding a royal flush. You still win off the progressive jackpot, though, which is why it's worth the extra dollar to enter it.

If the dealer does qualify and your hand beats hers, you win. Any pair pays one-to-one, two pair pays two-to-one and so on. A royal flush pays 100-to-one. A flush or better also wins some of the progressive jackpot, if you've entered it. A royal flush takes it all. The progressive pot starts at $20,000 and goes up from there, usually hitting at around $100,000. (The highest is said to be some $380,000.)

The odds say a royal will come up every 64,000 or so. Of course, you have a better chance of getting struck by lighting while being held hostage by a terrorist group than being dealt a royal—but think how you'd feel if it happened and you hadn't anted up a measly buck for the progressive pot.

Let It Ride

This newer game has caught on like wildfire; there are even slot machines offering it in some casinos. You play a basic five-card poker hand with the goal of getting the best possible hand. The dealer doesn't have a hand.

To start, you place three chips of equal value (usually $5 each) in their designated spots—but don't worry, you're not necessarily betting all three. You're dealt three cards, and two "community" cards are dealt facedown in the center of the table. If you like your three cards (you need a pair of 10s or better to win), place them under the first chip. If not, scratch your cards on the felt (as you do in blackjack) and you'll get that first chip back. When all players have made a decision based on their first three cards, the dealer flips over one of the two community cards. This counts as the fourth card in your hand. If you still like your hand, place your cards under the second chip. If not, scratch your cards on the felt, and you'll get that second chip back. When the whole table has made this decision, the dealer flips the fifth community card, which completes your hand.

A pair of 10s pays even money, two pair pays two to one and up it goes to the royal flush, which pays 1000 to one. Let It Ride is fun because at the worst, you lose only one chip. But if the cards are good to you, you'll win on all three.

Baccarat

Often the game of choice for high rollers, baccarat has relatively low house odds—1.17 percent betting banker and 1.36 percent betting player. It's played in a special area off the casino, usually quite classy looking and behind velvet ropes. The dealers usually wear tuxedos instead of the standard uniform. All this can be pretty intimidating to the average player, but anyone with money is welcome! The game is played by strict rules, so there are no decisions to make. Keep in mind, though, that table minimums usually start at $20 and go up from there.

The game is played with six to eight cards dealt from a shoe. Before the cards are dealt, you bet on either the player or banker; each gets two cards. The hand that goes closest to nine is a winner; zero (called a baccarat) is the worst score. No one wins on a tie.

Cards numbered two through nine are counted at face value, an ace equals one and the 10 and picture cards equal zero. Cards totaling 10 or more points have the first digit dropped (for instance, a 16 becomes a six).

A hand that equals eight or nine is called a "natural" and is an automatic winner, unless the opposing hand beats it. When the total is zero–five, the player hand gets a third card, but must stand on a total of six or seven. (No more than one additional card is ever dealt.) The bank hand always draws on zero, one or two. When the hand is worth three or more, it is subjected to an intricate list of rules. Whoever comes closest to nine wins—as a better, your only decision is to wager with the banker or player.

Baccarat pays even money. The banker position has slightly better odds, so a five percent commission is charged on each winning hand. This is paid up at the end, when you're ready to leave the table. (If you start to lose, make sure to save enough chips to pay the commission.)

Mini-Baccarat

Mini-baccarat is a great way to learn the game for those too timid to just plunk down at a regular baccarat table. The rules are the same, but it's played at a blackjack-style table and the bettor does not deal the cards.

You can wager with the player, banker or for a tie. The first two pay even money (minus the five percent commission on winning banker hands), while the latter pays nine to one.

Poker

Poker is one of the oldest and most popular casino games. It's played in the casino pretty much the same way you play with your friends around the kitchen table—but the jackpots in Las Vegas are probably a lot bigger than on your typical Friday night game.

In Las Vegas, poker is played with one deck of cards that is dealt by a professional dealer. No matter what the variation, you're trying for your best possible hand, one that will beat all the other players at the table. The rankings are: high card, one pair, two pair, three of a kind, straight (five cards in numerical sequence), flush (all cards of the same suit), full house (one pair and three of a kind), four of a kind, straight flush (all cards in numerical sequence and of the same suit), and royal flush (10, jack, queen, king and ace all of the same suit).

Many games use a "blind," a mandatory bet that must be made by the first player in the opening round of play, regardless of the cards. Others require an "ante," a uniform bet placed by all players into the pot before the cards are dealt.

Except when everyone must make a bet (usually the case in the first round), the first player to bet can: bet (place money in the pot), check (pass by making no bet) or fold (throw out his cards and sit that hand out). Once a bet is placed, you must either call (match the bet by putting an equal amount in the pot) or raise (call the bet and make an additional bet). If you don't like your cards and want to get out, you fold.

When the play comes back to the opening bettor (it goes clockwise around the table) he must call any previous raises to stay in the game. He can raise again if the raise limit has not yet been reached. The number of raises vary by casino, but is usually between three and five in any round—except if only two players are left. Then the sky's the limit. After all the betting rounds are concluded, it's "showdown" time, when everyone reveals their hands.

Here are some of the more common ways the game is played:

Draw Poker: Each player gets five cards facedown. There are two betting rounds, the first before the draw, when you can exchange up to all five cards for new ones (though if your hand is so lousy you need five new cards, you're better off folding). After the draw, there's a second round of betting before the showdown. The highest hand wins.

Lowball: Played like draw poker, but the lowest hand wins. The best possible hand is ace, one, two, three, four, five, called a "wheel."

Seven Card Stud: Each player receives a total of three down cards and four upcards. You don't get to draw, and make your bets based on your hand and the other players' upcards. The best five-card poker hand wins the pot.

Texas Hold'em: Each player receives two down cards, and five community cards are dealt face up in the center of the table. You use your two down cards with the community cards to come up with the best five-card hand at the table.

Omaha Hold'em: This game is just like Texas Hold 'em, except in the Omaha version, each player gets four down cards rather than two. You must use two of your four downcards and three of the five community cards to make the best five-card poker hand. (Pretty frustrating in the unlikely event you're dealt four of a kind.)

Pai Gow Poker

This increasingly popular game combines American poker and the ancient Chinese game of pai gow. It is played with a traditional deck of cards plus one joker, which is used only as an ace or to complete a straight, flush or a straight flush. The object is to have two poker hands that beat the banker's hands.

The dealer starts a game by rolling three dice. The total of the dice determines which player gets the first set of cards. Each player gets seven cards and creates two hands simultaneously, a "high hand" and a "second high hand." The player's high hand is made up of five cards and the second high hand made up of two cards. The low-card hand must be lower in rank than the five-card hand. The rankings are the same as traditional poker.

Both hands must be higher than the bank's hands to win. If one hand is higher and one hand is lower, it's a tie. If both hands are lower than the bank, the player loses. If either of the player's hands is the same rank as the banker's, the banker wins. Payoffs are even money and the house collects a five percent commission on all winning wages.

The house alternates with the players in serving as banker. If you want to bank, you must have enough money bet to cover all bets, including the house's bet. If you don't want to bank, the house will serve as banker for that hand.

Big Six Wheel

Probably the stupidest game you can play in a casino—the odds are way against you and it's lame to boot. The big six or money wheel is just like the old carnival wheel, only with real dollar bills inserted. The betting table uses real dollars, too.

To place a bet (often just a $1 minimum), put a chip on $1, $2, $5, 10, $20 or joker and house symbol. If it comes up, you win that amount. There are 23 $1 slots, 15 $2 slots, eight $5 slots, four $10 slots, two $20 slots, and one each of the joker and house logo. In the unlikely event it hits, it pays 40-to-one.

This is a game for people who don't know how to gamble. Why let everyone else in on that fact?

Keno

It's hard to escape keno in the casino. Those large electronic boards are everywhere, even in the coffeeshops. Each 10 minutes or so, a machine of bouncing balls (similar to bingo) selects 20 out of a possible 80 numbers.

To play, fill out a keno slip indicating how many numbers you want to play and for how much. You can play from one to 20 numbers on a "straight ticket" and two or more combinations (without duplicating any numbers) on a "split ticket." This is indicated by marking two or more sets of one to 15 numbers on a ticket, then separating them with a line or circle. Then just sit back and hope those numbers come up.

Keno is a decent enough way to kill time while waiting for lunch in the coffeeshop, but don't expect much. The odds are well in the house's favor—typically over 20 percent. On a brighter note, the top jackpot if you "catch" all numbers ranges from $25,000 to $50,000, and higher.

Video Poker

Video poker is by far the most addicting of the slot machines, so much so that it's earned the dubious title of "crack of the gamblers."

You can play from one to five coins for each game. The incentive is high to play all five, because the jackpot for a royal flush (10 through ace of the same suit) jumps from 1000 coins for four played to 4000 for all five. Many machines have a progressive jackpot in which a royal flush pays well over 4000 coins. Some progressives also reward four of a kind and straight flushes.

You're dealt five cards and have the option of holding or staying. To hold, push the button under that card. If you change your mind or make a mistake, just push it again. Make sure it says "hold" above the card before you push the "play" or "deal" button again. If all five cards make a winning hand, push hold under each. When you push the draw button, you'll get new cards for the ones you discarded; if you have a winning hand, the machine pays automatically.

A pair of jacks or higher pays even money, two pair pays double, three of a kind plays triple, a straight (all five cards in numerical sequence) pays four to one, a flush (all cards of the same suit) pays either six or seven to one, a full house (three of a kind and a pair) pays eight or nine to one, four of a kind pays 25 to one, a straight flush (all five cards in a numerical sequence in the same suit) pays 50 to one and a royal flush (10, jack, queen, king and ace of the same suit) pays 250 to one, unless you bet the maximum (usually five coins), when it pays 4000 coins.

Those payoffs are standard throughout casinos, but it varies on a flush and full house. Some pay six to one on a flush and eight-to-one of a full house; the better ones pay seven to one and nine to one, respectively. (Those in the industry refer to them as six-eights or seven-nines.) Obviously, you're better off with a seven-nine.

Here's some basic strategy for draw poker:

Always keep jacks or better, unless you're four to the straight flush or royal flush.

If you're dealt four to the royal flush, go for it, whether or not you already have a winning hand.

Don't go for flushes unless you have four of the same suit.

If you have a pair of jacks, as well as the possibility for a straight, stay with the jacks.

Always save picture cards and 10s of the same suit, and discard the others (unless you have jacks or better). For instance, if you're dealt a king and jack of spades, queen of hearts, three of diamonds and five of clubs, save only the king and jack. This way you're going for the royal (admittedly a long shot) as well as a flush.

Hold a low pair but don't try to get insurance by also holding a picture card in the hopes of jacks or better. It's stupid!

If your bankroll allows, always play the maximum coins. Nothing is more depressing than a royal with only two or three coins in.

Video poker also comes in variations with deuces wild, jokers wild and deuces and joker's wild. These require at least two pair to win and pay out lower across the board, unless you get a royal flush with no wild cards. They can be entertaining, though, because the wild cards mean more winning hands.

Slot Machines

One-armed bandits are everywhere in Las Vegas—as prevalent in laundromats and convenience stores as in the casinos.

Machines vary from the old fruit reels (becoming increasingly rare) to the cherries and bars types to red, white and blue sevens to symbols designed exclusively for a casino. Some of the newer ones are pretty nifty. On "Coral Reef," for example, reels move up or down if you get the right symbol, or spin wildly until they hit a winning combination.

Huge jackpots can be found on Megabucks, Quartermania and Nevada Nickels, all of which are linked to a slew of casinos throughout Nevada. In fact, the minimum jackpot for Megabucks has just been increased from $3 million to $5 million. The highest jackpot so far on that game is a cool $12 million, won in April 1997 by a local.

Many machines have multiple paylines that only pay off if you've inserted enough coins to light that line, so be sure to take a few seconds to study the machine before playing. I learned that the hard way when I stuck just $1 in a slot machine, watched gleefully as three bars lined up, and then heard...silence. It turns out I needed three coins in to get that $100 jackpot.

Payoffs vary by casino. It used to be that many predominantly displayed signs boasting of a 98 or 99 percent payback (the industry standard is 90 percent), but that's become rare. Instead, now they advertise how much is given away daily by the slots ($3.7 million daily, claims the Stardust, $2.6 million says Bally's).

The Stratosphere hawks over 98 percent return on its dollar slots and 100 percent return on so-designated video poker machines. Read the fine print at the poker machines, though: that 100 percent return is only with maximum coins wagered, and—the real killer— "optimum" play. That means you must play each hand absolutely correctly. And, that 100 percent payoff doesn't start until after 250,000 hands have been played right. (That's not to say that the machines don't pay off in the meantime, but probably not that promised 100 percent.) Play right for 249,999 hands but blow the last one, and the cycle starts all over again. Unless you have a huge bankroll and many, many hours to spend at one machine, it's a pretty meaningless promotion.

Race and Sports Book

Many casinos have elaborate (and not so) areas where you can bet on the ponies and virtually every sports event, from the World Cup to the World Series. These "books" range from small and tacky rooms (like at the Tropicana) to huge areas of electronic toteboards and plush seats where you can sit back and watch the action on large-screen TVs. They broadcast horse races live from a number of tracks, as well as whatever game is hot that day.

Sports betting is huge business—more than $70 million is bet each year on the Super Bowl alone.

Most books post similar odds for regular games in season, but odds vary widely for events far in the future. Take this example: In February 1994, the odds of the Denver Broncos winning Super Bowl XXX (11 months away) were only 18-to-one at the Tropicana, while just across the street at the MGM, they were giving 50-to-one odds. That means a $10 bet on the (very unlikely event) of the Broncos winning would pay only $180 at the Tropicana, but $500 at the MGM. The moral: Shop around!

Sportsbooks are found at: Aladdin, Bally's, Binion's Horseshoe, Caesars Palace, Excalibur, Fitzgeralds, Flamingo Hilton, Four Queens, Fremont, Golden Nugget, Jackie Gaughan's Plaza, Las Vegas Club, Luxor, MGM Grand, Mirage, Palace Station, Rio Suites, Riviera, Sahara, San Remo, Sands, Stardust and the Tropicana. The nicest and plushest are at the Las Vegas Hilton, Caesars, the MGM and Rio Suites.

Unlike the 24-hour casinos, most race and sports books open at around 8 a.m. and close by 6 or 7 p.m., or when the last event of the day is over. Exceptions are Caesars (open until at least 11 p.m. weekdays, 2 a.m. weekends), Golden Nugget (open until 11 p.m.), Sahara (open until 10:30 p.m.) and the Riviera (open 24 hours).

Slot Clubs

Slot machine players were once looked down upon by casino marketers, but no more. That's because the machines (including video poker) now make up the lion's share of casino winnings. To keep their slots customers loyal, most of the major casinos offer slot clubs that are free to join.

You're given a plastic card similar to a credit card. Each time you switch machines, insert the card. It keeps track of your level of play. If you play long enough (how long is long enough varies by casino), you'll earn free meals, show tickets and other perks—

sometimes even cash back. You may also get a reduced room rate or even a complimentary room.

If you play a lot of slots or video poker, it is well worth the minimal effort to join the slot club. Most reward players at the 25-cent level, though some, like Treasure Island and Golden Nugget, are only for $1 players.

Even if you don't get any comps out of your visit, you'll be put on the casino's mailing list and kept informed of special promotions and tournaments. Members are often entitled to reduced room rates. The more you play the more they'll covet your business, to the point where they'll not only put you in a suite, but reimburse your plane fare to boot.

Fun Books

Many casinos give out free "fun books" filled with useful (and not so) coupons. Barkers hand them out on the streets, or you can pick one up at the promotions desk. One coupon may be good for a free drink at the bar, another for a 50-cent Heinekin, still another for 20 percent off in the gift shop. There are also some nifty gaming coupons that give you a free bet at roulette, double your blackjack wager or give a free pull on a million-dollar-jackpot slot machine.

Drawing by S. Gross; ©1995 The New Yorker Magazine, Inc.

THE SHOWS

King Arthur's Tournament at the Excalibur features jousting knights on horseback.

I was never a great fan of the Las Vegas shows and used to avoid them in favor of spending every night in the casino. To research this book, I sat through virtually every one of them (once seeing eight shows in eight days) and to my happy surprise, found that I've been missig out on a lot. If it's your first time in Las Vegas, seeing a show is as *de rigueur* as trying the slot machines. If you've been here before and, like me, always considered them too hokey for words, think again. Even the corniest of productions has one huge advantage: You can't lose money while in the showroom.

Headliners are not as popular as in days past, but you can still see big stars perform at Bally's, Caesars Palace, Las Vegas Hilton, MGM Grand and the Sheraton Desert Inn. The Hard Rock Hotel books rock acts.

The best time to see a show is when it's the least crowded, typically Sunday through Thursday. Early shows are usually more popular on weekdays, while late shows fill up on weekends. Always reserve your ticket as far in advance as possible; this not only guards against disappointment but assures a better seat in theaters with assigned seating.

Many theaters don't have assigned seats, however. It's all up to the maître d', whose job it is to fill the showroom (or make it look full for the sake of the performers). Sometimes simply asking for a good seat—especially if you arrive early—is enough, but often you will have to tip if your heart is set on an upclose view. Do so with élan—have your money tucked discreetly into your palm with the denomination showing, and slip it casually to the maître d'. Better yet, use gaming chips from that casino, which shows you are a player in the house. You can try tipping the captain—the man who actually seats you—instead, but remember, the maître d' rules.

The Best Shows

Mystère (Treasure Island): This surrealistic circus from the famed Cirque du Soleil Troupe is as mesmerizing as it is astounding.

Legends in Concert (Imperial Palace): An infectious and unabashedly sentimental salute to musical greats.

EFX (MGM Grand): As dazzling and amazing as anything you've ever seen.

Enter the Night (Stardust): About as hip and happening as a traditional revue dares to venture.

The Goofiest Show

Jubilee (Bally's): No one comes close to the pageantry and spectacle at this "mother of all production shows."

The Most Un—Las-Vegas Las Vegas Show

Starlight Express (Las Vegas Hilton): Andrew Lloyd Webber's hit musical features rollerskating train cars—and not a single bare breast.

Best Show For Kids

King Arthur's Tournament (Excalibur): They get to eat with their hands, yell and scream and bang on the table—all at the same time.

Biggest Disappointment

Siegfried and Roy (Mirage): Yes, that was a lovely production number. Now may we please see some magic?

The following ratings are according to the readers of the *Las Vegas Review-Journal*—and who knows better than the locals?

Best Showgirls

Folies-Bergère (Tropicana).

Best Headliner

The locals pick Wayne Newton, but my vote goes to David Copperfield.

American Superstars ★★★

2000 Las Vegas Boulevard South, Las Vegas, ☎ (702) 380-7777. At the Stratosphere.

Five talented singers impersonate Madonna, Diana Ross, Gloria Estefan, Charlie Daniels and Michael Jackson in this high-energy show. There are also the Superstar Dancers (six beauties) and a live, seven-piece band. Especially noteworthy is Marva Scotta (Diana Ross), formerly the lead singer in Stardust's Enter the Night. Assuming you like the music of the featured "celebrities," this is a fun show for all ages. Showtimes are nightly, except Thursday, at 7 and 10 p.m. Tickets are reasonable at $22.95, including tax, for adults and $16.95 for kids 5 to 12.

An Evening at La Cage ★★★

2901 Las Vegas Boulevard South, Las Vegas, ☎ (702) 794-9433. Located at the Riviera Mardi Gras Plaza 3rd Floor.

If you're into men in drag, this is the show for you. It stars Frank Marino as Joan Rivers and has a cast of some pretty beautiful "women" who impersonate Dionne Warwick, Diana Ross, Tina Turner, Bette Midler, Cher... you get the idea. No one, including the performers themselves, takes it all too seriously—it's somehow sexy and sensitive at the same time. Shows are nightly except Tuesday at 7:30 and 9:30. There's also an 11:15 performance on Wednesday and Saturday. Tickets are $21.95, which includes two drinks but not tax or tip. Add $5.00 for "VIP seating."

An Evening in Vienna ★★★

3850 Las Vegas Boulevard South, Las Vegas, ☎ (702) 597-7600. Located at the Excalibur King Arthur's Arena.

The awesome white Lipizzaner stallions display their beauty and intelligence in this family-oriented show. Showtimes are 2 p.m. daily except Friday. Tickets are $7.95, which includes tax and gratuity. Kids under 12 and senior citizens pay $5.95.

Caesars Magical Empire ★★★

3570 Las Vegas Boulevard South, Las Vegas, 89109, ☎ (702) 731-7110. Located in Caesars Palace. Hours open: 11:30 a.m.–11:30 p.m.

It starts out great: Guests are transported down "100 feet" to a creepy and beautifully decorated chamber where dinner is served in one of 10 small and imaginatively appointed dining rooms. The three-course meal (a choice of fish, meat or vegetarian) is sparse but very tasty, and served with great pomp and circumstance by a sorcerer who occasionally bursts into song or performs a magic trick. Unfortunately, the slapstick and terribly corny humor during this segment distracts a lot from the otherworldly experience we've been set up to expect. After dinner, guests are set loose among the dramatic sets to watch live magic shows in two theaters or just relax at the bar. The magic is impressive, the decor electrifying, the food good—but the humor needs to be funnier, or, better yet, be cut out entirely. The entire experience takes from two to three hours and is open only to those over age 12. Shows are daily from 4:30 to 11:30 p.m.; reservations are required. Admission is $65 and $75, which includes dinner, tip, tax and the magic shows.

Catch a Rising Star   ★ ★ ★ ★

3799 Las Vegas Boulevard South, Las Vegas, 89109, ☎ *(702) 891-7777.*
Located at the MGM Grand.

Three comedians play week-long engagements here, and when they're hot, they're hot. Comedy is in the eye (or ear) of the beholder, but you can usually count on at least one of these professional-caliber comedians making you laugh. The price is a bit steep, since it does not include cocktails or tip. Shows nightly at 8:00 and 10:30. General Admission: $12.50.

Comedy Max   ★ ★ ★

160 East Flamingo Road, Las Vegas, ☎ *(702) 734-8550.*
Located at the Maxim Showroom.

This comedy nightclub features two or three young comedians. Usually good for a few yucks. Shows are at 7 and 9 p.m.; tickets are $16.25, which includes tax, tip, and two drinks. $19.95 also buys a buffet dinner.

Comedy Stop   ★ ★ ★ ★

3801 Las Vegas Boulevard South, Las Vegas, 89109, ☎ *(702) 739-2414.*
Located at the Tropicana.

This is a very good comedy show featuring three different comedians who perform twice nightly, at 8 and 10:30. Pay for the show at the Comedy Stop guest desk near the entrance of the showroom, and you can turn in your ticket stub at a self-service bar for two drinks, which makes this a better deal than Catch a Rising Star at the MGM. General Admission: $14.30.

Country Fever   ★ ★ ★ ★

129 East Fremont Street, Las Vegas, ☎ *(702) 386-8100.*
Located at the Golden Nugget Theatre Ballroom.

Country-western music lovers need look no further—this show is definitely impressive and high, high energy—"It clicks like a runaway train," says the *Las Vegas Review-Journal*. It features country star impersonators who look and sound like the real thing. There's also a great band, the Definitely Denim dancers and a gospel choir. Yeeha! Showtimes are 7 and 9:45 nightly, except Fridays. $22.50 buys the show, tax, a pitcher of beer, sangria or soda, and a basket of "county fixin's" including fried shrimp and chicken fingers.

Country Tonite   ★ ★ ★ ★

3667 Las Vegas Boulevard South, Las Vegas, ☎ *(702) 736-0419.*
Located at the Aladdin Showroom.

Wear your Stetson and head on down to the Aladdin Showroom, where this high-energy revue salutes all that is grand about country music. The show features singers, dancers, comics and a live band.

Among the highlights are performances by Shane Sutton, the 17-year-old grand prize winner of "Star Search"; 14-year-old fiddler Jasen Roller; and championship yodeler Karen Dee Brownlee. Named "Best Live Country Show in America" by the Country Music Association of America. Shows are at 7:15 and 10 nightly, except Tuesday. Adults pay $21.25 for show only, $26.20 with buffet; kids under 18 pay $15.35 show only, $18.55 for the show and buffet.

Crazy Girls—Sensuality & Passion ★★★

2901 Las Vegas Boulevard South, Las Vegas, ☎ *(702) 794-9433.*
Located at the Riviera Mardi Gras Plaza 2nd Floor.
This is billed as "Las Vegas' Sexiest Topless Revue," and I guess it is, but it's more R-rated than X. Lots of beautiful bodies, lots of dirty jokes, lots of horny conventioneers in the audience. Shows are nightly except Monday at 8:30 and 10:30; there's also a midnight show on Saturday. Tickets are $18.95, which includes two drinks, but not tax or tip. Add $5 for "VIP seating."

David Copperfield ★★★★★

3570 Las Vegas Boulevard South, Las Vegas, ☎ *(702) 731-7333.*
Located at the Caesars Circus Maximus Showroom.
Magician David Copperfield plays Caesars so much that he merits a mention in this book, although he is not on indefinite engagement like the other shows in this section. Copperfield is a master showman as well as one of the world's best illusionists and his boyish charm goes a long way. Some of his more famous tricks—flying about the stage, walking through his assistant—are amazing, but I still like the old cut-the-girl-in-half routines the best. He also does a neat trick in which he determines exactly what randomly chosen audience members predict he will draw. Copperfield can be a little too corny, such as when he demonstrates an old card trick taught by his late grandfather ("tonight, grandfather, I'll keep my promise and do that trick in my show" he says, gazing heavenward—like he doesn't do it every night?) but he's so darn cute that all is quickly forgiven. And the magic, set against a backdrop of pulsating rock music and sexy setups, is simply astounding. "How did he DO that?" is the refrain of the night. All seats are reserved in advance, though palming the maître d' $10 or so may help get you up front. I especially like the booths, which are slightly elevated for an unobstructed view. Tickets are about $60.

Debbie Reynolds Show ★★★

305 Convention Center Drive, Las Vegas, ☎ *(702) 733-2243.*
At the Debbie Reynolds Hotel & Casino.
Beloved entertainer Debbie Reynolds—who owns the hotel and casino in which this show takes place—holds court with singing, dancing, comedy acts and nostalgic film clips. Showtimes are Monday–Friday at 7:30 p.m. Tickets are $39.95, which includes tax, tip and two drinks. Not open to kids under six.

EFX ★★★★★

3799 Las Vegas Boulevard South, Las Vegas, 89109, ☎ *(702) 891-7777.*
Located at the MGM.
Closed: Tues.

Former teen heartthrob David Cassidy ("The Partridge Family") stars in this original $30-million production, which opened in 1995. He plays a hapless busboy who is kidnapped by magical masters who want him to recapture his imagination. The show is simply astounding in its special effects, and it's hard to imagine anyone coming away less than wowed all the way down to their socks. Just the smooth sounds from the six-member gospel choir One Spirit, which warms up the crowd, would be worth the price of admission, but there's more coming: much more. The show has a cast of 70 and fantastic music, primarily by Don Grady (another refuge from sitcomland, he was Robbie on "My Three Sons"). After a truly creepy opening featuring the disembodied head of James Earl Jones, Cassidy is whisked away, via the masters of magic, spirits, laughter and time, to other times and places. He meets Merlin and witnesses an intense dragon battle; plays P.T. Barnum in the "Intergalactic Circus of Wonders" (great costumes!); comes back from the dead as Houdini to comfort his grieving widow; and, as H.G. Wells, travels far back in time. That segment features a fantastically realistic 3-D movie. EFX (pronounced "Effects") may sound goofy, but it really works. Cassidy replaces Michael Crawford, who originated the role, and the word is Cassidy is much better. This show is highly recommended—even the theater is wonderfully atmospheric—and kids will love it. Well worth the high ticket price of $70, which includes tax, gratuity and one drink. Showtimes are 7:30 p.m. and 10:30 p.m. nightly except Sunday and Monday. A treat!

Enter the Night   ★ ★ ★ ★ ★

3000 Las Vegas Boulevard South, Las Vegas, ☎ *(702) 732-6325.*
Located at the Stardust Theatre.

Enter the Night is a great example of the Las Vegas revue, and manages to be hip enough to appeal to a younger crowd. The show has a little bit of everything, including lots of production numbers, topless dancers, impressive sets, tap dancing, specialty acts, and—my favorite part—professional ice skaters Cindy Landry and Burt Lancon doing amazing stunts on what has to be the world's tiniest ice rink. The singers are right on pitch, the comedy makes you laugh, the costumes are gorgeous and the laser light show is really cool. I also like the fact that some of the male dancers appear in G-strings—it's about time women in the audience got something to ogle besides bare breasts! Very high energy and very professional, I highly recommend this show for those too hip for Jubilee! or Folies Bergère. Shows are at 7:30 and 10:30 p.m. Tuesday through Saturday, 8 p.m. Sunday and Monday. Dark Friday. Open to adults only, tickets are $26.90, which includes two drinks, tax and tip.

Folies-Bergère   ★ ★ ★ ★

3801 Las Vegas Boulevard South, Las Vegas, ☎ *(702) 739-2414.*
Located at the Tropicana Tiffany Theatre.

Folies-Bergère has been around since 1961, making it Las Vegas' longest-running production show. This latest incarnation is billed as a "best of" show. It's modeled after the French spectacular from which it takes its name, and the theme is turn-of-the-century France. This is traditional Las Vegas all the way—topless girls in huge headdresses, elaborate costumes and the famed can-can finale. Among the variety acts are the Cavarettas, a couple who do an interesting gymnastic routine to the song "Lady in Red"; somehow, they manage to make this look both athletic and sexy at the same time. The show veers from its French theme for a lengthy "Tribute to American Music" that goes from gospel to rock and roll, with just about every musical fad covered in between. It gets overwhelmingly corny at times. Folies is certainly pleasant, but it lacks the absurd spectacle of Jubilee! and the hipness of Enter the Night. Most suitable for an older crowd. Shows are nightly, except Thursday, at 8 and 10:30. Slip the maître d' a few bucks if you want to be right up front.

Forever Plaid ★ ★ ★

3555 Las Vegas Boulevard South, Las Vegas, 89109, *(702) 733-3333. Located in the Flamingo Hilton.*

Here's the premise: in 1964, an accident kills a group of clean-cut, bow-tied young men on the way to their first gig. They go to heaven, but a hole in the ozone gives them one last chance to come back to Earth and do that concert. This lighthearted musical journey features songs of the 1950s like "Sixteen Tons," "Three Coins in the Fountain" and "Jamaica Farewell." Great for those who came of age when bobby socks and poodle skirts were all the rage. Shows are at 7:30 and 10 p.m. except Mondays. Tickets are $19.95 plus tax.

Great Radio City Music Hall Spectacular ★ ★ ★ ★

3555 Las Vegas Boulevard South, Las Vegas, ☎ *(702) 733-3333. Located at the Flamingo Hilton Showroom.*

This high-steppin' show stars the Radio City Music Hall Rockettes doing what they do best: marching about in amazing military-style precision—though they're certainly not wearing olive drab. "Special guest" Paige O'Hara narrates and also performs. There's also magic by Tim Kole and Jenny-Lynn, comedic juggler Nino Frediani and Stacy Moore with his "mess of mutts." The dinner show is 7:45 p.m. and costs $45.50, including tax and tip. The cocktail show is at 10:30 p.m.; $38.20 buys two drinks, tax and tip. Good for families.

Jubilee! ★ ★ ★ ★

3645 Las Vegas Boulevard South, Las Vegas, ☎ *(702) 739-4567. Located at the Bally Jubilee Theatre.*

This is what you think of when you think of a Las Vegas production show. The $10-million "Jubilee!" throws in everything but that old kitchen sink—if they could think of a song about it, they'd probably include that too. Lots of topless dancers with huge headgear, lots of corny songs, some variety acts and some astounding production numbers, such as the sinking of the *Titanic* (after a hapless passenger is nearly gang-raped in the engine room), the epic battle of Samson and Delilah (quite sexy) and airplane dogfights above the stage. The cast of 86 keeps things moving along at a jaunty pace. I've seen this show twice and laughed all the way through both times—it's not a comedy, mind you, just so over the top that giggles are spontaneous. Only recommended to those who really like splashy, glittery extravaganzas. Showtimes are 8 and 11 p.m. Tuesday through Saturday, and 8 p.m. on Sunday and Monday. Dark Fridays. Tickets are $49.50, including tax.

Kenny Kerr Show ★★

305 Convention Center Drive, Las Vegas, ☎ *(702) 733-2243.*
At the Debbie Reynolds Hotel & Casino.

Kerr and his "Women of Hollywood" is a lighthearted, adults-only show. Look out—those "women" are really female impersonators. Showtimes are 10:30 p.m. nightly except Sunday. Tickets are $19.95 plus tax.

King Arthur's Tournament ★★★★

3850 Las Vegas Boulevard South, Las Vegas, ☎ *(702) 597-7600.*
Located at the Excalibur King Arthur's Arena.

This dinner show is great for kids—they get to (actually, have to) eat with their hands and don't even have napkins! It's all great fun as the audience cheers on the Knights of the Round Table as they joust on horseback and fight an evil knight to the finish. The audience is separated into sections, each rooting for their own knight with the help of medieval maiden cheerleaders. Lots of table banging, yelling, screaming and fireworks. All the characters of Camelot are here, from King Arthur to Queen Guinevere to Merlin the Magician. Dinner consists of a Cornish hen and all the trappings. Showtimes are 6 and 8:30 p.m. nightly. Tickets are $29.95 including dinner, tax and tip. Children under three can sit on an adult's lap and share dinner. This show is highly recommended for families.

Lance Burton: Master Magician ★★★★

3770 Las Vegas Boulevard South, Las Vegas, ☎ *(702) 730-7000.*
At the Monte Carlo.

The good-looking Lance Burton has been playing Las Vegas for years; now he's really come into his own at the new Monte Carlo, where he has a beautiful showroom named for him and his own magic shop right next door. Spend one evening at his show and you'll agree such success is highly justified. Burton, who's been called "the magician's magician" and was awarded the gold medal of excellence by the International Brotherhood of Magicians, is a real charmer. (He also sounds a lot like Jack Nicholson, and his sly references to his over-rated competition, Siegfried and Roy, are a riot.) His excellent, self-effacing stage presence makes it all look so easy while he astounds the crowd with sleight-of-hand tricks and showy illusions that include levitation and disappearances. The comic antics of Michael Goudeau, a juggler whose claim to fame is keeping a burning torch, bowling ball and revved-up chain saw aloft (all at the same time), add just the right touch. The theater is quite lovely with its plush red seats and Victorian accents. Showtimes are 7:30 and 10:30 p.m. nightly, except Sunday and Monday. Tickets are a reasonable $34.95, which includes tax. Hint: If you want a drink at the show, you're better off bringing in one from the casino rather than waiting on the long line inside the theater. And here's a piece of trivia: Burton was once married to Melinda, "the First Lady of Magic," who plays downtown occasionally.

Legends in Concert ★★★★★

3535 Las Vegas Boulevard South, Las Vegas, ☎ *(702) 794-3261.*
Located at the Imperial Palace.

I admit that I approached this show with a feeling of dread, convinced it would be corny, obnoxious, and a big waste of a few hours. Was I ever wrong! It's tons of fun, and by the time "Elvis" leads the crowd in the "Viva Las Vegas" finale, I was stomping my feet and singing along with the best of 'em. The cast rotates occasionally—I saw impersonators of Neil Diamond, Liberace, Cher, the Blues Brothers, Hank Williams Jr., Sammy Davis Jr. and, of course, Elvis—in other words, someone for every taste. (Madonna, the Beatles, Marilyn Monroe and others are also sometimes featured.) Each performer looks and sounds amazingly like the real McCoy—Cher was particularly good. What's the point, then, of the big-screen TVs that run video of the real people while the performers are on stage? It only serves to distract and remind you that you are watching an impersonator. The performers all really sing (no lip syncing), and the live band, eight dancers, two back-up singers and cool light show add a lot. There's a lot of enforced clapping and cheering and it can be a bit too patriotic for non-Americans, but it's not hard to get into the spirit. Fun! Shows are nightly, except Sunday, at 7:30 and 10:30. Tickets are $29.50, $14.75 for kids under 12, which includes two drinks. Kids under eight may be bored, but their parents will love it. Note: the theater is nonsmoking.

MADhattan

3155 West Harmon Avenue, Las Vegas, ☎ *(702) 740-6969.*
At New York-New York.
Just opened in the summer of 1997, this show is meant to represent the "spontaneity, fast pace and high energy" of Manhattan in the middle of rush hour. Produced by Kenneth Feld, the man responsible for such high-profile hits as Siegfried & Roy, Walt Disney's World on Ice, and Ringling Bros. and Barnum & Bailey, it takes place in the new resort's 1000-seat theater. The show (not open for review at press time) is touted as a "moving, living collage of New York City," featuring "underground" dance and music talent. (Showtimes and ticket prices not available at press time.) Showtimes are 7:30 and 10:30 p.m. Dark Wednesday and Thursday. Tickets are $40 plus tax.

Mystère ★★★★★

3300 Las Vegas Boulevard south, Las Vegas, ☎ *(702) 894-7111.*
Located at Treasure Island.
Wow, what a show! Forget everything you remember about the big top as a kid—the pathetic animals, the sad clowns—and prepare to be blown away by this surrealistic circus by the famed Cirque du Soleil. The 70-member troupe hails from around the world and puts on an amazing show of acrobatics, stilt walking, pole climbing, trapeze swinging, modern dancing and more. Their costumes and makeup make the performers look like strange, humanoid creatures (I loved the overgrown baby), and the resident clown is a hoot! A live band and two singers make music as eerily enchanting as the performance. As the woman behind me murmured in a tone of awe, "Everything is so beautiful!" The theater, specially designed for Cirque du Soleil, is beautiful too, and the seats nice and plush. The stage rises and drops constantly, and the performers use virtually every inch of the theater in the show, often coming right into the seats to really wow the

crowd. I was thoroughly mesmerized, and you will be too. Kids under eight may get bored, though. Showtimes are nightly at 7:30 and 10:30, except Monday and Tuesday. Tickets are $64.90 for adults, $32.45 for kids under 11.

Riviera Comedy Club   ★ ★ ★

2901 Las Vegas Boulevard South, Las Vegas, 89109, ☎ *(702) 794-9433. Located at the Riviera.*

This is a very popular comedy show in Las Vegas and often plays to capacity crowds. The bill usually features at least three comics per week. Showtimes are 8 and 10 nightly. There's also an 11:45 p.m. show on Friday and Saturday. Admission includes tax and two drinks. The Riviera offers special deals when you buy tickets to more than one of their shows (the other two are "An Evening at La Cage" and "Crazy Girls—Sensuality & Passion"); inquire at the box office. General Admission: $14.95.

Showgirls of Magic   ★ ★

115 E. Tropicana Avenue, Las Vegas, ☎ *(702) 597-6028. Located at the Hotel San Remo.*

Three pretty, scantily clad women perform magic, with dance revues and the comedy of Los Latin Cowboys rounding out the show. Showtimes are 8 and 10:30 p.m. nightly except Monday; the late show is topless. Tickets are a reasonable $19.95, plus tax and tip.

The magnificent white Siberian tigers of Siegfried and Roy thrill audiences of all ages.

Siegfried & Roy   ★ ★ ★

3400 Las Vegas Boulevard South, Las Vegas, ☎ *(702) 792-7777. Located at the Mirage Theatre.*

I just don't get it. Siegfried & Roy have been playing Las Vegas for 25 years—Steve Wynn wooed them away from the Frontier when he built the Mirage—and everyone always carries on about what a great show this is. I went in with high expectations—after all, it costs a whopping $83.85 (Las Vegas' most expensive show by far) and it constantly sells out. In fact, it's the highest-grossing live show in history. What a disappointment! Sure, there are some neat tricks—

women turned into white tigers, white tigers turned into women, a disappearing elephant, a disappearing Siegfried, a reappearing Roy. But you wait a long time between ohhs and ahhs because this show is heavily padded with silly song and dance numbers. The cast is enormous and the production numbers impressive, but I came to see magic, damn it! All the other magic shows in town offer more magic per hour than this German duo does in their two shows nightly. The two try to prattle wittily with the audience, but they are showmen, not comics, and it falls flat. The highlight of the show, for me, was when they showed a videotape of their baby white tigers—cute!—and brought out a newborn white lion—adorable! But then, I'm a sucker for baby cats. Further adding to my unhappiness was the seating—everyone is jammed together at long tables and it's quite uncomfortable. And what's with those pants with the huge crotch padding that Roy wears? Is anyone really that well endowed? Having said all that, it's only fair to report that most of the audience seemed to be eating it up with a spoon. When Siegfried "floats," one of my table mates nearly fainted with excitement. The Associated Press calls it the "show of the century"—maybe I just caught them on a bad night. Siegfried & Roy have become an industry onto themselves—they even have their own gift shop in the Mirage, where you can buy everything from pajamas to calendars adorned with their heavily made-up faces. Showtimes are nightly at 7:30 and 11, except Wednesdays and Thursdays. The exorbitant admission fee at least includes two drinks, tax and tip. Insider's tip: Park with Mirage's north valet, rather than the one at the main entrance, to avoid a long wait after the show.

Spellbound   ★ ★ ★

3745 Las Vegas Boulevard South, Las Vegas, *(702) 369-5000.*
Located at the Harrah's Commanders Theatre.
Another of Las Vegas' many magic revues, this one stars a variety of master illusionists performing their best tricks. There's also singing and dancing between the gee-whiz effects and the amazing aerobatics of Human Design, who do their routine in slow motion, giving the illusion of ever-changing statues. Comic Jeff Hobson manages to combine yucks and sleight-of-hand at the same time. The showroom is quite nice. Shows are at 7:30 and 10 nightly, except Sunday. $27.70 buys one drink, tax and tip.

Splash II-The Next Wave   ★ ★ ★

2901 Las Vegas Boulevard South, Las Vegas.
Located at the Riviera Versailles Theatre.
The long-popular "Splash" reopened in the summer of 1995 after a major reworking. Though the theme is water, only the impressive opening number features the wet stuff. It includes synchronized swimmers, divers and, naturally, mermaids, in a 20,000 gallon transparent tank, as well as fountains and waterfalls. It's all pretty neat. The rest of the show is typical of what you'd expect from a Las Vegas revue: lots of singing, dancing and celebrity impersonating. "Michael Jackson" is especially good, and a dead-ringer for the pop star. There's also "Madonna" who supplements a greatest-hits medley with some scenes from *Evita*. I didn't much care for the antics of exotic bird trainer Clint Carvalho, but comedian Mark Konhauser is a

riot. The feats of four motorcyclists who race inside a 14-foot steel "Globe of Death"—a holdover from the original show—are as jaw-dropping as ever. "Splash's" best assets are its lavish costumes and great dancing, but the erratic shifts in mood can be unsettling. This production has won numerous Show of the Year awards, but it doesn't much do it for me. Showtimes are 7:30 and 10:30 p.m. nightly. The 10:30 show is topless, but even during the earlier show, much of the dancing is too suggestive for children. Tickets, which include one drink at any casino bar, are $39.50 plus tax for reserved seating and $49.50 plus tax for VIP seating.

Starlight Express   ★★★★

3000 Paradise Road, Las Vegas, ☎ (702) 732-5755.
Located at the Las Vegas Hilton Showroom.
"Starlight Express" is unlike any other show in Las Vegas. It is a full-scale musical play—story and all—by Andrew Lloyd Webber and has played around the world (although the critics hated it on Broadway). The plot is a little boy's dream of a race between a steam, diesel and electric train, with, naturally, a love story thrown in for good measure. The steam engine is the good guy while the other two are mean and cocky (guess who wins?). The cast, dressed in high-tech costumes, performs entirely on roller skates and it's quite dazzling to watch them roar around and somehow manage not to break their necks. The songs are forgettable, but are sung live and quite prettily at that. The theater was redesigned especially for the show and the seats are plush and comfortable. The time whizzes by as fast as the cast zips about the stage. I liked this play a lot, but if you're looking for Las Vegas-style glitz and glamour, you'll be happier at "Jubilee!" or "Enter the Night." Showtimes can vary, so call to confirm. The standard schedule is 7:30 and 10:30 p.m. Tuesday, Thursday and Saturday, and 7:30 p.m. on Monday, Wednesday and Sunday. Dark Fridays. Tickets are $19.50–$45.

Xtreme Scene   ★★

One Main Street, Las Vegas, ☎ (702) 386-2444.
At Jackie Gaughan's Plaza.
This adults-only show features high-energy dance numbers, magic by Dexion and excellent singing by Regina Powers. It's all suggestive as can be, though the producers insist it appeals to women just as much as men. Showtimes are nightly at 8 and 10 p.m. except Fridays. Tickets are $19.95, which includes tax and one drink.

NIGHTLIFE

Las Vegas owns the night, as its million-plus bulbs burst into blazing brilliance.

No matter how much Las Vegas woos kids with amusement parks and video arcades, the city will always be an adult's playground. Though it's a 24-hour town in the truest sense of the word, it's when the sun goes down that Las Vegas really shines—literally. The million-plus lightbulbs of the Strip and Glitter Gulch become blinding, the volcano at the Mirage starts spewing, the showgirls don their skimpy costumes and blush their nipples, Siegfried and Roy ready their rare white lions for yet another show.

And you, the visitor, have a ton of choices well beyond the obvious. Virtually every casino has live entertainment in at least one lounge—you can check out Rod Stewart (a.k.a. Rob Hanna) strutting his stuff nightly at the Stardust, boogy to the great bands at Treasure Island, line dance at the Gold Coast and Sam's Town.

You can also leave the sounds of the slots far behind at one of Las Vegas' happening nightclubs. With the exception of Club Rio, all the following are located outside casino-hotels, though some do have those ubiquitious video poker machines at the bar.

Beach, The

356 Convention Center Drive, Las Vegas, ☎ *(702) 731-1925.*
Located across from the Convention Center.
Hours open: 24 hours

The ocean may be far, far away, but that doesn't stop this club from playing up the theme to the max, with surfboards, coconuts and palms as prevalent as seagulls on a real beach. The first floor is given over to dancing to live music and D.J.-spun tunes; upstairs is a 24-hour sports bar with nearly 40 TVs, slot machines and video poker. A local hangout; come early to avoid the constant long lines. Cover charge is usually $10; women get in free Sunday and Monday.

Club Rio

3700 West Flamingo Road, Las Vegas, 89103, ☎ *(702) 252-7777.*
Located a few blocks off the Strip.

Club Rio in the Rio Suites Hotel and Casino is an especially happening place for the thirty-something crowd. Locals love this circular nightclub with D.J. music, a large dance floor and MTV-type videos. The tables are nice and spread out, and the atmosphere is pretty sophisticated. The dress code requires collared shirts and forbids baggy or torn jeans, hats, shorts, sandals, tennis shoes, flannel shirts and work boots. Women get in for free, but men must fork over $10. It's open from 10 p.m. to at least 3 a.m. Thursday through Saturday, and 9 a.m.–3 a.m. on Sundays.

Club Utopia

3765 Las Vegas Boulevard South, Las Vegas, ☎ *(702) 736-3105.*
Located on the strip, across from the Monte Carlo.
Hours open: at 10 p.m.

This newer spot has a huge dance floor, great light show and 20,000 watts of power to blow away your ear drums.

Drink, The

200 East Harmon Avenue, Las Vegas, ☎ *(702) 796-5519.*

Located at the corner of Harmon and Kovall.
Hours open: at 5 p.m.
Cigars are the big thing here at the atmospheric Drink—they sell a
good variety, and you're more than welcome to fire 'em up. Located
on two levels, with an outdoor dance floor in a courtyard and a pleasant balcony to catch a whiff of fresh air. There are six themed areas,
including psychedelic and tribal rooms and a vodka bar. The admission
charge is usually $5 after 9 p.m.; no cover on Tuesday and Wednesday.

Dylan's Dance Hall & Saloon

4660 Boulder Highway, Las Vegas, 89122, ☎ (702) 451-4006.
Located a few minutes off the Strip, near Sam's Town.
Hours open: 7 p.m.–late
Locals of all ages love Dylan's so much that they voted it best place to
dance in the 1994 *Las Vegas Review-Journal* readers' poll. The country-western dance hall is a rustic honky-tonk where cowboys and girls
come to line dance and do the West Coast swing. If you don't know
the steps, they'll teach you for free each day from 7:30-9 p.m. A great
place for those looking for love—eight couples met and got married
after meeting here in 1993 alone (two couples even tied the knot
right on the dance floor). You can munch on ribs and stuff, and $10
buys an unlimited mug of beer (you even get to keep the mug).

Fremont Street Blues & Reggae Cafe

400 Fremont Street, Las Vegas, ☎ (702) 594-4640.
*Hours open: 7 p.m.–3 a.m. Special Hours: until 5 a.m. Friday and Satur-
day.*
Musicians appear nightly at this high-energy club with two stages.
Despite the name, they also showcase rock, bluegrass and zydeco
bands, too. There's often no cover charge. For a recording of upcoming acts, call ☎ *(702) 594-4640.*

Gold Coast Dance Hall & Saloon

4000 West Flamingo Road, Las Vegas, ☎ (702) 367-7111.
Located at the Gold Coast Casino.
Hours open: at 7 p.m.
Dust off your boots and head on down to this giant club, which has the
city's largest dance floor. The Gold Coast, which also features rock
music and big band sounds, generally attracts an older (35-plus) crowd.
The schedule and cover charge varies (it's often free), so call first.

The Hard Rock's music club, The Joint, features top names in rock.

Hard Rock Casino

4455 Paradise Road, Las Vegas, ☎ *(702) 693-5066.*
Located a few blocks off the Strip.
Hours open: 25 hours

The casino is the coolest place in town, and the large circular bar in the center, under the giant globe, is where many partying locals begin their evenings out. The 1200-seat music club, The Joint, is the best place, bar none, to see live rock and other musical acts, but shows sell out quickly, so plan ahead.

Nightclub, The

3000 Paradise Road, Las Vegas, ☎ *(702) 732-5755.*
Located at the Las Vegas Hilton.

This nightclub just off the main casino in the Las Vegas Hilton is a class act, with art deco decor and a great light and sound system. The live music of Kristine W & The Sting—performing rock, jazz and Motown every night but Thursday—keeps the joint rocking. No cover charge, but there is a one-drink minimum.

Rockabilly's

3785 Boulder Highway, Las Vegas, ☎ *(702) 641-5800.*
Located near Boulder Station.
Hours open: 5 p.m.–late

Rockabilly's has the largest hardwood dance floor in Las Vegas at this country-western bar, so there's lots of room to swing and dip on its 2000 square feet. Free dance lessons begin at 7:30 p.m. nightly. There's no cover charge; $9 buys an all-you-can-drink mug of draft beer (turn the mug in at the end of the night for a $2 rebate).

Sand Dollar Blues Lounge

3355 Spring Mountain Road, Las Vegas, ☎ *(702) 871-6651.*
Located in southwest Las Vegas, at Polaris.
Special Hours: Open 24 hours; entertainment begins at 10 p.m.

You won't find more tourists at this off-the-beaten track venue for live blues. Don't judge this book by its cover—the atmosphere is laid-back and friendly, and the music couldn't get much better. When a cover is charged, it's usually less than $5.

Shark Club

75 East Harmon Avenue, Las Vegas, 89109, ☎ *(702) 795-7525.*
Located just off the Strip between Aladdin and MGM.
Hours open: 9 p.m.–3 a.m.

Named the best rock club by the readers of the *Las Vegas Review-Journal*, the multi-level Shark Club has a dazzling decor and three dance floors. Depending on the night, you'll groove to techno pop, hip hop, alternative and top 40 dance tunes. There's acoustic music on Sundays and blues on Tuesday, Friday and Saturday in the Atrium, while it's '70s retro every night in the Lava Lounge. Tuesdays and Wednesdays are ladies night (watch out for land sharks). The cover charge is $5 weekdays, $10 weekends.

TGI Friday's

1800 East Flamingo Road, Las Vegas, ☎ *(702) 732-9905.*
Located 2.5 miles east of the Strip, corner of Spencer.

THE place to celebrate the end of the work week is, appropriately enough, Friday's, where the locals jam the bar six deep and they pour some $6000 worth of booze from just 4–7 p.m. Named "best happy hour" and "best singles bar" in the *Las Vegas Review-Journal's* readers' poll, the restaurant attracts a diverse crowd from ages 25 to 50. Besides looking for love, they're looking for cheap eats: appetizers are just $1.99. If you're the kind of person who never knows what to order, you'll really be stumped by TGI Friday's selection of 300 drinks. Happy hour happens every night, but Fridays are when it really hops.

Tommy Rocker's Cantina & Grill

4275 South Industrial, Las Vegas, ☎ *(702) 261-6688.*
Located a block off the Strip.
Hours open: 24 hours

Headquarters for the Las Vegas Parrot Head Club (and if you have to ask, it means you're not much into Jimmy Buffett), you'll hear plenty of his music and the like at this kick-back, young locals' spot. Tommy Rocker does fun rock and roll sing-alongs on the weekends. There's no cover and no minimum.

"No more peanuts until you buy another round of drinks."

Drawing by Gahan Wilson; ©1995 The New Yorker Magazine, Inc.

SHOPPING

The "sky" changes often at Forum Shops, Caesar's Palace.

You've won all that money, so quick, go buy something before you give it all back. Las Vegas is happy to oblige in this endeavor—the city has several shopping malls and virtually every large hotel has a shopping arcade. The mall at Stratosphere—which you must pass through to get to the tower—is especially worth a look, as its shops are more affordable than most in the hotels.

Interesting specialty shops include **Bonanza Gift Shop** *(across from the Sahara at 2460 Las Vegas Boulevard South,* ☎ *(702) 385-7359)*, which claims to be the world's largest (tons of great tacky souvenirs); **Antique Warehouse** *(4175 S. Cameron, three blocks west of the Rio,* ☎ *(702) 251-3447)*, whose 100,000 square feet is crammed with antiques, collectibles and sports memorabilia; and the **Gamblers General Store** *(800 Main Street, downtown Las Vegas,* ☎ *(702) 382-9903)*, which has more than 5000 items for the gambler, including slot machines, dice, cards, chips and books. **The Gamblers Book Shop** *(630 South 11th Street, one block west of the Maryland Parkway,* ☎ *(702) 382-7555)* has the world's largest selection of books and computer software for gamblers and researchers. Call ☎ *(800) 522-1777* for a free catalog.

Unless noted otherwise, all the following have free valet parking.

Shopping Malls

Forum Shops at Caesars

3500 Las Vegas Boulevard South, ☎ *(702) 8934-4800.*
Located next to Caesars Palace.
The mall is open daily from 10 a.m. to 11 p.m., and stays open until midnight on Friday and Saturday. Though many of the shops are well beyond reach of the average consumer, a visit just to soak up the well-heeled ambience is a must.

They call it the "shopping wonder of the world" and the hype is actually justified. The Forum Shops are a must-see, whether you plan on actually spending any money or not. Attached to Caesars (and exited, of course, only through the casino), the mall, which recently doubled in size, is simply gorgeous. It's all made up to resemble a Roman village, with marble flooring, ornate statuary (some that even talks), spectacular fountains and imaginative facades. Overhead, the "sky" magically changes frequently—from sunrise to puffy clouds to dramatic sunsets and starry, starry nights. A variety of "sidewalk" cafes are perfect for people watching.

Every hour on the hour, the Festival Fountain comes to life as the robotic statues of Bacchus, Venus, Pluto and Apollo stage an impromptu party. This corny show is worth a glimpse if you're in the area, but not a special trip.

Among the upscale tenants are Gucci, Louis Vuitton and Christian Dior; there's also a neat store called Magnet Maximus with floor-to-ceiling magnets to put on your fridge. Another good stop is at the Museum Store, which features great gifts and curios. Among the eateries are Planet Hollywood, Spago and the Stage Deli.

Shopping Vegas-style is done in spectacular surroundings.

Fashion Show Mall

3200 Las Vegas Boulevard South, ☎ *(702) 369-8382.*
Located next to the Treasure Island.

Fashion Show is open Monday through Friday from 10 a.m. to 9 p.m., Saturday from 10 a.m. to 7 p.m. and Sunday from noon to 6 p.m.

The Fashion Show was Las Vegas' glitziest mall until the Forum Shops came along and stole its thunder. While it lacks the "gee-whiz" quality of The Forum Shops, it's still quite nice. There are 145 shops on two levels, and the mall is airy and light, enhanced by tasteful fountains, skylights and palm trees. There are even some plush couches for resting and live music from a white grand piano.

Major tenants include Neiman-Marcus, Saks Fifth Avenue, Macy's, Robinsons-May, and Dillard's. There are also the chain stores you expect to see in every mall across the land, including the Gap, the Limited, Banana Republic and Starbucks Coffee. Among the generous helping of restaurants is the submarine-themed Dive!, the upscale Chinese restaurant Chin's and one of the city's few sidewalk cafes, Sfuzzi.

Boulevard Mall

3528 Maryland Parkway, Las Vegas ☎ (702) 735-8268.
Located a few miles east of the Strip at Mayland Parkway and Desert Inn Road.
Boulevard Mall is open Monday through Friday from 10 a.m. to 9 p.m., Saturday from 10 a.m. to 8 p.m., and Sunday from 11 a.m. to 6 p.m.
This giant mall totals 1.2 million square feet and is touted as Nevada's largest, as well as its oldest. You'll see more locals than tourists shopping here than at the two more glamourous (and expensive) centers listed above. The 140-plus stores include Sears, JC Penney, Dillard's and Macy's. The 24,000 square-foot Panorama Cafe's food court has something for everyone.

Galleria at Sunset

1300 West Sunset Road, Henderson, ☎ (702) 434-0202.
Located in Henderson, about six miles from the Strip.
Open daily from 10 a.m. to 9 p.m., and 11 a.m. to 6 p.m. on Sunday.
The Galleria has one million square feet on two levels, with a nicely done Southwestern motif throughout. There are some 110 specialty stores as well as anchors J.C. Penney, Robinson/May, Dillard's and Mervyn's. The mammoth food court seats 600.

Belz Factory Outlet World

7400 Las Vegas Boulevard South, ☎ (702) 896-5599.
Located south of the Strip at Warm Springs Road.
Hours are Monday through Saturday from 10 a.m. to 9 p.m., and Sunday from 10 a.m. to 6 p.m. No valet parking.
This is America's largest factory outlet mall, with some 140 outlets under one roof. Center court features a carousel, and, because this is Las Vegas, the mall has a permanent laser show. Belz is Las Vegas' only nonsmoking mall.

Las Vegas Factory Stores of America

9155 Las Vegas Boulevard South, ☎ (702) 897-9090.
Located at the city's southern edge.
Open daily from 10 a.m. to 8 p.m., Sunday from 10 a.m. to 6 p.m. No valet parking. Call about bus transportation.
This Spanish-style open-air market, recently expanded, has more than 50 stores, including Adolfo II, American Tourister and Corning/Revere—as well as a bar where the ubiquitous video poker machines await.

Meadows Mall

4300 Meadows Land, ☎ *(702) 878-4849*
Located at U.S. 95 and Valley View, 15 minutes from the Strip.
Hours are 10 a.m. to 9 p.m. weekdays and 10 a.m. to 6 p.m. Saturday and Sunday. No valet parking.

This two-level enclosed complex has about 140 establishments, including anchor stores Macy's, Sears, Dillard's and JC Penney. There's also the Menagerie Carousel and a large food court.

Showcase Mall

3785 Las Vegas Boulevard South, Las Vegas, 89109, ☎ *(702) 597-3122.*
Located on the Strip next to the MGM-Grand Hotel and across from New York-New York.

This brand new complex opened in June 1997 and is anchored by a towering 100 ft. glass Coke bottle which encases a pair of elevators. Everything Coca-Cola is a Coke merchandise collector's dream come true with all sorts of Coca-Cola memorabilia and new logo products under one roof. A futuristic soda fountain and three-story wall of ice complete the "Things Go Better With Coke" theme. The complex also features a huge video game arcade operated by Sega Gameworks, a United Artists cinema, and the Official All-Star Cafe restaurant. Other retail stores and restaurants will open during the next year including Ethel M./M&M World, a chocolate extravaganza staged by the Mars Co.

SHOPPING

GETTING HITCHED

Getting married is the second most popular activity in Las Vegas. You can get hitched in a hot-air balloon, helicopter or your own car at a drive-through chapel.

Besides gambling, hitching couples is probably Las Vegas' biggest industry. Where else can you get wed while bungee jumping, or in medieval attire, aboard a hot-air balloon, hovering in a helicopter or in your car at a drive-in window?

Every six minutes, a couple is issued a marriage license in Las Vegas—in 1996, more than 104,000 tied the knot. No word on the number of corresponding divorces, though. Among the more famous Las Vegas marriages not to work out are those of Frank Sinatra and Mia Farrow and Jane Fonda and Roger Vadim. On a brighter note, Paul Newman and Joanne Woodward, Steve Lawrence and Edye Gorme and Ann-Margaret and Roger Smith all got married in Las Vegas, and are still together many years later.

The biggest days for Las Vegas weddings are Valentine's Day (for romantic reasons) and New Year's Eve (for tax reasons). Couples wait in line for hours on these days first to get a license, and then to have their turn in a production line-style wedding at one of the city's many chapels.

Getting married in Las Vegas is probably easier than anywhere in the world. There is no waiting period and no blood test is required. Those over age 18 do not need consent, but may be required to show proof of age (birth certificate or passport). If you're divorced, just tell them the date the divorce was finalized; you don't have to show papers.

If you're between 16 and 18, you're too young to get married—but if you insist, have your parent or legal guardian (for both the bride and groom) come in person when the license is applied for. If that's not possible, bring a notarized affidavit of consent containing the birthdate of the minor. If you're under 16 and want to get married in Las Vegas, you'll need the above as well as authorization from the Nevada District Court. Why not just spend the day at MGM Grand Adventures instead?

Licenses are issued at the **Marriage License Bureau** (☎ *(702) 455-3156* and *(702) 455-4415* after 5 p.m.) at the county clerk's office in the courthouse, downtown at *200 South Third Street.* They're open from 8 a.m. to midnight Monday through Thursday and around the clock from 8 a.m. Friday to midnight on Sunday. They're also open 24 hours on all state holidays. The fee is $35, payable only in cash or traveler's checks.

You can have the actual ceremony at the **Office of the Commissioner of Civil Marriages** at *136 South Fourth Street* (☎ *(702) 455-3474*), just a block from where you get your license. The charge is $35. Be warned, though, that this is hardly a dignified judge's chamber, as I had expected, but a really tacky office with cheap furniture and an ugly "congratulations" banner tacked over the thrift-store desk. There's even a cash register!

Much better to choose one of the 40 or so wedding chapels in town. The cheapest you'll get away with is about $100, including the license, and you can spend a lot more if you want all those little touches brides can't seem to live without. Every chapel mentioned here can take care of everything from witnesses to music to flowers to pictures to videotapes—for a fee. Prices quoted don't include your donation to the minister; $30 to $50 is the going rate, and it's always paid in cash.

One of the closest chapels to where you get your license is **A Chapel by the Courthouse** (*201 East Bridger Avenue,* ☎ *(702) 384-9099* and *(800) 545-8111*). This cute little building has ivy growing around a fence, a heart-shaped arbor and small chandeliers inside, and is far superior to the Commissioner's office. Fees start at $40 and go up to $199.

Another nice chapel is the **Candlelight**, across from Circus Circus *(2855 Las Vegas Blvd. South, ☎ (702) 735-4179 and (800) 882-3379)*. It's one of the more churchlike chapels, with a cute white-picket fence and arbor. Inside, the feeling is dignified with high beamed ceilings and spartan wood pews. The Candlelight has been around for 25 years and has married the likes of Whoopie Goldberg, Bette Midler and Michael Caine. Prices start at $55 and go as high as $419.

A Little White Chapel *(1301 Las Vegas Blvd. South, ☎ (702) 382-5943 and (800) 545-8111)* is another of Las Vegas' famous spots. It's here that you can have a drive-through wedding ($30); you don't even have to get out of the car, and you can both buy T-shirts to attest to that fact. But it's your wedding, for heaven's sake, so park the car and go inside. It's quite pretty with white pews accented with flowers, faux stained-glass windows, an electric candelabra at the altar and, unfortunately, claustraphobically low ceilings. Use of the chapel is $55, with packages as high as $499. Joan Collins and Michael Jordan were married here (not to each other); in fact, they each have packages named after them, despite the fact that Collins' marriage to the much-younger Peter Holm ended quickly in a nasty divorce.

A Little White Chapel also offers hot-air balloon weddings ("**Little White Chapel in the Sky**," ☎ *(702) 382-5943 or (800) 545-8111)* that start at $650 and soar as high as $1100. You can also choose a more economical ceremony in a helicopter hovering over the casino of your choice. That starts at $195.

You may have your heart set on taking your vows with an Elvis impersonator, but the poor guy can't get the appropriate license, so he can only do renewal of vows ceremonies. This takes place at the **Graceland Wedding Chapel** *(619 Las Vegas Blvd. South, ☎ (702) 474-6655 or (800) 824-5732)*, whose churchlike look is complete with real stained-glass windows and mauve and antique white furnishings. Weddings cost $50 to $180, while re-tying the knot with the King runs $150.

The only city chapel listed on the National Register of Historic Places is the **Little Church of the West** *(3960 Las Vegas Blvd. South, ☎ (702) 739-7971 and (800) 821-2452)*. They've been performing weddings here since 1942 and have married the likes of Judy Garland, Mickey Rooney, Dudley Moore and Richard Gere. Ann-Margaret and Elvis Presley said "I do" here in a scene from 1964's *Viva Las Vegas*. The cedar and redwood chapel, located on the grounds of the Hacienda Hotel, has the original wooden pews and four Victorian lamps believed to be from 19th-century railroad cars. Use of the chapel costs $55, while packages range from $179–$399.

Lots of celebrities have taken their vows at the **Silver Bell** *(607 Las Vegas Blvd. South, ☎ (702) 382-3727 and (800) 221-8492)*, some with happier results than others. If you want to be wed at the same place Melanie Griffith, Don Johnson, Diana Ross and Rodney Dangerfield were, head for this quaint little white building where you can have the ceremony outdoors by a waterfall and stream or inside the pink chapel. Packages run from $55 to $280.

The Chapel of the Bells *(2233 Las Vegas Blvd. South, ☎ (702) 735-6803 and (800) 233-2391)* is connected to the dumpy Fun City Motel, but it still manages to look pretty cute, with neon bells and lights and a tiny garden outside. The pretty chapel within has an arbor over the altar. Prices start at $45 and go to $325.

Just down the street, the **Chapel L'Amour** *(1901 Las Vegas Blvd. South, ☎ (800) 322-5683)* offers two rooms, one very small and simple, the other large with neat antique red velvet loveseats in lieu of pews, a wood-beamed ceiling and nice carpeting. The murals on the walls are pretty ugly, the flowers around the altar are obviously fake, but the windows look out onto the traffic on the Strip. Prices start at $55 for the small chapel, $95 for the large, with packages running from $150–$969.

The nearby **Little Chapel of the Flowers** *(1717 Las Vegas Blvd. South, ☎ (702) 735-4331 and (800) 843-2410)* is unusual in that the minister actually takes a few minutes to talk to each couple before performing the ceremony. There are three pretty Victorian-style chapels, all clean and airy with brass chandeliers, burnished cherrywoods and Impressionist paintings. Prices start at $149 and go up to $315.

Weddings with a genteel Victorian flavor can be had at **San Francisco Sally's** *(1304 Las Vegas Blvd. South, ☎ (702) 385-7777 and (800) 658-8677)*. The "old time wedding parlour" has crystal chandeliers, velvet draperies, deep rose carpeting and antique accouterments. You can carry the theme further by renting one of their many antique wedding gowns. The chapel fee is $45, plus $25 for the minister.

The **Long Fung Wedding Temple** *(4215 Spring Mountain Road in Chinatown Plaza, ☎ (702) 252-0400 or (800) 599-8228)*, opened in 1995, offers weddings with an Eastern twist. The Oriental chapel is done in red and ivory with a statue of Quan Yen, the Chinese symbol of happy marriages, front and center. Packages run from $288–$888. (Eight is the number for infinity, which keeps going and going and going, just as marriages are supposed to do.)

Perhaps the best deal in town is at the **Shalimar Wedding Chapel** *(1401 Las Vegas Blvd. South, ☎ (702) 382-7372 and (800) 255-9633)*, where $100 buys the ceremony, 12 photos, a videotape, limo service, flowers for the bride and groom, witnesses and music. The only other cost is the minister's donation.

Many casino-hotels also offer generally sophisticated wedding chapels. **The Island Wedding Chapel** at the Tropicana *(3801 Las Vegas Blvd. South,* ☎ *(702) 739-2451 and (800) 325-5839)* gets my vote for nicest. It's a tiki-style hut with skylights, wooden ceiling fans and a bamboo altar set above the Trop's fanciful pool, with lots of tropical foliage, fountains and waterfalls setting the mood. Night weddings are especially pretty when the tiki torches flicker merrily. Prices start at $250, which includes the ceremony, flowers and a few other extras including pictures, and go up to $975, which buys the works, as well as two nights at the hotel.

The two chapels at **Harrah's** *(3475 Las Vegas Blvd. South,* ☎ *(702) 369-5121 and (800) 392-9002)* are also quite nice, done up in pinks and mauves with pretty paned windows overlooking a garden. Use of the chapel costs $80–$150, with packages available from $250 to 975, which includes a gourmet dinner, one night's room, breakfast in bed and pampering in the health club.

Treasure Island *(3300 Las Vegas Blvd. South,* ☎ *(702) 894-7700 and (800) 866-4748)* has two wedding chapels, both quite pretty with floral wallpaper, gorgeous flower arrangements and blue padded pews. The only drawback is that they're right next to the meeting rooms, which could prove distracting if a big convention is taking place at the hotel. Prices start at $300 and go up to $475.

Circus Circus' Chapel of the Fountain *(2880 Las Vegas Blvd. South,* ☎ *(702) 794-3777 and (800) 634-6717)* is cute, with faux stained glass windows, a blue canopied ceiling and a large blue heart above the altar. Use of the chapel starts at $55 with packages reaching to $309.95.

You'll find more faux stained glass at the **Love at the Plaza Chapel** in Jackie Gaughan's Plaza Hotel *(downtown at One Main Street,* ☎ *(702) 386-0992 and (800) 392-5371)*. You enter the chapel through a whimsical round door; inside there are large arrangements of white silk flowers, mustard walls with white trim and chairs instead of pews. A stern sign admonishes: "Absolutely no rice in this building or on these premises." The chapel costs $55 and packages run from $189–$499.

There are even two wedding chapels in the new **MGM Grand Adventures Theme Park** *(3799 Las Vegas Blvd. south,* ☎ *(702) 891-7950 and (800) 929-1111)*. These gray and mauve rooms in the Central Park Wedding Chapels try too hard for a dignified look; they seem to me more suitable for a funeral. And do you really want to get married in a theme park? Prices start at $135 and go as high as $900, which includes two nights in an MGM spa suite.

The **Excalibur** *(3850 Las Vegas Blvd. South,* ☎ *(702) 597-7777* or *800 879-1379)* has two spots in which to tie the knot, Canterbury Wedding Chapel and Canterbury Gardens. Both are quite pretty; I especially like the Gardens, where the walls are painted as a blue sky with puffy clouds. What really makes this place unique, though, is that you can rent a medieval dress for the ceremony—a white and gold brocade, a rainbow brocade or a burgundy velvet gown. There's matching garb for the groom, too. This costs just $58.85 each, but you can only keep the fancy duds on while you're in the chapel. Wedding packages start at $247.22 and go up to $781.40 for the works, which includes two nights in the hotel, dinner and breakfast.

Divine Madness Fantasy Wedding Chapel *(1111 Las Vegas Boulevard South,* ☎ *(702) 384-5660 or (800) 717-4734)* lets you create your own fantasy wedding, with costumes and accessories that will make you into Tarzan and Jane, Caesar and Cleopatra, Rhett Butler and Scarlett O'Hara and more. Rentals go from $60 to $225 per person. The chapel also performs "alternative lifestyle commitments."

There are no special themes at **Bally's Celebration** *(3645 Las Vegas Blvd. South,* ☎ *(702) 739-4939* and *(800) 872-1211)*, just two somewhat elegant chapels with faux stained-glass and candelabra, that seat 50 and 20. Use of the chapel goes from $60 to $100, with packages that range from $235-$830.

The new **Orleans Hotel & Casino** *(4500 W. Tropicana Avenue, Las Vegas,* ☎ *(707) 365-7555 or toll-free (888) 365-7111)* has a pretty chapel with a marble altar area backed by a dreamy garden mural. Pew-like seats are covered in pink fabric, and the place is quite elegant. Packages start at $100 and go as high as $695, which includes two nights accommodations, a manicure and pedicure for the bride, breakfast in bed, a limo ride, photos, a video, flowers and other amenities.

The **Monte Carlo Resort & Casino**'s chapel *(3770 Las Vegas Boulevard South, Las Vegas,* ☎ *(800) 311-8999)* is also upscale. The minimum package is $285, which includes photographs, flowers and a bottle of champagne; splurge on the $850 package, and they'll throw in two nights in the hotel and lots of other goodies.

An art deco-style chapel themed like a penthouse overlooking Central Park (thanks to faux picture windows) awaits at **New York-New York** *(3155 West Harmon Avenue, Las Vegas,* ☎ *(702) 740-6969)*. The chapel is rich with gold pillars and accents and plush high-back chairs. Use of the chapel starts at $205; packages go as high as $1150, which includes two nights in a Jacuzzi room.

And what about that bungee wedding? You can really take the plunge at **A.J. Hackett Bungee** *(810 Circus Circus Drive,* ☎ *(702) 385-4321)*, where a spokesperson insists the weddings "are very lovely affairs." You take your vows atop a 180-foot-high tower while a sound system blares the song of your choice. Once you say you do, you're strapped together and off you go! Because you'll wind up upside-down, they encourage the bride to wear slacks or at least some interesting undergarments—one enterprising bride emblazoned her bloomers with "I Love Wesley." And forget a special hairdo—the idea is to dip into a pool before you pop back up. The price for this one-of-a-kind wedding starts at $300, which includes a video to show your grandkids.

Those Little Extras

You're in love, you've taken a spontaneous weekend trip to Las Vegas, you're winning at the tables—why not get married? Thousands do it that way every year—some more soberly than others. But what's a girl to do if she's only packed jeans? Why, rent a wedding gown, of course.

Designer Rentals for Her *(4559 West Flamingo Road,* ☎ *(702) 364-GOWN* or *(800) 249-5075)*, has more than 400 gowns in stock by the likes of Bob Mackie, Oleg Cassini and Jessica McClintock. Sizes run from 4-28, and prices go from $40 to $350. Similar services and prices can be found at **Rent-a-Dress & Tux Shop** *(2240 Paradise Road,* ☎ *(702) 796-6444)*, **Formal Affairs** *(4632 West Sahara Avenue,* ☎ *(702) 734-LOVE)*, **Irene's Bridal & Formal Wear** *(3049 Las Vegas Blvd. South,* ☎ *(702) 737-3858* or *(800) 889-4696)*, **Dolly's** *(3950 Las Vegas Blvd. South,* ☎ *(702) 597-5915)* and **Steppin' Out** *(1905 Las Vegas Blvd. South,* ☎ *(702) 732-7335)*. **San Francisco Sally's** *(1304 Las Vegas Blvd. South,* ☎ *(702) 385-7777* or *(800) 658-8677)* has a gorgeous collection of Victorian gowns, hats, boots, hair pieces—even earrings—for rent.

I get a kick out of the ad for **Wedding Singers** of Las Vegas: "Imagine what your friends will think when you tell them that a Las Vegas personality sang especially for you at your wedding." Imagine! Sixty dollars (and up) buys a real show girl or guy belting out a tune… "and, as proof of this event, [they] will provide you with a complimentary cassette of the actual performance." Wow! You can book as little as a day in advance, but you'll have to choose from a list of 23 songs that run the corny gamut from "Wind Beneath My Wings" to"Ava Maria" and the "Hawaiian Wedding Song." If you make reservations two weeks ahead, you get to request any song. Call ☎ *(702) 434-9775* or *(800) 574-4450*.

If you want to get to the church in style, virtually every chapel will fetch you in a limousine—for, of course, a fee.

GETTING HITCHED

SEX FOR SALE

If you're looking for love (or at least lust), Las Vegas is the place—but it will cost you dearly. Nevada is known for its legal brothels, but you won't find any in the city. (By law, only counties with less than 250,000 residents can have brothels.) The closest ones to Las Vegas are in Nye County, near Pahrump, about a 90-minute drive.

Las Vegas has very few streetwalkers, though you may glimpse a few in the downtown area. Most, however, ply their trade in the Yellow Pages under "Entertainers" and through sleazy magazines in newspaper vending machines. But keep in mind that prostitution is illegal in Las Vegas and the police take that law seriously. They bust some 40 to 50 unlucky would-be johns each month. Soliciting a prostitute is a misdemeanor that carries a six-month jail term and/or a $1000 fine. Beware: That alluring hooker may actually be an undercover cop whose only interest in handcuffs is slapping them on your wrists.

It's safer—both legally and health-wise—to try a brothel. If you're not up to the long drive (mainly over two-lane highways), just pick up the phone and they'll come get you in a limousine, free of charge.

Once you get there, you press a buzzer on the gate and a madame or hostess comes out to greet you and let you in. Depending on the house, anywhere from a few to several dozen girls will line up, and you select the one closest to your fantasies. She'll take you into a private room (or tiny trailer, as at the Chicken Ranch), where you negotiate her fee. (Money is not discussed prior to this point. These ladies can, and sometimes do, racially discriminate by demanding outrageous fees.)

Once you've agreed on exactly what you'll get and how much it will cost you, she'll closely inspect your genitals to make sure you're not carrying any obvious diseases. If you pass inspection (don't worry—she doesn't care about size), she'll wash your private parts and get down to business. Just don't expect her to kiss you on the mouth—it's never done.

You'll pay anywhere from $40.00 for a hand-job to at least $100 (and up to $200) to get laid. Condoms are mandatory, but if you are stupid enough to shun them and wave a lot of money under her nose, you may be able to pay for the privilege of contracting a venereal disease or AIDS. Wear a condom!

It's far from a glamorous life for these legal prostitutes. They undergo a complete health examination before being hired, and have weekly gynecological exams and tests for HIV, the virus that causes AIDS. They usually work in three-week shifts from 12 to 16 hours a day. If they're constantly passed over in the lineup, they'll have to try another house. The working girls are independent contractors; they pay the house half of each fee, plus a daily rent. Time is money to these girls—don't expect lots of foreplay, unless you're paying for it.

The closest brothels to Las Vegas: **the Chicken Ranch** *(the end of Homestead Road in Pahrump,* ☎ *(702) 382-7870),* **Cherry Patch Ranch** *(Ranch Road and Highway 160 in Crystal,* ☎ *(702) 372-5251)* and **Mabel's Whorehouse** *(Ranch Road and Highway 160 in Crystal,* ☎ *(702) 372-5468).* It takes a little over an hour to reach them. Farther out are **Cherry Patch II** *(86 miles north of Las Vegas in Amargosa Valley near the Route 373/Death Valley and the I-95 junction,* ☎ *(702) 372-5551)* and **Fran's Star Ranch** *(112 miles north of Las Vegas on I-95, north of Beatty,* ☎ *(702) 553-9986).*

The brothels are all pretty much the same, though Mabel's and the Cherry Patch Ranch are particular standouts, according to J.R. Schwartz, author of *The Official Guide to the Best Cat Houses in Nevada,* which has sold more than 147,000 copies. (To order, send $16.95 to *Box 1810, Boise, Idaho 83701.*) He calls Mabel's the "newest and nicest" in the entire state. The upscale Oriental-themed house has geishas who provide facials, manicures and pedicures, and what Schwartz called "exotic, beautiful women" to satisfy every whim, mainly to a Japanese clientele.

The Cherry Patch Ranch, according to Schwartz, offers everything from simple sex to Japanese baths to the electric chair and a dungeon for sadomasochistic types. Their ad features a menu with everything from enemas to spanking lessons to slave training, piercing, whips, ropes and chains.

There's also **Madame Butterfly's Bath and Massage** *(Highway 160, Crystal,* ☎ *(702) 372-5699),* which offers Japanese-style baths and massages by scantily clad or nude women. The official line is that there's no sex on the premises. Count on spending a minimum of $80 for a massage.

Those interested in the larger issues can visit the **Brothel Museum**, located at *Highway 160 and Ranch Road in the Crystal Springs Bar and Restaurant, Crystal* (☎ *(702) 372-9999).* Admission is free to these exhibits on the history of prostitution.

Those who don't want to go through the hassle of traveling at least an hour to get their thrills simply turn to the Las Vegas Yellow Pages' "Entertainment" section, which has more than 30 pages of ads for so-called escorts and entertainers, or pick up one of the thousands of sex brochures passed out day and night along the Strip and downtown. This leafleting is the bane of Las Vegas—besides being crude and crass, it causes lots of litter—but free speech rights keep them legal despite the city's efforts to wipe them out.

"These 'entertainment' services are all a front for prostitution," Lt. Bill Young of the Las Vegas Police Department's Vice Squad says flatly. "It will cost you $150 just to have her walk in the door, and that money all goes to the service. Then she will immediately negotiate a 'tip' for special services—which means sex. And that'll cost you from $300 to $500. If you don't want sex, she'll split immediately." (The same goes for the male escorts and dancers, who service both sexes.)

Despite such names as Naughty Girls, Las Vegas Playmates, Young Centerfolds and Dominant and Submissive Entertainment of Nevada, the services play it coy over the phone. They say the girls or guys only dance "for up to one hour" and insist that sex is not involved, though "tips are appreciated." That promised hour of dancing actually only lasts five or 10 minutes when it becomes apparent that no sex will be bought, Young says.

And consider this: At last count, 202 Las Vegas prostitutes tested positive for HIV. (Hookers are screened upon arrest; if they're HIV-positive and caught soliciting again, it becomes a felony.) Of those, 60 percent are female, 40 percent male. At least half of the hookers have a serious drug problem, Young says, and nearly 80 percent have pimps. These girls may make $2000 or $3000 a night, but it all goes to the boss.

You also should be careful about picking up a prostitute at the bar. Schwartz says you can spot a hooker if she's sitting alone at a casino bar late at night, nursing a drink or sipping coffee and making a lot of eye contact. He's "partied" (his euphemism for sex) with a number of Las Vegas prostitutes, paying about $100 to $150 a pop, and says the most beautiful women generally work right in Las Vegas rather than in a brothel.

But Young says men have to be on the lookout for women looking to "roll" them—going to their room with them under the pretense of having sex, but slipping a barbiturate or sleeping pill in the guy's drink before anything happens. The hapless bloke wakes up eight to 12 hours later to find his money and jewelry long gone. Some 12 to 18 men report this to the police each month, but the vast majority are too embarrassed to come forward, Young says. He adds that in April 1995, a man wearing nothing but a condom was found dead in his room at the Golden Nugget (one of the city's most respectable hotels), last seen in the company of two prostitutes.

Young says that often hookers looking to roll a guy will act as if they are tourists just looking for a good time. They'll make a beeline to a guy wearing lots of flashy jewelry and betting big at the tables. If you're fat and ugly and some cute young thing comes on to you, think twice before letting your pecker get you in trouble.

One of the biggest scams involves what Young calls "sex-tease clubs." Don't trust your friendly cabdriver who offers to take you to a place where you can have sex. You'll pay $40 at the door (which goes directly back to the cabbie), then enter a bar with nude or scantily clad young women. The bartender will try to sell you a "party package"—with prices starting at $1000 and going as high as $2500, inferring that the money will buy you sex. But once you go back into a room with a girl, all you'll get is a few minutes' conversation before she tries to get more money out of you. She'll keep talking as long as you keep paying, but you'll never get laid. Instead, once they've milked you dry, bouncers will come and throw your ass out.

The man who owns these clubs—Chaser's, Platos, Bare Babes—is currently under indictment, but the scam goes on, especially victimizing foreigners. The biggest tip-off that you're in a sex-tease club is that these places don't serve liquor because they can't get a license. They don't volunteer this fact, of course, and may actually pour you juice from a liquor bottle. Young advises looking for a tiny sign near the bar that says no alcoholic beverages are served.

That also holds true for strip clubs—if they do not serve alcohol, expect a scam. These places—Runway 69, the Can Can Room, Tally Ho—charge $5 or $6 for a glass of juice and $25 or $30 for a table dance. Often the girls are prostitutes who will go back to your hotel with you—for a price. You can bring your own booze in a paper bag as long as you keep it inconspicuously under the table.

There are some legitimate strip clubs where you can look but not touch. **The Palomino** (1848 Las Vegas Blvd. South, ☎ (702) 642-2984) is the only club in town that offers totally nude dancers and has a liquor license (that's because it is technically in North Las Vegas). It's open from 1:30 p.m.–4 a.m. and costs $10 to get in, plus a two-drink minimum ($6 each).

The Girls of Glitter Gulch (on Fremont Street across from the Golden Nugget, ☎ (702) 385-4774) only strip above the waist (and wear a tiny g-string below). There's no cover but you'll have to pay for at least two drinks at $5.75 each. They're open from 11 a.m.–5 a.m.

You can get cheap thrills at the **Crazy Horse Too Topless Saloon** (2476 Industrial Road, ☎ (702) 382-8003) which is open 24 hours and charges just $5 to get in, plus a one-drink minimum ($3.75). They're also open 24 hours at **Crazy Horse** (same name, different owners) and charge no cover until 7 p.m. Then it's $5 to get in and a one-drink minimum (about $3.50). They're at *4034 Paradise Road,* ☎ *(702) 732-1116.*

Other strip clubs that serve liquor:

Club Paradise

4416 Paradise Road, Las Vegas, (702) 734-7990.
The classiest of the topless bars. Open from 6 p.m. to 6 a.m. Cover charge is $10.

Lacy's

1848 Las Vegas Boulevard North, Las Vegas, ☎ *(702) 399-3144.*
Open from 9 p.m. nightly.

Satin Saddle Club

1818 Las Vegas Boulevard North, Las Vegas, ☎ *(702) 649-3590.*
Open from 5 p.m. nightly.

Olympic Garden

1531 Las Vegas Boulevard South, Las Vegas, ☎ *(702) 385-8987.*
Has a daily topless cabaret and the Dream Team Male Revue each Friday and Saturday night. Open 2 p.m. to 6 a.m.

Totally Nude Clubs (no liquor served)

Can-Can Room

3155 Industrial Road, Las Vegas, ☎ *(702) 737-1161.*
Open from 7 p.m. to 5 a.m. daily. $10 cover charge plus a two-drink minimum (drinks are about $5 each).

Tally-Ho

2580 S. Highland Drive, Las Vegas, ☎ *(702) 792-9330.*
Open 24 hours, admission $10.

Wild J's Book and Video

2923 Industrial Road, Las Vegas, ☎ *(702) 892-0416.*
Has a "Totally Nude Review" and monthly shows by porn stars. It's also "home of the 2 for 1 lap dance," and an ATM is thoughtfully provided on premises. Open noon–4 a.m.

Talk of the Town

1238 Las Vegas Boulevard South, Las Vegas, ☎ *(702) 385-1800.*
Has totally nude dancers plus fantasy booths in which you can buy a private dance (through glass). The video store is open 24 hours; dancers work from 4 p.m. to 4 a.m. No cover charge from 4–6 p.m. but a one drink ($3) minimum; after 6 p.m., there's a $12 cover charge, which includes one drink.

Realize that when you get in a taxi and ask the driver to take you to a strip club, he's taking you where he gets a kickback—usually $10 to $15 per person.

Finally, **Hot Spots of Nevada** (☎ *(702) 372-5522)* is a hotline that gives information on brothels, men's clubs, massage parlors, adult novelty shops and the like. And if you're feeling frisky but don't want to go too far, consider a trim at **A Little Off the Top**

(5720 West Charleston, Las Vegas, ☎ (702) 258-5411), which features women in lingerie cutting your hair.

So what if you really want to get laid, don't want to travel to Pahrump or Crystal and are smart enough to stay away from the hookers? "Bring your wife or girlfriend," Young laughs. "Or you can always find a tourist who is looking for a good time." Just be sure that self-proclaimed schoolteacher from Des Moines is not really a working girl with a pocket full of mickeys.

DAY TRIPS

To get back to nature, head out to nearby Red Rock Canyon where skies are blue, and there's not a neon sign in sight.

Las Vegas may be stuck out in the middle of the desert, but there are still many entertaining diversions far from the neon lights and clatter of coins. You can inspect ancient Indian petroglyphs, sweat out the hottest spot in the nation or ride the world's most daring roller coaster. It's doubtful anyone has ever done it, but Las Vegans like to brag that you can both snow ski and water ski in the same day—heading first to Lee Canyon for some downhill action, then over to Lake Mead and its lovely blue waters.

Mount Charleston

A whole other world awaits just 36 miles from the Strip. Mount Charleston, part of the Spring Mountain Range of the Toiyabe National Forest, looms 11,918 above sea level and offers year-round recreation.

You can ski and sled in its snow (man-made and natural) at Lee Canyon, a small gem of a ski resort where lift tickets are cheap

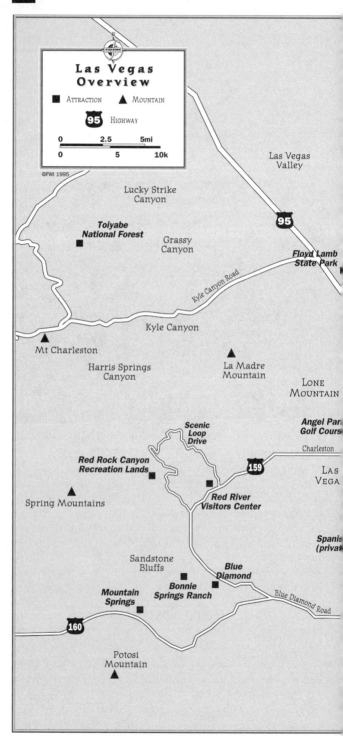

Las Vegas
Overview

■ ATTRACTION   ▲ MOUNTAIN

95 HIGHWAY

0   2.5   5mi
0   5   10k

©FWI 1995

Las Vegas
Valley

Lucky Strike
Canyon

*Toiyabe
National Forest*
■

Grassy
Canyon

95

*Floyd Lamb
State Park*

Kyle Canyon Road

Kyle Canyon

▲
Mt Charleston

Harris Springs
Canyon

▲
La Madre
Mountain

LONE
MOUNTAIN

*Scenic
Loop
Drive*

*Angel Par
Golf Cours*

Charleston

*Red Rock Canyon
Recreation Lands*
■

159

LAS
VEGA

▲
Spring Mountains

■
*Red River
Visitors Center*

Sandstone
Bluffs

*Blue
Diamond*
■

*Spanis
(privat*

■

*Mountain
Springs*
■

*Bonnie
Springs Ranch*

Blue Diamond Road

160

Potosi
Mountain
▲

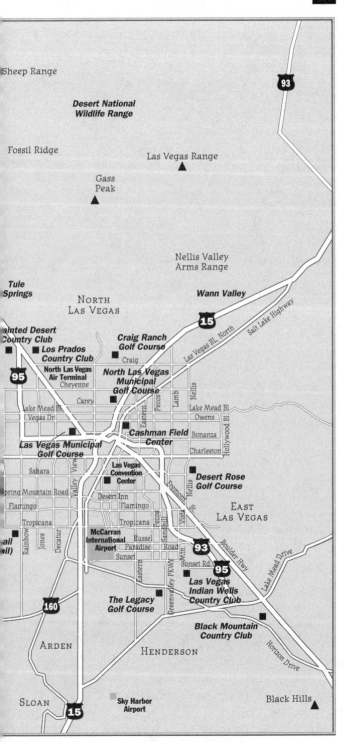

Sheep Range

Desert National Wildlife Range

Fossil Ridge

Las Vegas Range ▲

Gass Peak ▲

Nellis Valley Arms Range

Wann Valley

Tule Springs

NORTH LAS VEGAS

93

ainted Desert Country Club ■

Los Prados Country Club ■

95

Craig Ranch Golf Course

Craig

Las Vegas Bl, North

Salt Lake Highway

15

North Las Vegas Air Terminal ■
Cheyenne

North Las Vegas Municipal Golf Course ■

Carey

Lake Mead Bl.
Vegas Dr

Lake Mead Bl

Owens

Bonanza

Charleston

Nellis

Pecos

Lamb

Eastern

Hollywood Bl

Cashman Field Center ■

Las Vegas Municipal Golf Course

Sahara

Valley View

Las Vegas Convention Center ■

Desert Inn

Flamingo

Fremont St.

Nellis

Vista

Desert Rose Golf Course ■

EAST LAS VEGAS

pring Mountain Road

Flamingo

Flamingo

Tropicana

Tropicana

ail
il)

Rainbow

Jones

Decatur

McCarran International Airport

Russel
Paradise
Road

Sunset

Pecos

Sandhill

Eastern

Greenway PKWY

Mtn.

93

Sunset Rd.

95

Boulder Hwy

Lake Mead Drive

160

The Legacy Golf Course ■

Las Vegas Indian Wells Country Club ■

Black Mountain Country Club ■

ARDEN

HENDERSON

Horizon Drive

SLOAN

15

Sky Harbor Airport

Black Hills ▲

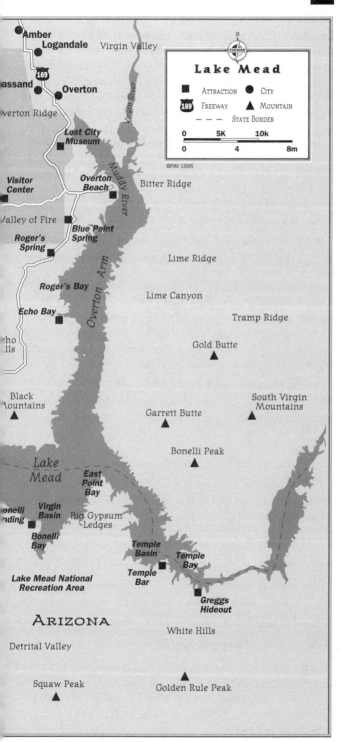

Amber
Logandale   Virgin Valley

assand   169   Overton

verton Ridge

Lost City Museum

```
                    N
              FIELDING
     Lake Mead
  ■  ATTRACTION    ●  CITY
 169  FREEWAY      ▲  MOUNTAIN
 - - -  STATE BORDER
 0        5K        10k
 0         4         8m
©FWI 1995
```

Visitor Center

Overton Beach   Bitter Ridge

Valley of Fire
Roger's Spring   *Blue Point Spring*

Roger's Bay   Lime Ridge

Overton Arm   Lime Canyon

Echo Bay   Tramp Ridge

ho
lls   Gold Butte ▲

Black Mountains ▲

South Virgin Mountains ▲

Garrett Butte ▲

Bonelli Peak ▲

Lake Mead

East Point Bay

onelli nding   *Virgin Basin*   Big Gypsum Ledges

Bonelli Bay

Temple Basin   *Temple Bay*

Lake Mead National Recreation Area   *Temple Bar*

Greggs Hideout

ARIZONA   White Hills

Detrital Valley

Squaw Peak ▲   Golden Rule Peak ▲

($27) and lines short. There are only two chairlifts (plus one for the bunny slope) and 10 runs—with names like Slot Alley and The Strip—but conditions are usually pretty decent. The season generally runs from Easter to Thanksgiving. Lee Canyon may be small, but it's still a full-service ski area. It has an extensive snow-making system, a rental shop, ski school, coffeeshop, cocktail lounge and sundeck. There's also night skiing until 10. Call ☎ *(702) 872-5462* for general information, ☎ *(702) 593-9500* for road conditions. The **Lee Canyon Bus** (☎ *(702) 646-0008*) makes daily trips from Jackie Gaughn's Plaza at 7 a.m. and the Santa Fe at 7:30 a.m., leaving the slopes at 4:30 p.m. The ride is free when you purchase a lift ticket. Understandably, this is quite popular, so make reservations as early as possible or at least three or four days in advance. (See "Attractions" for further details.)

The very atmospheric **Mt. Charleston Lodge** *(Route 157,* ☎ *(702) 386-5500)*, a bar and restaurant, offers sleigh rides each winter day from 10 a.m.–6 p.m., and occasionally later into the night during a full moon or holiday like New Year's Eve. Each sleigh holds up to nine people and is pulled by two magnificent Clydesdale or Belgian horses. The 25-minute scenic ride costs $8 for adults, $6 for kids. They also have several brand-new cabins that cost $95 to $200 per night, depending on the season. The rates include a Continental breakfast served in your room.

The **Mt. Charleston Hotel** *(2 Kyle Canyon Road,* ☎ *(702) 872-5500 or 800-794-3456)* is a pretty alpine-style stone structure with great views from the comfortable guestrooms. The sights are stunning from the glass-enclosed Cliffhanger Lounge where a roaring fire keeps folks toasty. And, of course, there's a slot casino. Rates are $59–$62 on weekdays, $69–$79 weekends. Suites with a balcony and fireplace go for $155.

When the snow melts, Lee Canyon becomes a haven for hikers, fishers and picnickers. The Mount Charleston National Recreation Trail ascends the 11,918-foot summit of Charleston Peak, Nevada's fourth-highest peak. There are several less-strenuous trails as well.

Camping is permitted from May 1 to September 30 at $8 per day. Some are first come, first served, while others can be reserved from 10–120 days in advance. Call ☎ *(800) 280-2267* for reservations. You can also do walk-in snow camping if your car can be parked safely off the highway.

To get to Mt. Charleston, take the I-15 north to the Kyle Canyon Turnoff, then Kyle Canyon Road (Route 57) for another 15 minutes. Driving time from Las Vegas is about one hour. For general information on Mt. Charleston, call the Ranger Station at ☎ *(702) 872-5486.*

Hoover Dam

A few years ago, I went to Las Vegas with my family. One day I was happily sunning at the Flamingo Hilton's pool when my dad got the bright idea to visit Hoover Dam. No one wanted to go, so I reluctantly dragged myself from my lounge chair, got dressed and went along to keep him company.

Dad died shortly afterwards. I'll always remember my mom saying, "Aren't you glad you went to Hoover Dam?"

And how! But actually, though it was agony to leave the sun and my piña colada behind, the tour was well worth the time and effort. Hoover Dam is one of the easier day trips to take from Las Vegas. It's only 34 miles away and guided tours of the facility are conducted every few minutes. The dam is considered one of the seven engineering wonders of the world and is truly an awesome sight. And the surrounding area, crowned by Lake Mead, is splendidly scenic.

Hoover Dam was authorized by Congress in 1928 as a way to control the rampant flooding of the Colorado River and to maintain a controlled and reliable source of water. The dam's construction included the creation of Lake Mead, which supplies water to some 25 million people, including Las Vegans.

More than 5000 people were employed on the project; 96 workers perished on the site. The entire project used some 4.4 million yards of concrete, enough to build a two-lane highway from San Francisco to New York. It cost about $60 million to build and—get this—was finished two years ahead of schedule.

Dedicated by President Franklin Roosevelt on September 30, 1935, Hoover Dam is 726 feet high. Its 17 generators produce four to five billion kilowatt-hours of electricity each year—enough power to supply half a million homes, and to keep the neon lights of Las Vegas glowing. The arch-gravity dam is 660 feet thick at its base, and its spillways are 50 feet in diameter.

More than 30 million visitors have toured the dam since its opening. The 35-minute tour takes you deep into the bowels of the dam, past its giant generators and through one of the original tunnels blasted out for its construction. It costs $6, $5 for seniors and $2 for kids 6–16. A one-hour, behind-the-scenes hard-hat tour is $25.

To get to Hoover Dam, take I-93/95 south to I-93 south. You'll pass through Henderson (site of the Kidd Marshmallow Factory, Cranberry World West and the Ethel M Chocolates Factory—see "Attractions") and Boulder City, a small town born during the dam's construction that is listed on the National Register of Historic Places.

Lake Mead

Gorgeous Lake Mead was created in the building of Hoover Dam, and back then, the government sure knew how to do things right. The man-made lake is enormous (twice the size of Rhode Island), with 550 miles of craggy shoreline and lots of private, sheltered coves for peaceful boating and fishing. It begins about 25 miles from Las Vegas and extends far east to Arizona and south to Cottonwood Cove, where Lake Mohave begins. The surrounding desert is comprised of spectacular canyons and jagged mountains that are home to bighorn sheep, mule deer, coyotes, kit fox, bobcat, ringtail cat, desert tortoise and lots of birds, lizards and snakes (including rattlers).

A good place to start out your visit is at the Alan Bible Visitor Center, four miles northeast of Boulder City on I-93, open daily from 8:30 a.m.–4:30 p.m. Here you can watch an introductory movie, browse through the exhibits and talk to the rangers. There's a neat botanical garden here with some of the area's most interesting desert trees, shrubs and cacti.

Lake Mead has several developed areas with visitor services. Those closest to Las Vegas are Las Vegas Bay, Boulder Beach and Callville Bay. **The Lake Mead Lodge** *(322 Lakeshore Road, Boulder City, NV 89005,* ☎ *(702) 293-2074)* at Boulder Beach provides lodging right near the water. This peaceful retreat has basic rooms (no phones) for $53–$65. One suite has a fireplace and kitchen for $125 a night. Also worth checking out is **Echo Bay Resort** *(☎ (702) 394-4000)*, a peaceful little oasis, with pretty views of Lake Mead from some rooms. The on-site bar is a great place to wax poetic about the desert. Rooms go for $70–$85.

RVs can spend the night at **Callville Bay** *(☎ (702) 565-8958)*, where they have hookups, or at any of the campgrounds in the developed areas, which have no hookups. Camp sites are available on a first-come, first-served basis and cost $8 per night. Because of fluctuating water levels, all the campgrounds are located well off the lake, but usually within walking distance.

While the entire area is open to hikers, there are few developed trails. One of the best is the 2.6-mile **Historic Railroad Trail**, which traces part of the route of an old railroad built for the construction of Hoover Dam. The trail passes by many rock tunnels and was the site of a scene from the Clint Eastwood film *The Gauntlet*. Temperatures well over 100 degrees make hiking in the summer impractical—if not suicidal.

The best way to experience Lake Mead is to be on it (and in it in the warmer months, when the water temperature hovers around 80 degrees). You can take a lunch or dinner cruise, rent a motorboat or set sail for a few days on a houseboat.

SilverLine (☎ *(702) 733-8283)* offers a three-hour sunset cruise on a triple-deck steamwheeler that includes dinner, dancing and round-trip transportation from your hotel for $55. **America's Travel Company** (☎ *(702) 456-1355)* conducts an all-day tour of Hoover Dam and a 1.5-hour cruise on Lake Mead for $33, while **Ray & Ross Transport** (☎ *(702) 646-4661)* offers a similar tour for $31.90. Check the tourist magazines for other options and frequently offered two-for-one coupons. Finally, **Lake Mead Cruises** has the *Desert Princess*, an authentic paddlewheeler that can be combined with a tour of Hoover Dam. Call ☎ *(702) 293-6180.*

For houseboating, try Forever Resorts at **Callville Bay Marina** (☎ *(800) 255-5561)*. This company rents houseboats that sleep up to 10 and include everything from linens to fully equipped kitchens to barbecue grills. Prices start at $795 for three or four nights during the winter season (November 1–May 6) and go as high as $1895 from June 14–September 5. **Seven Crown Resorts** (☎ *(800) 752-9669)* also rents houseboats for three to seven days.

Finally, you can float down the Colorado River on Lake Mohave with **Black Canyon Raft Tours** (☎ *702) 293-3776)* (see "Attractions" for details).

To get to the visitor's center, take I-95 (Boulder Highway) to I-93 east. For general information on Lake Mead, call the Superintendent's Office at ☎ *(702) 293-8906* or write to *601 Nevada Highway, Boulder City, NV 89005.* The entrance fee to the park is $5.

Valley of Fire State Park

Valley of Fire State Park offers Native American stone carvings dating back to 300 B.C. and dramatic sunset views of the sandstone rock formations.

Those who appreciate the subtle beauty of the desert love Valley of Fire, a large state park located 52 miles northeast of Las

Vegas. It occupies a basin some six miles long and three to four miles wide. Its jagged walls contain formations of eroded red sandstone that appear to be ablaze when reflecting the sun's rays—hence the name. Petroglyphs (stone carvings) in the area date from 300 B.C. to A.D. 1150. They are the legacy of the Basketmaker people and later, the Anasazi Pueblo farmers. Take the quarter-mile Mouse Tank trail for a good view of the petroglyphs and petrified wood. A new six-mile road runs from the Rainbow Vista lookout point to the White Domes area, a series of giant sandstone formations once submerged under an ancient inland sea. If you're lucky, you'll spot bighorn sheep and wild burros.

The visitor center, located on SR 169, is open daily from 8:30 a.m.–4:30 p.m. and offers trail maps and exhibits on the park. Call ☎ *(702) 397-2088* for details.

Admission is $4 per vehicle and can be paid at the visitor center or at honor boards at the park's entrance.

To get to Valley of the Fire, take I-15 north about 45 miles to the state park exit. If you're visiting in the late spring or summer months, come early in the morning; the afternoon heat often tops 100 degrees and is very oppressive.

While in the area, check out the interesting **Lost City Museum**, which contains artifacts from the Anasazi Indians who once lived along the Muddy River. The grounds include several Pueblo-type houses constructed of wattle and daub. (See "Attractions" for details.)

Red Rock Canyon

It only takes about half an hour to get to Red Rock Canyon, a strikingly beautiful slice of nature that is the perfect antidote to the smoky, crowded casinos in town. The canyon was formed by a thrust fault—a fracture in the earth's crust where one rock plate is trust horizontally over another. The red sandstone and gray limestone formations have been carved to dramatic perfection over the eons by the ever-present wind. The area was once home to the Paiute Indians. Red Rock, a national conservation area, is being expanded to more than 100,000 acres thanks to a congressional act.

A 13-mile scenic loop winds through high-desert terrain; you may catch a glimpse of bighorn sheep and wild burros. (Frequently posted signs warn of big fines for feeding the burros—plus, as the signs add, they bite!)

Numerous hiking rails will take you to the ruins of an old homestead, a spring and a waterfall. Stop by the visitor center (☎ *(702) 363-1921*) for trail maps and exhibits on the area. Admission is free.

Spring Mountain Ranch State Park lies within the boundaries of Red Rock Canyon. The 500-acre ranch has great views and a great roster of former owners, including Howard Hughes and German actress Vera Krupp. Special events and activities take place here throughout the year; call ☎ *875-4141* for information. Park entry is $4 per vehicle; hours are 8 a.m.–dusk.

In the summertime, the **Theater Under the Stars** *(☎ (702) 594-7529)* holds concerts on the lawn in front of the 1869 ranch house; call for a schedule.

While you're in the area, you may want to stop by Old Nevada, a nicely done re-creation of an old Western mining town (see "Attractions"). Right next door is the **Bonnie Springs Ranch**, where there's a decent restaurant (open 8 a.m.–11 p.m.), a free petting zoo and stagecoach rides on weekends and holidays ($5 adults, $3 children.) They also offer one-hour trail rides on horseback from 9 a.m. to 5:45 p.m. in the summer, 9 a.m. to 3:15 p.m. in the winter. The cost is $16.50.

Bonnie Springs Motel offers the only lodging in the immediate area. Rooms run the gamut from standard motel units ($55-$75) to one-bedroom kitchen suites ($85–$95) to theme rooms with in-room Jacuzzis and Chinese, Spanish, American Indian or Gay '90s decor. These cost $110–$125 per night.

To get to Red Rock, take I-15 south to Route 160 to Route 159 north.

Death Valley

It sure doesn't sound like much, but Death Valley is actually quite fascinating. More than a million people learned that in 1993, the first time the 62-year-old park broke the one million visitor mark. Until 1994, Death Valley was a designated national monument; it's now a national park. The valley began forming some three million years ago when the Earth's crust broke into blocks, some of which tilted and rotated to create the area's alternating mountain and valley pattern. Large salt deposits, left during the ice ages when lakes occupied the basin, are still visible today. The valley was home to several Indian tribes.

Death Valley is 120 miles long and from four to 16 miles in width. Everything is a study in contrasts. There are sculpted rocks, undulating sand dunes, Indian petroglyphs, hot springs and volcanic craters and more than 900 species of trees and plants in the park, 21 that are unique to the valley, including Death Valley sage and rattleweed. Bristlecone pines, thousands of years old, grow at 10,000-foot elevations on Telescope Peak. In the springtime, the wildflowers are legendary, especially after a rainy winter. The lowest point is 282 feet below sea level—the lowest point in the entire Western Hemisphere—while Telescope Peak, the highest point, soars to 11,049 feet.

More than 500 miles of roadways traverse the park, and there are lots of opportunities for hiking. It's best visited anytime but summer—temperatures of 100 degrees are common then, and once, in 1913, it soared all the way to a hellish 134 degrees.

The **Furnace Creek Visitor Center** (☎ *619-786-2331*) is open daily from 8 a.m.–7 p.m. Stop by to pick up a trail map, peruse the exhibits and view a short film on the park. Admission to the park is $10 per vehicle.

Other spots worth visiting in the park: the **Borax Museum**, near the visitor center, which showcases tools once used in extracting and refining borax and other minerals; the spectacular scenic view from **Dante's View**; and the five- to 10-million-year-old lake beds at **Zabriskie Point** and **Ubehebe Crater**, an 800-foot-deep depression created 3,000 years ago by a volcanic explosion. And don't miss **Scotty's Castle** in the northern part of the park, where rangers costumed in 1930s garb conduct tours of the elaborately furnished Spanish-Moorish mansion. Admission is $6.

Death Valley has three choices for overnight lodging. The most luxurious is the **Furnace Creek Inn** (☎ *619-786-2361*), located a mile from the visitor center. Amenities include an 18-hole championship golf course (214 feet below sea level!), four tennis courts, a full health club, an archery range and palm-studded terrace gardens. Rates at this very special site are $210 to $350, and it's open only from October to May. The nearby **Furnace Creek Ranch** (☎ *619-786-2345 or 800-528-6367*), open all year, is also quite nice and much more affordable, with rates in the $65–$100 range. Both facilities offer horseback riding, hayrides and carriage rides.

The motel-style **Stove Pipes Wells Village** (☎ *619-786-2387*), located 24 miles northwest of the visitor center, is also open year-round. It has a pool and restaurant but little else in the way of amenities. (In fact, the water in some of the rooms is unsuitable for drinking.) Rates are $50–$70.

It's believed that the valley got its macabre name in 1849, when men flush with gold fever mistakenly took it for a shortcut and got lost. There is actually only one confirmed death of a pioneer from those days, though it's believed that a party of nine may have also perished in the valley.

To get to Death Valley, take I-95 north to Lathrop Wells, then turn at the Death Valley junction. SilverLine Tours offers day trips to Death Valley that stop at Furnace Creek Ranch, Dante's View and other highlights, then swings by the Pahrump Winery for a tour and lunch on the way back to Las Vegas. It costs $99.50 per person; call ☎ *(702) 733-8283*. Wild West Tours offers a similar package; call ☎ *(702) 731-2425*.

Grand Canyon

Considered the greatest natural wonder of the world, the Grand Canyon is a bit of a stretch for a day trip—it's 300 miles away and takes six hours to get to the South Rim—but some folks spend a few days in its natural splendor, then head for Las Vegas for its man-made splendors (or vice versa).

You'll have to plan this far in advance if you have any hope of getting a hotel room at or near the canyon. If that's not possible and you're dying to see the canyon, take one of the flyovers detailed in the "Attractions" section.

The South Rim is open all year, while the North Rim is usually accessible from mid-May to mid-November, depending on the weather. Though the two rims are only 10 miles apart as the crow flies, the road separating them is more than 215 miles long and takes five hours to drive. Entrance to the park is $10 per vehicle.

All lodging within the South Rim is handled through **Grand Canyon National Park Lodges** (*P.O. Box 699, Grand Canyon, AZ 86023;* ☎ *520-638-2401*). Accommodations range from rustic cabins to basic motel rooms to swank suites; prices range from $37 to $300 per night. RV campers can hookup at **Trailer Village** for $16 per night; call ☎ *(520) 638-2401* for reservations. Tent campers can reserve sites by calling **MISTRIX** (☎ *800-365-2267 and 619-452-8787*) no more than eight weeks in advance, or cross their fingers and hope to get into one of the first-come, first-served sites for $10 per night.

Sixteen trails and numerous obscure routes provide access to the inner canyon. Most are recommended only for the most seasoned of hikers; 10 people fell to their deaths in 1993 alone.

Accordingly, the most popular way to see the inner canyon is on mule. You can take a half-day trip or one that lasts two days and includes overnight lodging at the **Phantom Ranch**, set all the way on the canyon bottom. These trips are in great demand and sell out fast. You can make reservations 11 months in advance by calling **Grand Canyon National Park Lodges** (☎ *520-638-2401*). Riders must be over four feet seven inches and, for the sake of the poor mules, weigh less than 200 pounds. One-day trips cost $105.61 while the overnighter goes for $261.77. Hikers are welcome to spend the night at the Phantom in a dormitory ($22.27) or cabin ($56.21).

Nearly 20 companies run river trips on the Colorado through the Grand Canyon that last anywhere from one day to several weeks. Among them: **Aramark-Wilderness River Adventures** (☎ *800-992-8022*), **Canyon Explorations** (☎ *800-654-0723*), **Diamond River Adventures** (☎ *800-343-3121*), **Grand Canyon Dories** (☎ *209-736-0805*) and **Outdoors Unlimited** (☎ *800-367-7238*).

To get to the South Rim from Las Vegas, go southeast on I-93 to Kingman, then east on I-40 to Williams, and north on Route 64. For general information, call ☎ *(520) 638-7888* or write to *P.O. Box 129, Grand Canyon, AZ 86023.*

Laughlin

For years just a tiny speck on the map (if it even made it onto the map), Laughlin has become Nevada's boom town. Why? Gaming, of course. A man named Don Laughlin, a true visionary, started the town up less than 30 years ago, though it didn't really start taking off until the late 1980s. Today, Laughlin is the state's fastest-growing city, boasting 11 large casino-hotels and more than 11,000 rooms.

Set on the banks of the Colorado River some 90 miles south of Las Vegas, Laughlin is just a stone's throw from Bullhead City and Lake Havasu, Arizona; ferries carry gamblers back and forth between the two states. The town lures some five million visitors each year, mainly a blue-haired crowd of retirees. Buffets, nickel slots and has-beens (or never-wills) in the lounges are the big thing here.

There's some golf and tennis, boat rides and jet skiing, and hiking and fishing, but the real reason people flock to Laughlin is to gamble—and take advantage of the town's incredibly cheap rates. Rooms on weekdays go in the neighborhood of $15, and you can pay as little as $28 even on the weekends. It goes up from there, but rooms are always a good deal, even when they reach as high as $75, which is rare. And the limits at the tables are low, low, low.

The road from Las Vegas to Laughlin winds through some pretty desert scenery, but the town is not really special enough to warrant a day trip. It can be a decent place to spend a few (cheap) nights, but Las Vegas it ain't. Young hipsters will be bemused—and a bit bored.

Among the better casino-hotels are the **Colorado Belle** (☎ *(702) 298-4000* and *800-458-9500*), **Flamingo Hilton** (☎ *(702) 298-5111* and *800-352-6464*), **Golden Nugget** (☎ *(702) 298-7111* and *800-237-1739*) and **Harrah's** (☎ *(702) 298-4600* and *800-427-7247*).

To get to Laughlin, take I-95 south to Route 163 east—or better yet, catch one of the buses that not only take you there for free, but throw in a buffet and discount coupons too. Reservations are necessary; call **One Stop Travel** (☎ *(702) 898-9800*) or **Teddy Bear Express** (☎ *(702) 737-6062*).

For general information, contact the **Laughlin Visitors Bureau** at *1555 Casino Drive,* ☎ *(702) 298-3321* and *(800) 452-8445.*

Mesquite

Located some 80 miles northwest of Las Vegas, Mesquite is quickly becoming one of Nevada's new boomtowns. The population is expected to double every five years at its current rate of growth. Hopefully it won't grow too much, though, as the area's charms lie in its small-town feel. It's pretty and laid-back, accommodations are a bargain, there are four golf courses with greens fees of just $20 to $80, and the atmosphere is much more relaxed than the frenetic pace of Las Vegas.

The premier property in town is **Players Island** (☎ *(800) 896-4567 or (702) 346-7529)*, a resort so lavish it seems somewhat out of place in this unassuming community. Rates are high for the area—$45 to $89—but a real steal compared to what you'd pay for comparable accommodations in a more established destination. The resort is quite lush with a great swimming pool and upscale spa.

Other Mesquite properties include the **Oasis** (☎ *(800) 621-0187 or (702) 346-5232)*, whose rooms are $29 to $59, and the **Virgin River Hotel Casino** (☎ *(800) 346-7721 or (702) 346-7777)*, where rates start at just $24 on weeknights.

Primm

There was never much reason to visit Primm (formerly known as Stateline) unless you were already passing it en route from Southern California, but now this border town, 42 miles south of Las Vegas, is attracting lots of day-trippers with the **Desperado**, the world's largest and fastest roller coaster. If you're really into dips, swirls and heart-stopping plunges, it's worth the 50-minute drive to Buffalo Bill's. More sane types can ride the free choo-choo or Ferris Wheel next door at the **Primm Valley Resort & Casino** (formerly the Primadonna). Across the freeway at **Whiskey Pete's**, they proudly display the authentic car—complete with shattered glass and scores of bulletholes—in which Bonnie and Clyde met their demise.

Stateline became Primm in 1997 to honor Ernest J. Primm, who founded the area that today houses three casinos and two golf courses, all operated by Primadonna Resorts. (Hey, if Don Laughlin can name his town after himself, why not Ernest?)

Teddy Bear Express (☎ *(702) 737-6062)* will take you to Primm for free and even throw in lunch. They want you to gamble, of course, but no one will know if you sneak off to the rides instead.

Where to Stay in Primm

Las Vegas is located some 43 miles from the California border, but you can start gambling as soon as you cross the state line. This area is coming into its own as a destination, thanks to the company that owns the three large casino-hotels there. Whiskey Pete's is the oldest and nothing to get excited about, but across the I-15 freeway (and connected via a free monorail) there's tons to do at the Primm Valley and Buffalo Bill's, including free Ferris wheel and train rides, a bowling alley and the world's biggest roller coaster.

Rooms here at Primm (formerly called Stateline) are much, much cheaper than in Las Vegas, and there really is enough to do to fill a weekend happily.

Buffalo Bill's $23–$43   ★★★★

I-15 at the California border, Primm, 89193, *(800) 367-7383, (702) 382-1111, FAX: (702) 874-1749.*

Located next to the Primadonna. Double: $23–$43.

I am really impressed with this $90 million resort, which was opened in August 1994 by the same folks who own the nearby Primm Valley and Whiskey Pete's. The outside resembles a huge red barn—that strange yellow thing wrapping around it is "The Desperado," the world's largest and fastest roller coaster. Everything inside is themed to the rafters, and it all looks quite grand, with colorful Old West facades, large trees, a river running through, miners working on overhead tracks—you get the idea. Besides the roller coaster, there's a log flume ride; both hurl through the casino at various stages (see "Attractions" for more on these rides). Kids are also kept happy at motion simulator theaters, a video arcade, the carnival-style midway and waterslides outside in the buffalo-shaped pool. There's also the Star of the Desert arena, a 6500-seat indoor theater; four restaurants; numerous lounges with country-western bands; and comfortable, Western-style guest rooms. All this for rates that start at $23 on weekdays and $43 on the weekends! This place is so successful that immediately after opening, it added another 600 rooms—and I wouldn't be surprised to see it keep expanding. The best out-to-town choice by far. 1214 rooms. Credit cards: A, CB, DC, D, MC, V.

Primm Valley Resort & Casino $23–$43   ★★★

I-15 at the California border, Primm, 89193, *(800) 367-7383, (702) 382-1212, FAX: (702) 874-1749.*

Located next to Buffalo Bill's. Double: $23–$43.

Drivers heading to Las Vegas from Southern California often make a pilgrimage stop at this large resort 43 miles south of Vegas. There's a ton of free stuff to keep you happy here, including a Ferris Wheel (especially fun at night), carousel and monorail to Whiskey Pete's across the freeway. Inside, there's a huge kiddie arcade and small bowling alley. The Victorian-themed casino, formerly known as the Primadonna, gets quite crowded on the weekends; come-ons such as 50-cent shrimp cocktails entice many to drop in. Guest rooms are surprisingly large and nice and include the always-welcome coffeemaker, but the low-market restaurants are merely adequate. The pool is situated in a pleasant courtyard. The hotel is owned by the same folks who have the neighboring Buffalo Bill's and Whiskey Pete's. Together, the three offer enough diversions to keep you happy for a few days, and it's much cheaper than Las Vegas. Amenities: conference facilities. 661 rooms. Credit cards: A, CB, DC, D, MC, V.

Whiskey Pete's $23–$43 ★★

I-15 at the California border, Primm, 89193, ☎ *(800) 367-7383, (702) 382-1212, FAX: (702) 874-1749.*

Located across from the Primm Valley Resort and Buffalo Bill's. Double: $23–$43.

This is a popular place for California motorists heading home to try their luck one last time. As a result, the casino gets very crowded, especially on weekends. Whiskey Pete's is a sister property to the Primm Valley Resort and Buffalo Bill's, both located across the freeway and connected via monorail (though you can probably walk across the underpass in the same time it takes to wait in line). It should be considered the third choice, as the other two offer more bells and whistles for about the same price. Pete's biggest claim to fame—and it milks it for all it's worth—is displaying the actual car, bullet holes and all, in which Bonnie and Clyde were gunned down. Like its sister properties, the guest rooms are basic but comfortable and the restaurants cheap but nondescript. 777 rooms. Credit cards: A, CB, DC, D, MC, V.

Jean

There's not much to the tiny town of Jean, located 34 miles south of Las Vegas, except a prison and two casinos, the Nevada Landing and the Gold Strike (neither worth a special trip). Eight miles northwest of Jean is the historic mining town of Goodsprings, now a virtual ghost town but worth a visit for its Pioneer Saloon, established in 1913 and one of Nevada's oldest operating bars.

Where to Stay in Jean

Jean's two casino-hotels, the Gold Strike and Nevada Landing aren't very impressive, but the rates are cheap and it's usually easy to snag a room. They'll also let you stay just a Saturday night, which is virtually impossible anywhere else.

Gold Strike $19–$39 ★★★

1 Main Street, Jean, 89193, ☎ *(800) 634-1359, (702) 477-5000, FAX: (702) 874-1583.*

Located across from Nevada Landing. Single: $19–$39. Double: $19–$39.

Situated right on I-15 opposite the Nevada Landing, this Wild West-themed hotel is 34 miles south of Las Vegas. Lots of eager gamblers driving in from Southern California stop by the casino to warm up on their way to the Strip. The very reasonable rates make it a good alternative to Vegas on the crowded weekends, but don't come expecting the same high-tech glitz. The Western-themed casino is nothing special, but the betting minimums are low and the excellent live bands add a partying atmosphere. If you like the one-arm bandits, sign up for their slot club; it takes no time at all to earn free meals and a comp room for the future. Guest rooms are quite basic but surprisingly spacious. Such low-frills amenities as plastic drinking cups and soap the size of a pat of butter reflect the rates—as does the Burger King off the casino. But the Steak House restaurant is a real find and quite unexpected in this blue collar haven (see "Restaurants"). Better than the Nevada Landing, but not as good as the hotels in Primm. 800 rooms. Credit cards: A, DC, D, MC, V.

Nevada Landing $21–$34   ★ ★

2 Goodsprings Road, Jean, 89193, ☎ *(800) 628-6682, (702) 387-5000, FAX: (702) 874-1399.*

Located on the I-15, across from the Gold Strike. Double: $21–$34.

Designed to look like a giant paddlewheeler (never mind this is the middle of the desert), Nevada Landing is 34 miles south of Las Vegas, making it a popular spot when Vegas sells out, as is often the case on weekends. It's all a bit run down, but the casino seems to always be hopping, and it's tough to beat the rates. Rooms are spartan but comfortable enough. The restaurants are as low frills (and cheap) as everything else; the Steak House across the freeway at the Gold Coast is far superior to anything here. I'd try Buffalo Bill's or the Primm Valley first, though. Amenities: conference facilities. 303 rooms. Credit cards: A, CB, DC, D, MC, V.

FIELDING'S CHOICE AGENDAS

From roller coasters to fabulous shops, Las Vegas offers something for every visitor.

For Those Who Would Rather Be Anywhere Else

Stay at the very elegant Alexis Park, which has nary a slot machine.

See Starlight Express *at the Las Vegas Hilton–a real play with not one showgirl.*

Enjoy a civilized afternoon at Tricia's Teas.

Dine at one of Las Vegas' many independent gourmet restaurants.

Rent a car and head for the scenic hills and canyons that surround the city.

For Kids Who Never Grew Up

Stay at Circus Circus, where there are free acts daily under the big top.

Head out to Primm and ride the world's biggest roller coaster.

Try the magic motion machines at the Excalibur.

Giggle at the nearly naked ladies in a production show.

When Money Is No Object

Book a Fantasy Suite at Caesars Palace, the swankest resort in town.

Be pampered at the Bacchanal dinner feast at the same hotel.

Rent a Corvette convertible, or hire a stretch limo.

Fly over the Grand Canyon.

Rent a private helicopter for a buzz over the Strip.

Shop till you drop at the tony Forum Shops.

Impressing a Date

Book a Jacuzzi suite at the Mirage.

Have a romantic meal at the Stratosphere's Top of the World.

Instead of just hanging at the pool, rent one of the Mirage's private cabanas.

Buy tickets to Siegfried and Roy, the most expensive (but not best) show in town.

Sip champagne in a hot-air balloon.

Play the $100 slots, available at finer casinos everywhere.

Nature Lovers

Rent a convertible.

Monday: Check out the eerie rock formations at Valley of Fire State Park.

Tuesday: Ride horseback at Bonnie Springs Ranch, then hike around awesome Red Rock Canyon.

Wednesday: Rent a boat and zip around Lake Mead.

Thursday: Take an air tour of the Grand Canyon.

Friday: Collapse by the pool.

Elvis Aficionados

Stay at the Aladdin, where Elvis married Priscilla in 1967.

Check out the mini shrine in the Las Vegas Hilton, then ride elevator number one, which goes to floors 15-30. That little door on the left was built so the King could go right from his suite to the showroom and bypass the always-present mobs of fans.

Elvis Aficionados

Take a picture of the Normandie Motel, a dump on the lower Strip at 708 Las Vegas Blvd. South, where the marquee proudly proclaims "Elvis Slept Here." (Obviously before he hit it big.)

Groove to the Elvis impersonator in the Imperial Palace's "Viva Las Vegas" show.

Drop by the Silver Bell Wedding Chapel (607 Las Vegas Blvd. South), where Elvis married Ann-Margaret in Viva Las Vegas.

For those itching to spend their winnings, casino gift shops offer plenty of temptations.

Wild & Crazy Types

Bungee jump at A.J. Hackett.

Ride the world's biggest roller coaster at Buffalo Bill's.

Careen down the huge water slide at Wet 'n Wild.

Ski the black-diamond Slot Alley run at Lee Canyon.

Put your entire bankroll on red at roulette. (One guy once did just that, starting with $25,000 and walking out with $250,000.)

Hipsters

Stay at the Hard Rock Hotel, the grooviest place in town.

Dance the night away at the Shark Club.

Rub elbows with the locals at the Friday happy hour at TGI Friday's.

Take in a few yucks at the Tropicana's Comedy Stop.

Have a loud meal at Planet Hollywood, the rock and roll cafe in the Forum Shops.

Don your finest duds and head for Club Rio.

If you must see a show, make it "Enter the Night" at the Stardust.

Stay away from Laughlin.

When the Casino's Taken All Your Dough

Move over to Circus Circus, where the rooms are cheap.

Take in the free pirate show at Treasure Island.

Ooh and ahh as the volcano erupts in front of the Mirage.

Eat only at buffets.

Enjoy the free street entertainment at MGM Grand Adventures theme park.

Walk around the Forum Shops at Caesars—but stay out of the stores.

Consider enrolling in Gamblers Anonymous.

Coping with the Kids from Hell

Set them loose in Grand Canyon Adventuredome.

Make them ride the roller coaster until they cry.

Buy them five consecutive rides on the Magic Motion machines at the Excalibur.

Take them to MGM Grand Adventures, but don't let them go on any rides.

Bring them to Treasure Island's pirate show, then lose them in the crowd.

Drawing by M. Stevens; ©1995 The New Yorker Magazine, Inc.

CONCLUSION

The skyline of Las Vegas is changing quickly with the addition of several mega-resorts and new hotels.

What's Ahead?

Las Vegas is sort of like the Energizer rabbit—it keeps going, and going and going. And the building boom of the last decade shows no signs of abating. Here's what to expect in the next few years.

Steve Wynn, the visionary behind the Mirage, Treasure Island and Golden Nugget, is currently constructing Bellagio on the site of the old Dunes, which will become Las Vegas' most costly and sophisticated resort when it opens in September 1998. Designed to recall the Italian village of the same name, the resort will overlook a 12-acre man-made lake complete with a $30-million choreographed water ballet. Guestrooms will be luxurious with European antiquities and artwork and lots of marble. Wynn is spending $1.3 billion on this resort, a remarkable figure considering the hotel will have "only" 3000 rooms. (MGM Grand cost $1 billion, but has 2000 more rooms.)

Another entry into the upscale market is Four Seasons Regent Hotels and Resorts, the luxurious Toronto-based chain. The company has signed an agreement to manage a 400-room, non-gaming property on the Strip—the first Strip hotel to lack a casino. Room rates will exceed $300 per day. It's expected to open in 1998.

Another highroller, Ritz-Carlton, is coming to the area in the form of a 526-room hotel-casino in the northwest area of the Las Vegas Valley.

Hyatt, another Las Vegas newcomer, will debut in Henderson's Lake Las Vegas in 1998. The 500-room hotel will be set within a championship, Jack Nicklaus-designed golf course. The site will also be home to the Grand Bay Hotel & Resort, a 400-room, 210-condominium resort.

Don't let the influx of luxury chains worry you; Las Vegas will still be as goofy as ever. Witness the planned CountryLand USA, located on the site of the shuttered El Rancho, which will be marked by a 35-story-high sign in the shape of cowboy boots. And the upcoming $750-million, 3000-room Paris will boast a 50-story replica of the Eiffel Tower, as well as reproductions of the Arc de Triomphe, Paris Opera House and the Louvre. Opening in 1999, it will be located adjacent and south of Bally's. (Hilton is now the world's largest gaming company after acquiring Bally Entertainment Corp. for $3 billion in December 1996.)

The site of the old Sands will become the $1.8 billion Venetian, an ambitious project by multimillionaire Sheldon Adelson. The first phase of the 6600-suite Venice-themed resort will open in 1999, with the second phase planned for the year 2000.

Plans for a $830-million, 4300-room Planet Hollywood Hotel have been delayed by partner ITT. Originally set to open in 1999, construction was not scheduled to begin until early 1998 at press time. The resort will be adjacent to the Sheraton Desert Inn and be stocked with movie memorabilia.

It's a safe bet the city will be thriving well into the 21st century. Viva Las Vegas!

LIST OF ATTRACTIONS

Attraction	Rating	Pg.
24-Hour Fitness Centers		125
A.J. Hackett Bungee		123
American Superstars	★★★	149
An Evening at La Cage	★★★	149
An Evening in Vienna	★★★	149
Angel Park Golf Club		117
Baby-sitters		20
Beach, The		160
Belz Factory Outlet World		167
Bikes USA		122
Black Canyon Raft Tours	★★★★★	124
Black Mountain Country Club		117
Bonnie Springs Ranch		123
Boulder City Municipal Golf Course		120
Boulder City/Hoover Dam Museum	★★★	126
Boulevard Mall		167
Buffalo Bill's	★★★★★	110
Caesars Magical Empire	★★★	149
Can-Can Room		181
Catch a Rising Star	★★★★	150
Cinema Ride	★★★★	110
Circus Circus	★★★	102
Clark County Heritage Museum	★★★	126
Club Paradise		181
Club Rio	★★★★★	160
Club Utopia		160
Comedy Max	★★★	150
Comedy Stop	★★★★	150
Country Fever	★★★★	150
Country Tonite	★★★★	150
Craig Ranch Golf Club		120
Cranberry World West	★★★	102
Crazy Girls—Sensuality & Passion	★★★	151
David Copperfield	★★★★★	151
Debbie Reynolds Show	★★★	151
Debbie Reynolds' Movie Museum	★★★★	126
Desert Rose Golf Club		120
Don Pablo Cigar Company	★★	102
Dream Flights Company	★★★★	122
Drink, The		160
Dylan's Dance Hall & Saloon	★★★★★	161
EFX	★★★★★	151

Attraction	Rating	Pg.
Enter the Night	★★★★★	152
Ethel M Chocolate Factory Tour	★★★	102
Excalibur's Fantasy Faire	★★★★★	111
Fashion Show Mall		166
Floyd Lamb State Park	★★★	116
Folies-Bergère	★★★★	152
Forever Plaid	★★★	153
Forum Shops at Caesars	★★★★★	103
Forum Shops at Caesars		166
Fremont Street Blues & Reggae Cafe	★★★★	161
Fremont Street Experience	★★★★★	103
Galleria at Sunset		167
Gold Coast Dance Hall & Saloon		161
Gold's Gym		125
Grand Canyon Tours	★★★★	113
Grand Slam Canyon	★★★★	107
Great Radio City Music Hall Spectacular	★★★★	153
Guinness World of Records Museum	★★★	127
Hard Rock Casino		162
Highland Falls Golf Club		120
Holy Cow! Brewery Tours	★★★★	104
Hoover Dam	★★★★	114
IMAX Theatre	★★★★★	111
Imperial Palace Automobile Museum	★★★	127
Jubilee!	★★★★	153
Kenny Kerr Show	★★	154
Kidd Marshmallow Factory Tour	★★★	104
King Arthur's Tournament	★★★★	154
King Tut's Tomb and Museum	★★★★★	127
Lacy's		181
Lake Mead Recreation Area	★★★★★	114
Lance Burton: Master Magician	★★★★	154
Las Vegas Art Museum	★★★★	128
Las Vegas Athletic Clubs		125
Las Vegas Factory Stores of America		167
Las Vegas Golf Club		120
Las Vegas Helicopters	★★★★★	115
Las Vegas Hilton Country Club		120
Las Vegas Mormon Temple	★★★	128
Las Vegas Motor Speedway		123
Las Vegas Natural History Museum	★★★	128
Las Vegas Racquetball Club		123
Las Vegas Sporting House		126
Las Vegas Stars-Baseball		122
Lee Canyon Ski Area	★★★★	124
Legacy Golf Club		121
Legends in Concert	★★★★★	154

Attraction	Rating	Pg.
Liberace Museum	★★★	128
Lied Discovery Children's Museum	★★★★	112
Los Padres Country Club		121
Lost City Museum	★★★	128
MADhattan		155
Magic and Movie Hall of Fame	★★★★	129
Manhattan Express	★★★★	112
Masquerade Show in the Sky	★★★★★	104
Meadows Mall		168
MGM Grand Adventures	★★★★★	107
Mirage Dolphin Habitat & Secret Garden	★★	129
Mirage Volcano	★★★★	104
Mount Charleston	★★★★	115
Mystère	★★★★★	155
National Finals of Rodeo	★★★	130
Nevada Banking Museum	★★	129
Nevada State Museum & Historical Society	★★★	129
Nightclub, The		162
North Las Vegas Community Course		121
Old Nevada	★★★★	108
Olympic Garden		181
Omnimax Theatre	★★★★	112
Painted Desert Country Club		121
Performing Arts at UNLV	★★★★	130
Red Rock Canyon	★★★★★	116
Riviera Comedy Club	★★★	156
Rockabilly's	★★★★★	162
Sand Dollar Blues Lounge		162
Santa Fe Ice Arena		123
Satin Saddle Club		181
Scandia Family Fun Center	★★★	112
Secrets of the Luxor Pyramid	★★★★★	108
Shark Club	★★★★★	162
Sheraton Desert Inn Golf Course		121
Showboat Hotel-Bowling		122
Showcase Mall		112
Showcase Mall		168
Showgirls of Magic	★★	156
Siegfried & Roy	★★★	156
Southern Nevada Zoological Park	★★★	116
Spellbound	★★★	157
Splash II-The Next Wave	★★★	157
Sports Hall of Fame	★★★★	130
Star Trek: The Experience	★★★★★	109
Starlight Express	★★★★	158
Stratosphere Tower	★★★★	109
Sunset Stampede	★★★★	104

Attraction	Rating	Pg.
Talk of the Town		181
Tally-Ho		181
Tennis at the Hotels		124
TGI Friday's	★★★	162
Tommy Rocker's Cantina & Grill		163
Treasure Island Pirate Battle	★★★★★	105
University of Nevada, Las Vegas-Tennis		125
Valley of Fire State Park	★★★★	117
Wet 'n Wild Water Park	★★★★	113
White Tiger Habitat	★★★	106
Wild J's Book and Video		181
Wildhorse Golf Club		121
Wildlife Walk	★★	106
World Gym		126
Xtreme Scene	★★	158

LIST OF HOTELS

Hotel	Price	Rating	Pg.
Aladdin Hotel & Casino	$45–$195	★★★	33
Alexis Park Resort	$95–$175	★★★★	48
Bally's	$85–$225	★★★★	38
Barbary Coast	$75–$200	★★★★	38
Best Western Mardi Gras	$50–$120	★★★	50
Best Western McCarran Inn	$65–$140	★★★	51
Binion's Horseshoe	$28–$60	★★★	54
Blair House Suites	$45–$125	★★	49
Boomtown RV Resort	$18–$20	★★★	62
Boomtown	$45–$75	★★★★	59
Boulder Lakes RV Resort	$19	★★★★	62
Boulder Station	$29–$189	★★★	56
Bourbon Street	$40–$175	★★★	39
Buffalo Bill's	$23–$43	★★★★	198
Caesars Palace	$89–$500	★★★★★	39
California Hotel	$50–$80	★★	56
Carriage House	$89–$275	★★★	49
Casino Royale Hotel	$45–$85	★★	40
Center Strip Inn	$50–$250	★	51
Circus Circus Hotel	$39–$79	★★★	40
Circusland RV Park	$16–$18	★★★	52
Comfort Inn Central	$65–$95	★	52
Continental Hotel and Casino	$35–$95	★★	41
Courtyard by Marriott	$80–$140	★★★	50
Days Inn Downtown	$36–$175	★★	58
Debbie Reynolds' Hotel and Casino	$49–$175	★★★	41
Emerald Springs Holiday Inn	$70–$200	★★★	51
Excalibur Hotel	$59–$250	★★★	26
Fairfield Inn by Marriott	$50–$80	★★	51
Fitzgerald's	$38–$90	★★★	56
Flamingo Hilton	$69–$205	★★★	41
Four Queens	$48–$59	★★★	56
Frontier Hotel & Casino	$35–$95	★★★	42
Gold Coast Hotel	$55–$75	★★★	42
Gold Strike	$19–$39	★★★	199
Golden Nugget	$59–$300	★★★★★	57
Good Sam's Hitchin' Post	$18	★★★	63
Hard Rock Hotel	$85–$300	★★★★★	42
Harrah's	$50–$259	★★★★	43
Holiday Inn Casino Boardwalk	$49–$149	★★★	44
Holiday Inn Crowne Plaza	$79–$109	★★★	49
Hotel San Remo	$89–$149	★★	44

Hotel	Price	Rating	Pg.
Imperial Palace	$49–$129	★★★	44
Jackie Gaughan's Plaza	$30–$140	★★★	57
KOA Kampgrounds	$28	★★★	63
La Quinta Motor Inn	$50–$80	★★	51
Lady Luck Casino Hotel	$40–$80	★★★	57
Las Vegas Club	$40–$50	★★	58
Las Vegas Hilton	$95–$275	★★★★★	26
Luxor	$69–$159	★★★★	28
Maxim Hotel	$42–$96	★★★	45
MGM Grand Hotel Casino	$69–$259	★★★★	29
Mirage	$79–$380	★★★★★	30
Monte Carlo	$60–$200	★★★★	31
Nevada Landing	$21–$34	★★	200
New York-New York	$89–$129	★★★★	32
Orleans	$49–$350	★★★★	59
Palace Station Hotel	$49–$109	★★★	45
Primm Valley Resort & Casino	$23–$43	★★★	198
Quality Inn Hotel & Casino	$49–$59	★★	45
Residence Inn by Marriott	$95–$219	★★★	49
Rio Suites Hotel	$95–$150	★★★★★	60
Riviera Hotel	$35–$250	★★★	45
Royal Hotel & Casino	$45–$85	★★	46
Sahara Hotel & Casino	$85–$115	★★★	46
Sam Boyd's California Hotel RV Park	$12–$12	★★★	59
Sam Boyd's Fremont	$36–$52	★★★	58
Sam's Town RV Resort	$16–$16	★★★★	52
Sam's Town	$50–$100	★★★	62
Santa Fe Hotel	$49–$89	★★★	62
Sheraton Desert Inn	$89–$220	★★★★★	46
Showboat Hotel	$49–$69	★★★	58
Somerset House	$40–$50	★★	52
St. Tropez Suite Hotel	$95–$300	★★★	50
Stardust Resort	$32–$150	★★★	47
Stratosphere	$39–$229	★★★★	32
Sunrise Suites	$40–$85	★★★	50
Town Hall Casino Hotel	$35–$74	★★	47
Travelodge Downtown	$40–$50	★	58
Travelodge South Strip	$49–$99	★	52
Treasure Island	$59–$249	★★★★★	33
Tropicana Resort & Casino	$49–$159	★★★★	47
Vacation Village Hotel	$35–$175	★★★	48
Westward Ho	$37–$76	★★	48
Whiskey Pete's	$23–$43	★★	199

LIST OF
RESTAURANTS

Restaurant	Price	Rating	Pg.
Ah-So	$$$	★★★★	79
Aladdin Marketplace	$	★★★	67
All American Bar & Grille	$$$	★★★★	95
Alpine Village Inn	$$	★★★★	80
Alta Villa	$$	★★★★	80
Andre's	$$$	★★★★★	80
Antonio's	$$$	★★★★	80
Aristocrat, The	$$$	★★★★	92
Bacchanal	$$$	★★★★★	80
Bally's Big Kitchen	$$	★★★★★	67
Bally's Steakhouse	$$$	★★★★	81
Bally's Sterling Brunch	$$$	★★★★★	67
Barronshire	$$$	★★★	81
Beijing	$$	★★★★	81
Benihana Village	$$$	★★★★	81
Bertolini's	$$	★★★★★	82
Big Dogs Cafe & Casino	$$	★★★★	74, 95
Billy Bob's Steakhouse	$$$	★★★	92
Binion's Steak House	$$$	★★★	78
Bistro Le Montrachet	$$$	★★★★★	82
Bistro, The	$$$	★★★★	82
Boison's	$$$	★★★	92
Boomtown's Blue Diamond Buffet	$	★★★	73
Bootlegger	$$	★★★	93
Boulder Station's The Feast	$	★★★	68
Bourbon Street Buffet	$	★★★	68
Brittany's	$$	★★	96
Brown Derby	$$$	★★★★	82
Buccaneer Bay Club	$$$	★★★★	83
Buffet of Champions	$$	★★★★★	68
Burgundy Room	$$$	★★★	78
Caesars Palace's Palatium	$$	★★★★★	68
Cafe Michelle	$$$	★★★	95
Camelot	$$$	★★★★	83
Celebrity Cafe	$	★★★	68
Center Stage Restaurant	$$	★★★	78
Chin's	$$$	★★★★	83
Cipriani	$$$	★★★★	83
Circus Circus Buffet	$	★★	68
Claudine's	$$$	★★★★	83
Continental's Florentine	$	★★	69
Country Star American Music Grille	$$	★★★★	74
Coyote Cafe	$$	★★★	84
Desert Inn Sunday Brunch	$	★★★★	69

Restaurant	Price	Rating	Pg.
Dive!	$$	★★★	74
Embers	$$$	★★★★	84
Emeril's New Orleans Fish House	$$$	★★★★★	84
Empress Court	$$$	★★★★★	84
Excalibur's Round Table Buffet	$	★★★	69
Fisherman's Broiler	$$$	★★★	85
Flamingo Hilton's Buffet	$$	★★★★	69
Fremont Paradise Buffet	$$	★★★	66
Garden of the Dragon	$$$	★★★	85
Garlic Cafe	$$$	★★★★★	93
Ginza	$$$	★★★	85
Gold Coast Buffet	$	★★★	69
Golden Nugget's Buffet	$$	★★★★★	66
Golden Steer Steak House	$$$	★★★	85
Great Moments	$$$	★★★★	96
Guadalajara Bar and Grille	$$	★★★	75
Hamada Sushi Bar	$$$	★★★★	86
Hard Rock Cafe	$$	★★★★	75
Harrah's Galley Buffet	$	★★★★	69
HIPPO & the Wild Bunch	$	★★★	75
Holy Cow!	$$	★★★	75
House of Lords	$$$	★★★★	86
Ho-Wan	$$$	★★★★	86
Hugo's Cellar	$$$	★★★★	78
Imperial Palace's Emperor's Buffet	$	★★★	69
Isis	$$$	★★★★	86
Isis	$$$	★★★★★	86
Kokomo's	$$$	★★★★	87
Lady Luck's Buffet	$	★★★★	66
Lance-a-Lotta Pasta	$	★	76
Leilani's Island Cafe	$	★★★	74
Lilly Langtry's	$$$	★★★★	79
Lone Mountain Buffet	$	★★★★	73
Luxor's Manhattan Buffet	$	★★★	70
Mama Ilardo's Pizzeria	$	★★★★★	76
Marrakech	$$$	★★★★	87
Maxim's Grand Buffet	$	★★★	70
MGM Grand Sunday Brunch	$$	★★★★	70
MGM Grand's Oz Buffet	$	★★★★	70
Michael's	$$$	★★★★★	87
Mirage Buffet	$$	★★★★★	70
Mizuno's Teppan Dining	$$$	★★★★★	87
Molly's Country Buffet	$	★★★	66
Monte Carlo	$$$	★★★★★	87
Monte Carlo's Buffet	$		70
Morton's of Chicago	$$$	★★★★	88
Motown Cafe	$$	★★★	76
Nippon	$$	★★★	88
Official All-Star Cafe	$$	★★★	76

Restaurant	Price	Rating	Pg.
Palace Court	$$$	★★★★★	88
Palace Station's The Feast	$	★★★	71
Palm, The	$$$	★★★★	88
Pamplemousse	$$$	★★★★★	88
Pasta Pirate	$$	★★★	79
Pegasus	$$$	★★★★★	89
Philips Supper House	$$$	★★★	89
Piero's	$$$	★★★★	89
Planet Hollywood	$$	★★★	77
Plank, The	$$$	★★★★★	89
Portofino	$$$	★★★★	89
Redwood Bar and Grill	$$$	★★★	79
Rio's Carnival World Buffet	$	★★★★★	71
Riviera's World's Fare	$	★★★★	71
Rosewood Grille	$$$	★★★★	90
Ruth's Chris Steakhouse	$$$	★★★★	90
Sahara Buffet	$	★★★	71
Sam's Town Great Buffet	$	★★★★	73
Seasons	$$$	★★★★	90
Sfuzzi	$$	★★★★	77
Shalimar	$$	★★★★	90
Showboat's Captain's Buffet	$	★★★	66
Sir Galahad's	$$	★★★	91
Spago	$$$	★★★★★	91
Stardust's Warehouse All-You-Can-Eat	$	★★★	71
Steak House at Circus Circus	$$$	★★★★	91
Steak House, The	$$	★★★★	93
Stefano's	$$$	★★★★	79
Stratosphere Buffet	$		72
Swiss Cafe	$	★★★	94
TGI Fridays	$$	★★★	96
Tillerman	$$$	★★★	93
Tokyo	$$	★★★★	91
Tony Roma's	$$	★★★★	74
Top of the World	$$$	★★★★	91
Treasure Island Buffet	$	★★★★	72
Tricia's Teas	$	★★★★	94
Tropicana's Island Buffet	$$		73
Vacation Village Buffet	$	★★★	73
Venetian Ristorante	$$	★★★	95
Vineyard	$$	★★★	77
Wild Bill's	$$	★★★	96
William B's	$$$	★★★★	92
Wolfgang Puck Cafe	$$	★★★	77

INDEX

Order Your Guide to Travel and Adventure

Title	Price	Title	Price
Fielding's Alaska Cruises and the Inside Passage	$18.95	Fielding's Indiana Jones Adventure and Survival Guide™	$15.95
Fielding's America West	$19.95	Fielding's Italy	$18.95
Fielding's Asia's Top Dive Sites	$19.95	Fielding's Kenya	$19.95
Fielding's Australia	$18.95	Fielding's Las Vegas Agenda	$16.95
Fielding's Bahamas	$16.95	Fielding's London Agenda	$14.95
Fielding's Baja California	$18.95	Fielding's Los Angeles	$16.95
Fielding's Bermuda	$16.95	Fielding's Mexico	$18.95
Fielding's Best and Worst	$19.95	Fielding's New Orleans Agenda	$16.95
Fielding's Birding Indonesia	$19.95	Fielding's New York Agenda	$16.95
Fielding's Borneo	$18.95	Fielding's New Zealand	$17.95
Fielding's Budget Europe	$18.95	Fielding's Paradors, Pousadas and Charming Villages	$18.95
Fielding's Caribbean	$19.95	Fielding's Paris Agenda	$14.95
Fielding's Caribbean Cruises	$18.95	Fielding's Portugal	$16.95
Fielding's Caribbean on a Budget	$18.95	Fielding's Rome Agenda	$16.95
Fielding's Diving Australia	$19.95	Fielding's San Diego Agenda	$14.95
Fielding's Diving Indonesia	$19.95	Fielding's Southeast Asia	$18.95
Fielding's Eastern Caribbean	$17.95	Fielding's Southern California Theme Parks	$18.95
Fielding's England including Ireland, Scotland and Wales	$18.95	Fielding's Southern Vietnam on Two Wheels	$15.95
Fielding's Europe	$19.95	Fielding's Spain	$18.95
Fielding's Europe 50th Anniversary	$24.95	Fielding's Surfing Australia	$19.95
Fielding's European Cruises	$18.95	Fielding's Surfing Indonesia	$19.95
Fielding's Far East	$18.95	Fielding's Sydney Agenda	$16.95
Fielding's France	$18.95	Fielding's Thailand, Cambodia, Laos and Myanmar	$18.95
Fielding's France: Loire Valley, Burgundy and the Best of French Culture	$16.95	Fielding's Travel Tools™	$15.95
Fielding's France: Normandy & Brittany	$16.95	Fielding's Vietnam including Cambodia and Laos	$19.95
Fielding's France: Provence and the Mediterranean	$16.95	Fielding's Walt Disney World and Orlando Area Theme Parks	$18.95
Fielding's Freewheelin' USA	$18.95	Fielding's Western Caribbean	$18.95
Fielding's Hawaii	$18.95	Fielding's The World's Most Dangerous Places™	$21.95
Fielding's Hot Spots: Travel in Harm's Way	$15.95	Fielding's Worldwide Cruises	$21.95

To place an order: call toll-free 1-800-FW-2-GUIDE
(VISA, MasterCard and American Express accepted)
or send your check or money order to:
Fielding Worldwide, Inc., 308 S. Catalina Avenue, Redondo Beach, CA 90277
http://www.fieldingtravel.com
Add $2.00 per book for shipping & handling (sorry, no COD's),
allow 2–6 weeks for delivery

Favorite People, Places & Experiences

ADDRESS:	NOTES:

Name

Address

Telephone

Name

Address

Telephone

Name

Address

Telephone

Name

Address

Telephone

Name

Address

Telephone

Name

Address

Telephone

Name

Address

Telephone

International Conversions

TEMPERATURE

To convert °F to °C, subtract 32 and divide by 1.8. To convert °C to °F, multiply by 1.8 and add 32.

WEIGHTS & MEASURES

LENGTH

1 km	=	0.62 miles
1 mile	=	1.609 km
1 meter	=	1.0936 yards
1 meter	=	3.28 feet
1 yard	=	0.9144 meters
1 yard	=	3 feet
1 foot	=	30.48 centimeters
1 centimeter	=	0.39 inch
1 inch	=	2.54 centimeters

AREA

1 square km	=	0.3861 square miles
1 square mile	=	2.590 square km
1 hectare	=	2.47 acres
1 acre	=	0.405 hectare

VOLUME

1 cubic meter	=	1.307 cubic yards
1 cubic yard	=	0.765 cubic meter
1 cubic yard	=	27 cubic feet
1 cubic foot	=	0.028 cubic meter
1 cubic centimeter	=	0.061 cubic inch
1 cubic inch	=	16.387 cubic centimeters

CAPACITY

1 gallon	=	3.785 liters
1 quart	=	0.94635 liters
1 liter	=	1.057 quarts
1 pint	=	473 milliliters
1 fluid ounce	=	29.573 milliliters

MASS and WEIGHT

1 metric ton	=	1.102 short tons
1 metric ton	=	1000 kilograms
1 short ton	=	.90718 metric ton
1 long ton	=	1.016 metric tons
1 long ton	=	2240 pounds
1 pound	=	0.4536 kilograms
1 kilogram	=	2.2046 pounds
1 ounce	=	28.35 grams
1 gram	=	0.035 ounce
1 milligram	=	0.015 grain

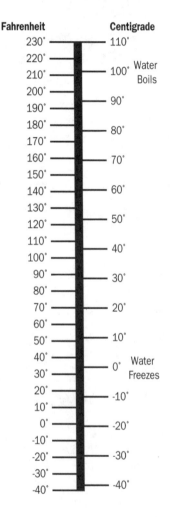

Fahrenheit — Centigrade thermometer scale:

Fahrenheit	Centigrade	
230°	110°	
220°		
210°	100°	Water Boils
200°	90°	
190°		
180°	80°	
170°		
160°	70°	
150°		
140°	60°	
130°		
120°	50°	
110°		
100°	40°	
90°	30°	
80°		
70°	20°	
60°		
50°	10°	
40°		
30°	0°	Water Freezes
20°	-10°	
10°		
0°	-20°	
-10°		
-20°	-30°	
-30°		
-40°	-40°	

cm 0 1 2 3 4 5 6 7 8 9

Inch 0 1 2 3